ASSYRIAN HISTORY CULTURE AND TRADITIONS

Venesia Yacoub

To order additional copies of this book, contact:
Xlibris
844-714-8691
www.Xlibris.com
Orders@Xlibris.com
836230

To peace in the world
To writing without limitations
To speaking freely
To dreaming endlessly

ASSYRIAN
HISTORY
CULTURE AND
TRADITIONS

Special Dedication

This book is dedicated to all the children of Assyria around the world; it is love for our language and our ancient traditions that binds us. Our traditions have been practiced for centuries, and it's because of your diligence and perseverance that they will remain in our lives and hearts forever.

Welcome to Ashur

Contents

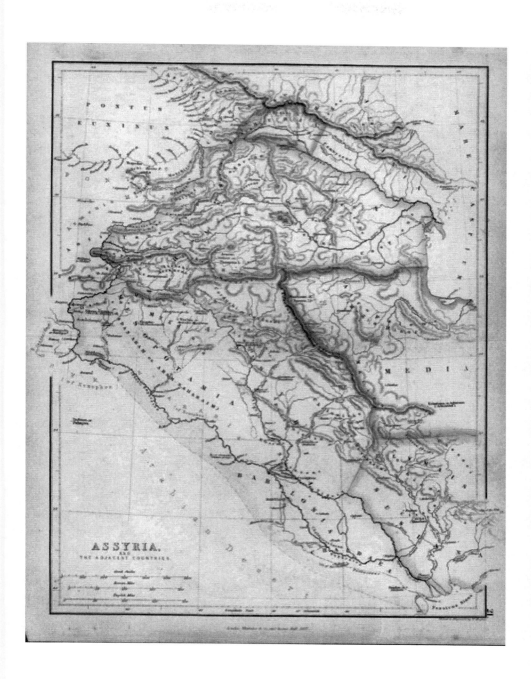

ASSYRIA,
AND
THE ADJACENT COUNTRIES.

LIST OF FIGURES AND ARTIFACTS

1. Ancient map of Assyria
2. Picture of the city of Ashur
3. Royal Symbol, part of the Babylon Ishtar Gate
4. First map of the world found in Babylon
5. Map of Assyrian Empire
6. Cuneiform symbol Akkadu
7. Aramaic cuneiform tablet
8. Assyrian alphabet
9. Assyrian king Ashurnasirpal, reign 668–627 BC
10. Assyrian deities
11. Babylon Ishtar Gate
12. City of Ashur, current day in Iraq
13. Ziggurat of Ashur, current day
14. Religious stone carvings, King Ashurnasirpal II, 883–859
15. Ziggurat reconstructed model and current day
16. Ashurnasirpal II, 883–859 BC, sold at Christie's auction
17. Stele of the Assyrian Tree of Life
18. Stele of King Ashurnasirpal II, currently housed in the British Museum, 883–857 BC
19. Shalmaneser III and Marduk-Zakir Shumi Stone Dias, 846–845 BC
20. Syriac traditions and Assyrian influence

A ROYAL SYMBOL FOR ALL OF YOU

J want to thank my precious children, I know you have been very patient with me as I wrote this book and that it took time away from you, but one day you will understand the importance of this book.

To my mother and my best friend, you are my guiding light and my mentor; you have been there for me every step of the way my entire life. I could sit for hours just listening to the sound of your voice and to hear your comforting thoughts and words. You always managed to make things better, even when they were not. You have always taught me to see the brighter side and the good in everything. I want to thank you for all the guidance you have given me throughout my life and all the unconditional support I have received. You are truly a remarkable person, and I could have never done it without you. I love and cherish you dearly.

I have to mention my grandmother Axania and my great-grandmother Shakre, and even though you are not with us anymore, I want my children to know that you have shaped my life in many ways, and although I grew up miles away from you and the memory of your faces is very faint, it was your voices that always seemed to follow us and echo everywhere we went. We still heard all the stories you told, and each story will be cherished and remembered for a lifetime.

I want to thank Unna, for the priceless stories that you shared with me; and each time you shared a memory, it took me back to a different time and a different place, and I could imagine exactly what you meant. I will forever treasure our talks.

I want to thank Jounsun Magsoud. You have been an integral part of this process and provided vital information that I used in this book. Thank you for helping translate some complex history and archaeological data. Your wisdom never seizes to amaze me.

A special acknowledgment and thank-you to all my friends that helped translate a lot of historical and archaeological data. You are truly a gift, and your ability to read between the lines and translate complex historical data is inspirational. You know who you are.

A special acknowledgment goes to those Assyrians who have worked tirelessly to bring light to archaeological, historical scripts and ancient texts that display the antiquity and continuity of the Assyrian people. You have been instrumental in debunking radical theories by some individuals that have attempted to justify in wiping out the existence of an entire nation for their own personal gain. You have provided creditable and invaluable information that no one can dispute or deny. You are modern heroes.

I also want to thank all the Assyrian writers and advocates who support or write our stories to be shared with the world; your passion and dedication to the Assyrian people is priceless.

My deepest gratitude also goes to the Assyrian Cultural Foundation, the Ashurbanipal Library – Chicago, the Assyrian Cultural & Social Youth Association Inc. (ACYSA), the Assyrian International News Agency, the Mar Shimun Foundation, and all Assyrian groups for all the work you do. You are the pillar of light at the end of a very dark road. Thank you for all your hard work and your perseverance in telling our stories. Thank you to those who preserve ancient Assyrian texts, and all the volunteers that teach the Assyrian language today; and if it weren't for all of you, a lot of history, the Assyrian language and culture would be lost and forgotten.

A special mention and thank-you to the Oriental Institute University of Chicago for spending ninety years establishing the *Assyrian Dictionary* and capturing specific details of the oldest language in the world. The project was started in 1920 and completed in 2010, given its complexity.

Thank you to those who manage and contribute to the global registry of cuneiform tablets, and for the preservation and the translation of these ancient texts at the University of Cambridge, University of California, Los Angeles, Harvard University, Yale University, Oxford University, the Max Planck Institute of History and Science Berlin, University of Heidelberg, University of Helsinki, and the Chicago University. I couldn't possibly put into words my gratitude for all the work you do in the preservation of the ancient cuneiform tablets; your translations and work toward making them available for study, adding to the understanding of ancient Assyrian and Babylonian history, is priceless. To allow us to read what happened thousands of years ago when writing was only carved in stone using wedge-shaped letters is truly remarkable and a gift that you have given the world.

I am so grateful to those behind the Open Richly Annotated Cuneiform Corpus Project and the cuneiform digital library initiative, to all the contributors, the translators, the professors, the Assyriologists, and the administrators for making the cuneiform tablets available to allow researchers to study them, to allow Assyrians to look into their past and to further understand their ancestors, their ancient culture, heritage, traditions, and history. Your contribution to education and research is a lesson for us all, and your work is simply invaluable. Thank you!

A special mention and thank-you to all the museums around the world, especially in Britain, France, Germany, Finland, Russia, Australia, China, Japan, America, Canada, Iraq, Iran, Israel, Turkey, Syria, Armenia, Jordan, and Lebanon for housing Assyrian artifacts and for preserving and protecting them, which allows us to still enjoy and learn from them as they tell their story from thousands of years ago until today. Your preservation of these artifacts has never been so vital, especially with the recent destruction of Assyrian artifacts in their homelands. If I missed any museums, please accept my apologies—this is a growing research project to locate all Assyrian artifacts worldwide. Thank you to all of you.

INTRODUCTION

A legacy unforgotten, its history is engraved in the very fabric of the earth in the Middle East, within the four corners of their ancient lands, hidden and tucked away like little gems in the very same soil for thousands of years; a history that, through time, slowly starts to unravel and unveil itself magnificently. A culture so rich and ancient, where urbanization and religion emerged, and which predates the Bible by thousands of years. Known in world history as the Cradle of Civilization and history of the world.

I had to limit myself in this book, as the information and research on this topic is so overwhelming that it would be difficult to complete in a whole lifetime. Given Assyrians have over seven thousand years of continuous history, this was certainly not an easy task for one person to write; therefore, learning, researching, and updating is an ongoing process. This book contains information about Assyrian culture and traditions that link their ancient cultic rituals to modern times. This documentation is even more vital now, as the Assyrians continue to be under threat and at the brink of extinction in their native homelands.

The idea of this book developed in July 2014 when livestream videos in social media began to circulate of the ISIS terrorist group and invasion of modern-day Iraq. I will never forget that day because I witnessed some of the most shocking and unimaginable events taking place in the Middle East in modern history—innocent people were removed from their homes and being massacred for being who they are. The entire world stood silent and did nothing.

It was difficult to comprehend the previous genocide attempts against the Assyrian people throughout history, which we all heard and several stories were told about it but this one; no one could say they didn't know. With today's technology, we all saw it livestreaming—it happened in 2014, and continued to happen for years. The world knew, everyone knew the atrocities committed to innocent people, and nothing was done until several years later.

Iraq and parts of Syria, Turkey, and Iran are native Assyrian homelands, and the Assyrian people in Mosul, northern Iraq, and Syria today are the survivors of the last genocide that occurred in 1915 Seyfo and in 1933 Simele, Iraq. The descendants of those survivors are here again today, experiencing the same thing, as did their grandparents, which certainly was difficult to think about at the time or even comprehend.

As the months went by, and there were more developments on the ongoing genocide, I sadly realized that my nation was slowly being wiped out, physically, culturally, politically, historically, and religiously—and all this right in front of the watch of the whole world. Whether terrorists did it or by ordinary people, the attempts to try and erase a nation and their people, I could just not understand. Assyrian history is one of the richest and most plentiful in the ancient world; its existence is through scientific facts such as archaeological data and old texts, and here we are again learning of people trying to destroy it along with its people.

This book will uncover traditions that have been practiced for thousands of years, and some will be linked directly to cuneiform stone tablets dating back to an estimated 1000 BC. As new archeological discoveries are made, it will provide new insights that cities of Assyria are even older than this estimated timeline. This book will also explain some of the misconceptions and translate some of the historical complexities of the Assyrian nation from an insider's viewpoint.

OVERVIEW AND BRIEF HISTORY

*S*everal genocide attempts have occurred against the Assyrian people throughout the centuries, with the most recent occurrence in modern history initiated in June of 2014. Similarly, to other state-sponsored massacres, the Assyrian people received a letter to disarm and turn their weapons into the local government with the promise that the government would protect them. That promise of protection again did not happen

Assyrians received word from family members that Islamic State of Iraq, a terrorist group of the Levant, also known as ISIL, or ISIS, would be coming, and they needed to leave their homes or risk facing severe harm or death. ISIS came to each home in northern Iraq, marking the door with the letter *N* in Arabic, which refers to *Nazarene*, meaning "Christian" in the Arabic language. This was done to all the Christian homes. While members of ISIS went to each home and told the people of the households they have three choices: (1) pay a jizya tax (this is an additional tax that Christians have to pay in an Islamic country), (2) convert to Islam, or (3) die by the sword.

This backward extremism came as a shock to the entire world as we all watched from our homes, scared for their lives an estimated 250,000 Assyrians were forced to flee their homes. Those who had cars packed up the women and children first, leaving their personal belongings and taking only the necessities. Those who didn't have cars walked in groups, for days and months in the scorching heat, sleeping on the cold ground at night, some finding shelter in nearby towns and churches.

Assyrians in the main villages of Nineveh province, also known as Mosul, Tel Keppe, Qaraquosh, Bartella, and Karamlish, were all forced to flee. On February 25, 2015, ISIS invaded Assyrian towns in Syria, such as Khabour; and again, thousands fled. Those who could not flee due to medical reasons stayed, and some opted to stay to protect the ones who could not leave.

The world stood silently watching while Assyrians around the world were outraged and held protests and meetings, to no avail. Almost a year later, ISIS was still getting stronger, with no one to stop them. There was no outcry from anyone except those who were being persecuted, such as the Assyrians and Yezidis, other groups such as Shia Muslims who were also being murdered.

How do we fail humanity like this? When did we lose our moral judgment and not step in to stop such atrocities when they are happening? How did the world ignore this? They can start a war in a matter of days, yet it takes years to help stop one—after millions have lost their lives, millions have lost their homes and lands, after the entire country has been destroyed and turned to rubble. When humanity fails, it must be the responsibility of everyone; it should be on everyone's conscience, because the world could not be a better place if we continue to turn a blind eye.

The terrorist group was caught removing Assyrian artifacts and digging Assyrian archaeological sites; some were caught selling massive numbers of priceless artifacts to black markets around the world. Some sites were wired with explosives and destroyed permanently after they took what they could, while others were destroyed using hammers and chainsaws while being recorded for the world to watch online. The Assyrian people were stripped of their lives, their homes, their possessions, their dignity, their culture and their history. All of this while under the so-called watch of the US and other governing bodies.

The Assyrian and Yezidi girls were given the option of converting to Islam or suffering daily rapes. They refused, and so many lost their lives senselessly. The world stood silent, watching thousands of people being murdered, persecuted, and raped; women and children were being sold as slaves, beheaded, crucified—even children were crucified with no remorse. The terrorists group hung thousands of people. So many lost their lives, and thousands were displaced. Even today, some of those people are still living in tents—from 2014 to now, 2021. It was not until late 2019 that a coalition was formed to take out the terrorist group.

Up to February 2020, 51 Assyrian children, 84 women, and 95 men remained in captivity, held by the ISIS terrorists. The Assyrians have been treated like this for centuries, while slowly they are resorted to flee to diaspora while others profit off their lands and homes. The last mass exodus was one hundred years ago—750,000 Assyrians were murdered. Others were raped or forced to convert to Islam. Some killed themselves because they couldn't live like that. Some children were kidnapped, and although they are living in Islamic families, they were children when they were taken, and now the children of the last genocide are the great-grandmothers from the last genocide. Some women have been known to put a cross on dough when making bread; this is what Assyrians do today. When these Islamic grandmothers were asked why they put the sign of the cross on the dough, they said they don't know why, but this is what they remember to do. These grandmothers were Assyrian children that were kidnapped in the last genocide, and this is what their mothers did, so they do the same.

The neighbouring countries around Iraq and Syria did nothing; the internal governments did nothing. Since the US invasion of Iraq in 2003, thousands of innocent lives have been lost, and now, splitting the Iraq government has created even bigger problems, with more strife and separatism; extremists are coming from all over the world to cause havoc there.

ASSYRIA

It lies abandoned and forgotten where history began to make its mark and some of the greatest human achievements were recorded on stone tablets, and once the Garden of Eden flourished, but now lies hidden, buried underground in that same soil just waiting to be unveiled. With only minimal accounts written by Greek and Latin historians, and with some mentions in the Bible, today this civilization's memory faces a new threat of destruction with some biased and unmerited accounts of Assyria being documented; today, terrorists and local governments destroy what is left of these ancient historical sites and artifacts while forcing Assyrians to flee their historical homelands.

Assyrians are currently scattered around the world, and while they still practice some ancient traditions until today, sadly they have stopped practicing some very old traditions in recent years; the reason being there isn't a strong presence of them left in their homeland, so we will review their ancient traditions and customs— from those they still practice today to the ones that have sadly stopped in recent years.

We go back in time where it all started in the Fertile Crescent, where the city of Assur and its capital Nineveh, once thrived over seven thousand years ago; it flourished and gradually became the biggest and first empire in the world. Each Assyrian king that ruled at the time made vast contributions to their country and to their people. They wrote extensively about their creations, their power, their military strength, religion, their cultural diversity, and their

1

vast diplomatic administrations. Today some superpowers still follow the same concepts. Luxury and opulence defined their everyday life; they lived in vast and lavish palaces decorated with elaborate hues of blue, tinges of yellows, extravagant golds, bewildering silvers, and mystifying reds. Each city had a religious temple called ziggurat; these temples were built high to the sky so that the people were close to the heavens when they prayed to their god.

Their buildings—showing remarkable engineering for their time, some still standing today—they were built by hand using sunbaked bricks. They had slabs of limestone or alabaster with intricately carved stone reliefs; each carving depicted a special scene, which displayed cuneiform writing with each stele telling a story. These impressive wall carvings were in the entranceways of the palaces. Just moving the massive limestone blocks was a feat on its own, let alone the hand-carved details and writing on them before the world had an alphabet. The grand colossal Lamassu greeted you while you walked in; they were carved out of alabaster and were placed at each entryway of the citadel to protect the people of the city from wrongdoers, and their buildings were surrounded with large-scale citadels, also for protection.

Assyrian merchants established the first trading routes; this allowed for their lavish lifestyles, which built their wealth, and eventually gave them access to many different luxuries from their visits to various countries far and wide. These trade routes, called the Royal Roads, eventually extended east to China and west to Europe; later the trading routes became known as the Silk Road. This helped establish their kingdoms and allowed them to share their language, religion, and culture with the world, as they knew it then. They traded in gold, silver, tin, copper, precious stones, grains, silk, and wool. Their trading taxes and other charges were documented on cuneiform tablets, and some of which are over five thousand years old. Traders brought back spices and the finest textiles, perfumes, and oils from their journeys.

They created hand-carved masterpieces on stone that depicted their god and mystical beings, each piece telling its story to the viewer, to this day.

Their mystical beings were half human, half animal, and had wings; they were known as Apkallu, which is what we know as demigods or angels today. These creations, of great imagination and artistry, bring us some of the first stories ever told.

The Assyrian kings had grand and lavish gardens filled with exotic animals and birds, using the first ever built canals, aqueducts, and advanced watering systems. The palaces and gardens were built, according to King Sennacherib, to be "a wonder for all people," which they were, with the famous Hanging Gardens of Nineveh still known today as one of the seven wonders of the ancient world. The gardens had fragrant roses, gardenias, and jasmine; and they brought fruits and plants from all around the world.

They were some of the first people to make wine and beer, and they enjoyed dates, figs, and pomegranates, to name just a few of their favorites. They had medicinal planets and herbs, grooming systems, makeup and perfume; and in each home, there were bathing areas with washrooms, built an estimated three thousand years before these were "invented" by others.

The kings that ruled these lands were immaculately groomed, with each piece of curly hair precisely placed in their beards. They were adorned with glorious earrings and elaborate jewelry, and they wore the finest fabrics, woven by hand, and sewn with perfectly placed stitches. They wore handcrafted leather shoes with some that tied all the way up to the knees.

They enjoyed music and singing and had a great appreciation for the arts, and art was displayed all over their palaces. The Assyrian kings had grand-scale events and festivals that included watching the famous lion hunts. They had schools and vast libraries—one of the most famous one is Ashurbanipal's library which housed over hundreds of thousands of carved stone tablets. Their library in Nineveh housed some of the most important pieces of literature in the world, such as the world's first story ever told—the Epic of Gilgamesh, the world's first poem, and the original f lood story, just to name a few.

Archaeologists and historians have found meticulously documented religious prayers, letters of governance, royal letters, contractual documents, and administrational, medicinal, mathematical, magical, and healing instructions—all carved in stone using the ancient writing technique of cuneiform.

Assyrian society was diverse in all aspects, and the people lived together with other nations, allowing each person to practice their own beliefs. They had the first laws ever created to maintain law and order; they gave women their due rights. They prepared elaborate sacrificial meals to their gods and planned their events around the moon and stars, which they watched using the first lens ever created. They had the first map of the world—carved in stone—and they used mathematical concepts that are still in use today. They had special healers that treated the ill; they used a lot of medicinal herbs and treated medical conditions naturally.

Shortly after King Ashurbanipal's death, it didn't take long for the Babylonians and Medes to join forces with the Chaldeans to sack the city of Nineveh, and that was the end of the glorious Assyrian rule—this happened around 612 BC. One of the greatest cities ever created in ancient times, the city of Nineveh, was sacked and burned to the ground; and since then, it has never been the same, and it has been detrimental to the Assyrian people.

Map of the world, 1500–539 BC, found in Babylon
and currently housed at the British Museum.

The Assyrian kings named the city of Assur/Ashur, after their nation's primary god; and the people were named after their god Ashuraye or Ashurian by their kings, meaning "the people of Ashur," and later the Greeks called them Assyrians, which came from the name Assyria.

The city name Nineveh, or Ninua, was near the Tigris river, which was known for its abundance of fish.

The city named Arbela, or Arba-il, which means four gods in Assyrian. The city of Kalhu, which Assyrian kings referred to in many tablets, is called present-day Nimrud; the name *Kalhu* translates to mean "bride" in the Assyrian language.

Eventually, Assyriology was created, which includes the study of archaeological antiquities, historical and linguistic study of Assyria and the rest of ancient Mesopotamia. Several prestigious universities worldwide teach Assyriology, which includes the study of Sumer, Akkad, and Babylonia. These scholars divide the Assyrian historical period into three main sections, plus a fourth, called prehistory. The date ranges of these periods vary depending on the scholarly source, but they are estimated as follows:

Prehistory: 2400 BC+
Old Assyrian period: 2400–1600 BC
Middle Assyrian period: 1601–910 BC
Neo-Assyrian: 911–612 BC

In the past as they do today, people were named after the towns they lived in before there were countries and states.

The Sumerians and Akkadians are Assyrian ancestors, they called people Sumerians because they lived in the city of Sumer, and the people who lived in the city of Akkad were called Akkadian. In the same way, the people who lived in the city of Babylonia were called Babylonians, and the people who lived in the city of Nineveh were called Ninevites, but they were all part of the same civilization and the same people. There were people of other nationalities living in Assyria, so not everyone was Assyrian in nationality, but 80 percent were. This is similar to how countries of today are formed. They practiced the religion of Ashurism; while they had multiple gods, with the representation of the different aspects of nature, each city had a principal god, the nation's primary god, the creator of all gods and the universe, was Ashur. The one-god concept at the time laid the foundation for monotheism in Judaism, Christianity, and Islam. They later accepted Christianity readily because they already believed in the one-god concept, and they heard about the miracles performed by Jesus, so it was easy for them to convert; however, Assyrians practiced their ancient religion beyond the time of Jesus, and some still do up to today.

In AD 33, the Assyrians became one of the first people to accept Christianity.

In AD 50, some Assyrians, a smaller portion, started to follow the religious practice of Judaism;[1] and until today, there are still some Assyrians that adhere to this religion.

Some Assyrians are known as Nestorians because they follow the teachings of Nestorius and mainly adhere to the Church of the East and the Holy Apostolic Catholic Assyrian Church of the East. Some Assyrians also follow the Orthodox Church and the Roman Catholic Church.

Many centuries later after its destruction, Assyria appeared in the Bible and in the work of ancient historians. Most, however, portrayed it negatively, never encompassing its greatness. It was not until archaeological discoveries were made that a different picture began to emerge. Many historians, however, limited their knowledge of Assyria to its military methods and conquests, and researchers today confirm scholars have underestimated the Assyria's technological expertise.

It was not until the 1800s when Austin Henry Layard was tasked by the British government to find, uncover, and excavate some of the ancient cities of Nineveh, Babylon, and Kalhu based on the accounts of the biblical stories, to prove the existence of them. The journey

---

[1] Assyrian News Agency

began, and the fact-finding became a sensation for the British people and Europe. It was often publicized in grand events and in the local papers. This created a new sensation, and once again, the once forgotten Assyria was seen for its original light and glory, which paved the way to amazing discoveries, which they only heard and read about sparingly.

These discoveries uncovered contributions and achievements to world history that eventually earned them the name of the Cradle of Civilization. Historians and scholars named the area the Cradle of Civilization because it was there that the first agriculture and urbanization of the world started. This is where they engineered the first great cities and citadels. These cities were Uruk, Sumer, Assur, Nineveh, Kalhu, Arbela, and Babylon, to name a few. They built homes and roads; there was merchant trading; they used the first writing systems; they discovered how they established to tell time, which we still use today. They discovered Hammurabi's code of laws, these were the first laws ever created; they discovered indoor plumbing, the use of medicinal herbs, maps, mathematical concepts still in use today, libraries, astronomy, the mailing system, the wheel, the army, and the first monarchs of the world. There was evidence of their love for music and art, some of the first poems ever written.

They divided land into territories and the monarchs ensured they had appointed administrations in each area. They founded the first university, called Nisibis, this is where writing, theology, philosophy, science, and medicine were taught. They had knowledge of the first religions of the world. There were various scientific and medical tablets found, which were later translated and written by Hunayn Ibn Ishaq in AD 950; these textbooks would remain a definitive source until the 1800s. They had thousands of cuneiform tablets from around the region in their library of all various subjects, and when papyrus was invented, they had thousands of manuscripts documenting their way of life. There was great interest in this ancient world, and people were eager to learn more about it.

The excavations that were done in the 1800s once again glorified Assyria as it once was—the first empire of the world and one of the greatest empires that ever existed. It created excitement about what they would find next and whether they could confirm the stories written by historians in the Bible and through the centuries.

In the nineteenth century, the Middle East was ruled by the Ottoman Empire. It was not until the Europeans and the Western diplomats; government officials and merchant traders travelled to this land while exploring all the ancient ruins discovered some of the oldest civilizations in the world.[2] Their stories and discoveries were brought back with them to Britain and France, which raised interest in expanding their political gains in the Middle East. A British archaeologist named Claudius Rich, between 1787 and 1820, conducted one of the earliest expeditions, and it was at this time when the first extensive antiques were collected from Mesopotamia and shipped to Britain, which began to establish the Mesopotamia collection at the British Museum. Between 1802 and 1870, a Frenchman named Paul-Emile Botta conducted some major excavations that in 1842 included the city of Nineveh, present-day Mosul in Iraq; this was an ancient city of Assyria, and later he went on to excavate another ancient city of Dur-Sharrukin..

The various excavations conducted in ancient Dur-Sharrukin were in the following timeframes 1842–1844, 1852–1855, 1928–1935.

The first major discovery was the palace of King Sargon II (reign 721–705 BC); this is where they found the famous Assyrian slabs of alabaster with carved reliefs along the palace walls. This is also the time they discovered the massive colossal Lamassu guarding the entryways of the palace. In 1846, Paul-Emile Botta quickly shipped many of these antiques and enormous monuments to France. This was the start of the Mesopotamian collection at the Louvre Museum in Paris, France. These finds made by the Frenchman created a lot of excitement, but it was not until an Englishman, Austen Henry Layard, and his Assyrian assistant, Hormuz Rassam, began their

---

[2] Department of Ancient Near Eastern Art, "The Rediscovery of Assyria," in *Heilbrunn Timeline of Art History* (New York: The Metropolitan Museum of Art, 2000), http://www.metmuseum.org/toah/hd/rdas/hd_rdas.htm, (October 2004).

excavation of Kalhu, present-day Nimrud, between 1817 and 1894, that was ordered by the British Museum that created the awareness of these majestic sites.

Their team, which consisted of over a hundred of people, discovered many stone carvings and the palace of the Assyrian king Ashurnasirpal II (reign 883–859 BC); they also found the remains of many palaces built by the various Assyrian kings that reigned for hundreds of years in Assyria. They uncovered various temples at Kalhu, including royal buildings; and in Nineveh, they discovered the palace built by Assyrian king Sennacherib (reign 704–681 BC) and the famous Ashurbanipal library.

In the city of Nineveh, they discovered over two miles of hand-carved stone slabs. The majority of the antiques uncovered were shipped to the British Museum, some went to other institutions, some across Europe, some were acquired by American missionaries working in Iraq at the time, and other pieces found their way in private collections, including J. P. Morgan, which six of the antiques are now in the Metropolitan Museum. Layard sent several reliefs to his cousin's manor in Doresetshire, England, which were installed as a Nineveh Porch, which had cast-iron doors featuring the Lamassu and inspired stained glass windows depicting the wall paintings found in Kalhu and ceiling painted using cuneiform writing.

There they had a collection of twenty-six Assyrian sculptures displayed on the walls, and the British Museum was adorned by several antiquities. In 1851, Layard concluded his excavations and went back to Britain.

Eighteen of the sculptures were sold in 1919 to the private collection of John D. Rockefeller Jr., who later donated them to the Metropolitan Museum in 1932. Hormuz Rassam continued to dig in Nineveh and, in 1853, discovered the palace of Assyrian king Ashurbanipal (reign 668–627 BC). This is where they found the famous stone carvings of the lion hunting scenes and various other art pieces and sculptures. The French under Victor Place (1818–1855) worked in Dur-Sharrukin. The antiques they found were all shipped to the British and French museums. The next major archaeological discovery was of the royal tombs at Kalhu conducted by Iraq's archaeologists in 1988–1989, which found mounds of gold, often referred to as the Nimrud treasure, which consisted of crowns, jewelry, gold vases, and the skeletal remains of the Assyrian kings, queens, and their servants.

The map of the Assyrian empire:

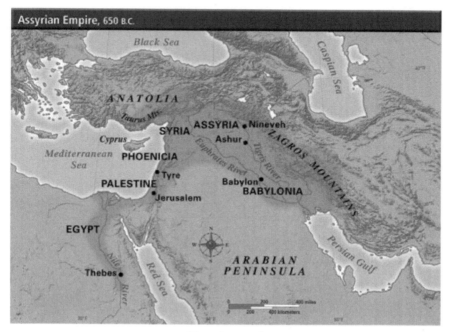

(Google maps)

After the various conquests of Assyria, the Assyrian people remained in their homelands; these areas today are broadly identified as modern-day Iraq, parts of Iran, Turkey, and Syria, with the heartland being northern Iraq. This is where the ancient cities of Assur, Nineveh, Arbela, and Kalhu still exist today; with the exception of Arbela, most of the cities are covered in mounds of dirt through the ages and hidden under the ground while some peaks of the citadels are still visible today. The Greek historians called Assyria "Mesopotamia," meaning "the land between two rivers," which refers to the Tigris and Euphrates rivers; however, the name

Mesopotamia does not encompass all of Assyria. Assyria extended beyond the land between the two rivers at its peak.

The Assyrians in the past used the different phases of the moon to establish the start of their year at the first sight of spring. Today they use a solar calendar and based the start of their year using a date that was set as the baseline of their year in the 1950s, which marks the date that the first temple of Ashur was built in 4750 BC. Spanning the following years, 4750 (starting point) + 2021 (current year) = 6771 is what was established as their year; however, archaeological finds that have recently been translated confirm the date ranges are much older. As more information becomes available, their date will continue to change.

Some of the darkest aspects of Assyrian history is they are one of the most-targeted people in the world; this is evident by the fact that 80 percent of them live outside their native homelands. This number is very telling, and it speaks to how dire their situation is in their homelands.

Assyrians have been forced out of their native homelands because of who they are and because of their religious beliefs, and some have been uprooted so that others can take their lands and homes. Highlighting a recent and major incident that is well documented, is the example of the ISIS invasion in 2014, during which several Assyrians were uprooted and their archaeological sites were completely destroyed, presumably to wipe out any history of their existence and to create major demographic changes in the area of their historical home grounds.

In the ISIS invasion, the terrorist group forced 250,000 Assyrians to flee from their homes and land. Some fled to neighbouring countries such as Iran, Jordan, Syria, and Turkey because it had become difficult to get into Western countries to seek asylum.

When the Assyrians fled, their neighbours took possession of their lands and homes occupying them without any legal justification. If the neighbours didn't take possession of Assyrian homes the local government would move other people in Assyrian owed homes. These vast demographic changes of once Assyrian-dominated regions, and throughout time this systematic persecution changes the demographic of the area and now, as a result, the Assyrians are considered the minority in ancestral lands that they have lived in for thousands of years. The attempt to wipe them out is very clear with these actions.

Since the fall of the Assyrian empire and more recently throughout modern history, the various governments in the Assyrian homelands would often start confiscation tactics targeting Assyrian homes, lands, belongings, or churches. Their lands and homes would be sold or resettled by other people with no legitimate justification. Some cases are still in courts today fighting a losing battle to get their lands and homes back.

The genocide attempts on the Assyrian people are a vast subject, occurring from the fall of their empire in 612 BC until modern times. Some main documented dates are as follows: in 350 BC, Assyrians attempt to establish autonomy, but the Persians castrated 400 members of the Assyrian ruling families. In AD 448, 153,000 Assyrians were massacred by an order from the Sassanid king Yesdegerd II. In 1843, Kurdish Badr Khana- Bek massacred about 50,000 Assyrians.[3] Between 1914 and 1918, also known as the year of the sword, which Assyrians call Seyfo, the Ottoman Turks and Kurds massacred 750,000 Assyrians along with thousands of Greeks, Yezidis and Armenians, the Assyrians within that area comprised of 75 percent of their population that were massacred. In 1933, the Assyrians were massacred by the Iraq army, which is known as the Simele massacre. The start of the US invasion of Iraq in 2003 until now caused havoc in the area, which created a sort of lawlessness state, and resulted in terrorists coming from around the world to Iraq and systematic ethnic cleansing that continues to occur by their neighbours and the local governments. In 2014, the well-documented ISIS invasion created the uprooting of 250,000 Assyrians; kidnappings, destruction of Assyrian antiquities, and massacres played while live streaming it for the entire world to watch.

---

[3] Assyrian News Agency

Years of research and historical evidence will never encompass all of the genocides—it would require an entire book strictly dedicated to this subject alone. The massacres and assassinations of the Assyrian people are well documented, and well-preserved evidence still exists in their historical sites until today.

In 2014 and onward, the ISIS destruction of Jonah's tomb, which was blown up on July 24, 2014, and later in 2019 in Nineveh they uncovered a 2,600-year-old palace belonging to Assyrian king Esarhaddon, which had never before been excavated. Seven slabs were inscribed with texts of King Esarhaddon, and some inscriptions were upside down. ISIS had dug various tunnels while destroying and looting Assyrian artifacts to be sold in the black market. They left behind several marble cuneiform inscriptions, stone sculptures of demigods, and various carved reliefs that were too big to carry out. Farther in the tunnel, a relief was uncovered; it was of four ladies wearing long dresses, holding a cup on the left hand, and holding the famous Assyrian religious symbol on the right hand. What they couldn't carry out, they destroyed by blowing up, such as the ancient site of Kalhu, modern-day Nimrud. The British Institute for the Study of Iraq and various international institutions rushed to provide their assistance in preserving the sites and to study the remaining treasures.

From 2019 to 2020, a team of Italian and Iraq archaeologists uncovered rare stone reliefs of the Assyrian procession of the gods, which are estimated to be about 2,700 years old and belong to the reign of the mighty Assyrian king Sargon II and, since 1845, have never been found until now.

Procession of the gods.

Many Assyrians thought that when the US invaded Iraq in 2003, this would bring good change and bring more freedom and peace in the region and some thought the Assyrians would be given their legitimate rights to have their own state to govern and protect themselves, but that did not happen, and they became more endangered and persecuted.

Instead, the 2003 US invasion made matters worse because of the corrupt people that planted themselves in governmental positions, and this resulted in more Assyrians being targeted and forced to f lee.

Today, as a result of their historical demise, the Assyrians are scattered all around the world with their main populations being in the US, such as in the areas of Chicago and Arizona, California and in the countries of Australia, Canada, Sweden, Switzerland, France, Germany, Russia, Armenia, Jordan, Turkey, Iran, Syria, and Israel. There are Assyrians still living in their native homelands which are current-day Iraq, Iran, Syria, and Turkey, but their numbers are dwindling annually.

Assyrians normally reside where the majority of their people live, and they tend to find each other wherever they go, even on social media. The majority of Assyrians form close communities, and they automatically become friends with one another; even though they don't know each other, there is an automatic special bond because of who they are.

The Assyrians have adapted well in other diaspora countries, but they are in what is called melting pots, and they are slowly losing touch of their native lands, which results in slowly losing their ancient roots, traditions, culture, and language as a result. This is why it's of vital importance to document and save their culture, heritage, and traditions. This book was written to capture their daily customs so that they can be preserved and passed on to their future generations for centuries to come.

It's very evident that Assyrians need to be given a state of their own in their heartland; they need to preserve themselves to connect to their lands, and continue to practice their ancient traditions in their homelands; they need to govern themselves and have their rights; they simply cannot rely on others to protect them. This has been clear throughout history and become more evident in recent years. The vast persecutions they have faced have brought them to the brink of extinction and all on the so-called watch of others to protect them. The Assyrians don't need anyone to protect them; they can protect and govern themselves.

Despite its ultimate demise, Assyria still speaks today, slowing unveiling herself for the world to see and to remind us of her glorious past.

THE ASSYRIAN LANGUAGE AND ALPHABET

The Akkadian language was the universal language in ancient Assyria, and scribes documented all their daily activities using cuneiform tablets. The writing system used at that time was comprised of wedge-shaped characters to denote meaning in the ancient writing styles. This was the preferred language of the Assyrian kings. It was written on soft clay tablets using a stylus-writing tool, which then were dried in the sun to harden. It is thanks to these cuneiform tablets that have survived through the ages that we know so much about the Assyrian people today and their vast empire in the ancient past.

For centuries, these stones lay beneath the earth, just waiting to be discovered. Over the centuries, over 230,000 cuneiform tablets have been dug up and brought to Britain, France, and other countries to be translated. It's thanks to these countries, they still silently tell the Assyrian story, while destruction and conquests engulfed them throughout time in their homelands. Their conquerors have attempted to destroy everything that makes up of their memory and history in various historical events that have occurred throughout time and up to the present day.

Today Assyrians refer to Akkadian as their ancient language, *listana teequa*, and meaning "old language." The Assyrian people still speak this ancient language, but in a modernized and evolved form, which today is known as Assyrian.

Thorough history and modern times, clergy, historians, and scholars have given various other names to the Assyrian language as a result of the fall of the Assyrian empire. These misnomer labels for their language include Babylonian, Aramaic, Syriac, Suryoyo, Chaldean, and Surit. However, it's important to note Surit is derived from Asurit.

According to some scholars, Aramaic was the second language spoken at that time, which was accepted by the Assyrians and quickly became the lingua franca at around 600 BC. It became the official language of the Persian dynasty around 550 BC; however, this topic still needs to be researched in more depth. Many ancient peoples of the time who spoke the language were of different ethnicities, and each group like to refer to the same language by a different name

Some professors argue that the language is called Aramaic, while others say it's Assyrian. New names for their language have popped up throughout time, and it's become more alarming in recent years. This just confirms that the continuation to wipe out a people's true name and their language is real. It is of utmost importance for the people of Assyrian descent to learn more about their history and language and, most importantly, to preserve their ancient language. It's become imperative to house more of their historical data so that Assyrians can research and understand more about their glorious past. These misnomer names for their language and identity are becoming a vital problem because they are distorting facts and true history. Assyrian history is scattered around the world in various museums and schools, with some in the possession of private collectors, which makes it difficult for Assyrian people to learn more about their history. However, it's thanks to these museums that have preserved their artifacts over time that today we can see and trace back their lineage to thousands of years ago.

Scholars have consistently written that Aramaic replaced Akkadian language, and some even go as far as saying the Akkadian language is dead and the language has vanished. Yet that is not the case completely; the Assyrian people still use over fifteen hundred words of Akkadian as part of their language today, so this is clear evidence that the language is not completely dead or replaced. There are various cuneiform tablets that include references that show that Akkadian was still spoken up to 530 BC. Examples are the clay tablets in Cyrus II, Darius II, and Xerxes I[4]. The official language in these tablets is Akkadian, so this contradicts the Aramaic timeline.

In the book *Glossary of Akkadian-Assyrian Words Still Used in Qaraqosh Dialect*,[5] author Mazin Zara brilliantly documents over fifteen hundred Akkadian words still used in the modern Assyrian language today. This book is currently only published in Iraq and Qaraqosh is a dialect of Assyrian; the Assyrian language has various dialects like other languages in the world, all languages have different dialects. So given that there are about fifteen hundred words of Akkadian (ancient Assyrian) still in use today and spoken in modern Assyrian language, this alone is proof enough that the language was never replaced.

The written language with wedge-shaped characters was replaced with the alphabetical system to make it easier to memorize and write. Their spoken language evolved over time, while still maintaining hundreds of their original words they still use Today and can be clearly traced back to cuneiform stone writings. This development of going from cuneiform letters to script-style writing has led some to believe that the Assyrians replaced their language, when that is not the case. As with other languages in the world, they evolve over time; especially a language that is over seven thousand years old, it will certainly evolve. For example, when comparing Old English to modern English, they seem very different, and we would find it very difficult to understand or speak Old English, but we still call it English.

---

[4] https://cdli.ucla.edu.

[5] Mazin Zara, *Glossary of Akkadian/Assyrian Words Still Used in Qaraqosh Dialect* (2020).

Assyrian language today is written from left to right, and the six hundred Akkadian cuneiform symbols were written left to right as well. The modern Assyrian alphabet consists of an easier alphabetical system of twenty-two characters, which the Assyrians call Alap-Bet, and the English letters that followed is called by the similar name of *alphabet.*

The Jewish people, who are also an ancient people, use the same writing style and alphabet as Assyrians; however, their alphabetic symbols have a more square shape format, but the pronunciation of their alphabet is the same as the Assyrian alphabet. The Hebrew formal name for their alphabet is called "Ktav Ashurit," literally meaning "writing Assyrian." However, they call their language Aramaic, or Hebrew. There are various same words used by both peoples, and linguistic scholars would be more versed in the intricacies of these two languages.

The Assyrian people speak two main dialects. They are identified as the Eastern Assyrian dialect and the Western Assyrian dialect. Examples of these dialects would be as follows: *hello* in Eastern Assyrian is "shlama," and in Western Assyrian, it's "shlomo." There are several other Assyrian dialects within these two main dialects, and the dialect spoken is dependent on their geographic location.

The University of Chicago spent ninety years and millions of dollars documenting the ancient Assyrian language with the help of scholars worldwide. More information can be reviewed at the University of Chicago website. Today, Assyrians speak a modernized version of the language while still maintaining some ancient words. (https://oi.uchicago.edu/research/publications/assyrian-dictionary-oriental-institute-university-chicago-cad).

Stone carvings using cuneiform writing confirm that Assyrian kings called their language Līšānu Akkadītu, which translates exactly to "language Akkadian."

The Akkadian cuneiform inscriptions of King Sargon of Akkad and the kings that followed called their language līšānu aššūrītu, literally "language Ashurian," today called Assyrian by the Greeks.

Today Assyrians still refer to their language as Lishanu Asurit or Lishanu Ashuraya or Lishanu Surit, which all translates to "Assyrian language."

Assyrian king Ashurbanipal was a known scholar, and on tablet 002, he indicates specifically the languages he knew, which were Sumerian and Akkadian.[6]

This is an unedited version of his entire cuneiform tablet that has been translated by scholars.

Neo-Assyrian Period (668–631 BC)
Provenience—Nineveh
Language—Akkadian

Cuneiform Tablet, Ashurbanipal, 002 Translation

[I, Ashurbanipal, great king, strong king, king of the world, king of Assyria, king of the four quarters (of the world)],

missing 8 lines

[military governor of B]abylon, king of [the land of Sumer and Akkad, grands]on of Sennacherib, [great] kin[g, strong king, king of the world, king of Assyria], [de]scen[de]nt of Sargon (II), gre[at] king, [strong king, king of the world, king of Assyri]a, [military governo]r of Babylon, king of the land of S[umer and Akka]d —

[(The god) Aššur], the father of the gods, a roya[l] destiny [determined as my lot] while (I was) in my mother's womb; [the goddess Mul]lissu, the great mother, called [my name] for ruling over the land and people; [the god] Ea (and) the goddess Bēletilī skillf[ully] fashioned a form fit for lordship; [the god] Sîn, the pure god, made a favorable sign visible

---

6   Ashurbanipal Assyrian Tablet 002 [via RINAP/RINAP5, http://oracc.org/rinap/Q003772/.

regarding my exercising kingship; [the gods Šamaš (and) Adad] placed at my disposal the lore of the diviner, a craft that cannot be changed; [the god Mardu]k, the sage of the gods, granted me a broad mind (and) extensive knowledge as a gift; the god Nabû, the scribe of everything, bestowed on me the precepts of his craft as a present; the gods Ninurta (and) Nergal endowed my body with power, virility, (and) unrivalled strength.

I learned [the c]raft of the sage Adapa, the secret (and) hidden lore of all of the scribal arts. I am able to recognize celestial and terrestrial [om]ens (and) can discuss (them) in an assembly of scholars. I am capable of arguing with expert diviners about (the series) "If the liver is a mirror image of the heavens." I can resolve complex (mathematical) divisions (and) multiplications that do not have a(n easy) solution. I have read cunningly written text(s) in obscure Sumerian (and) Akkadian that are difficult to interpret. I have carefully examined inscriptions on stone from before the Deluge that are sealed, stopped up, (and) confused.

With (carefully) selected companion(s), this is how I spent all of my days: I cantered on thoroughbreds, rode stallions that were raring to go; I [h]eld a bow (and) made arrows fly as befits a warrior; I threw quivering lances as if they were javelins; I took the reins (of a chariot) like a charioteer (and) made the rims of the wheels spin; I . . . arītu shields (and) kabābushields like a engineer. I am proficient in the best technical lore of all specialists, everyone of them.

At the same time, I was learning proper lordly behavior, becoming familiar with the ways of kingship. I stood before the king who had engendered me, regularly giving orders to officials. N[o] governor was appointed without me, no prefect installed without my consent.

The father who had engendered me constantly saw heroism that the great gods had determined for me. By the command of the great gods, he (Esarhaddon) greatly preferred me over the assembly of my <<older>> brothers. With regard to my exercising kingship, he appealed to (the god) Aššur — the king of the gods (and) the lord of everything — beseeched the goddesses Mullissu (and) Šērū'a — the queen of goddesses (and) the lady of ladies — prayed to the gods Šamaš (and) Adad — the diviners of heaven (and) earth, judge(s) of the (four) quarters (of the world) — (and) [prayed devo]utly to the gods Nabû (and) Marduk — the ones who give scepter (and) throne, the ones who firmly establish kingship — [saying] "Proclaim one of my sons as [my] succes[sor in] your assembly. [. . .]

Lacuna

[Before] the great gods of the heavens [and netherworld], he (Esarhaddon) reinforced, wrote out, (and) establi[shed tr]eaties [for future days]. In the month Ayyāru (II), the month of the god Ea — the lord of humankind, the one who fashioned [the physique of my royal majesty] — I entered the House of Succession, a place of instruction and coun[sel], and by the command of (the god) Aššur — the father of the gods — (and) the god Marduk — the lord of lords (and) the king of the god[s] — he (Esarhaddon) elevated me above the (other) sons of the king (and) called my name for king[ship].

Upon my entry into the palace, the entire camp rejoiced, it was filled with joyous celebrations. Nobles and eunuchs were happy, they heeded the words of [my] li[ps]. Before the king, the father who had engendered me, I would intercede on their behalf, I would annul (their) si[ns].

The great gods looked with pleasure upon my good deeds and, by their exalted command, I gladly sat on the throne

23

of the father who had engendered me. Nobles (and) eunuchs required my lordship; they loved my exercising kingship. Being happy at the mention of my venerated name, the four quarters (of the world) rejoiced.

Kings of the Upper (and) Low[er] Sea(s), servants who belonged to the father who had engendered me, kept sending glad tidings to m[e] regarding my exercising the kingship. The enemies' readied weapons eased to rest, they dissolved [their] well-organized battle array. They laid their sharpened axes to rest, they unstrung their ar[med] bows. Brazen men who devised war against those who did not bow down to them calmed down.

Within city and household, no one took anything from his neighbor by for[ce]. Throughout the entire land, not a single young man commit[ted] a crime. A traveler on his own walked in safe[ty] on remo[te] road(s). There were no thieves (or) murderers, violent cri[mes] did not occur.

The lands dwelt in peace[ful] abode(s), the four quarters (of the world) were placid [li]ke the finest oil. The Elamites sent me mes[sages] to inquire about my well-being and they were . . . By the command of the god Marduk, [the great] lord, I had no rival, no one to oppose me.

ruling rest is missing

During my first regnal year, [whe]n the god Marduk, the lord of everything, [placed] in my hands dominion over [. . .], I took hold of the garment of his great divinity, was assiduous towards his places of worship, (and) constantly appealed to (and) beseeched his great divinity regarding the journey of his divinity, (saying):

24

"Remember Babylon, which you yourself destroyed in your anger. Relent (and) turn [your] att[ention] back to Esagil, the palace of your lordship. You have abandoned your city for too long (and) have taken up residence in a place not befitting you. You are the supreme one of the gods, O Marduk. Give the command to travel to Šuann[a] (Babylon). At [your ho] ly command, which cannot be changed, may your entry into Esag[il] be established. Who [. . .]?"

missing lines

[(5) m]e, [Ashurbanipal . . .]. (9) Exorcist(s) . . . [. . .], (10) lamentation-singers [. . .] with man[zû-drums (and) ḫalḫallatu-drums], (11) singers with lyres [were singing] the praise of [his] lordshi[p]. (7) Šamaš-šuma-ukīn, (my) favorite brother whom I dedica[ted to the god Marduk], (8) taking the hand of his great divinity, was marching be[fore him].

(13) From the quay of Baltil (Aššur) to the quay Babylon, wherever they stopped for the n[ight], sheep were butchered, bulls were slaughtered, armannu-aromatics were scattered, . . . [. . .] . . . They brought bef[ore him] everything there is for morning (and) evening meals, and (then) piles of brushwood were lit (and) torches ignited. [The]re was lig[ht] for each league. All of my troops, like a rainbow, were arranged in a circle, there were festivities day and night.

The deities the Lady of Agade, Nanāya, Uṣur-amāssa, Hanibiya, (and) Adapa, had taken up residence on the bank of the river, waiting for the king of the gods, the lord of lords. The god Nergal, the most powerful of the gods, came out of Emeslam, his princely residence, approached the quay of Babylon amidst a joyous celebration, drawing near in safety. The god Nabû, the pre-eminent heir, took the direct ro[ad] from Borsippa. The god Šamaš rushed from Sippar, emitting radiance onto Babylon. The gods of the land of Sumer and Akkad, like tired foals, looked exhausted.

Among the fruit trees of the luxuriant gardens of Karzagina, a pur[e] place, before the stars of heaven — Ea, Šamaš, Asalluḫi, Bēlet-ilī, Kusu, the [. . .] gods — through the craft of the sage, "the wa[shing of] the mouth," [. . .], he (Marduk) entered [inside] it (Esagil) and took up residence on (his) [eternal] d[ais].

Be[fore him], I offered [choic]e prized bulls (and) fattened sheep. I presented to him f[ish and bird(s)], the abundance of the apsû. I made [. . .], honey, (and) oil flow like a downpour. As my gifts, I presented (him) with [. . .] (and) extensive gifts.

I placed at their service [ramku-priests], [p]ašīšu-priests, ecstatics. [. . . those who] have mast[er]ed (their) [entire] craft.

[. . .] . . . was pleased [. . .] like [. . .]

Lacuna

At that time, I had a stele bearing my name made and I engraved image(s) of the great gods, my lords, on it (and) placed before them an image of my royal majesty beseeching their divinity. I had the praise of the god Marduk, my lord, and my good deeds inscribed upon it and I [left] (it) for the future.

As for m[e, Ashurbanipal], he determined [a favora]ble [destiny] as my lot.

. . . [. . .]
From Eḫur[saggalkurkurra]
Remnants [. . .]
The gods of the land of Sumer [and Akkad]

His neck
M[e], Ashurbanipal
He approached
Šamaš-šuma-ukīn
[The hand of] his divinity
[E]xorcist(s)
[Lamen]tation-singers
[Sin]gers
[. . .] Maumuša
[From the quay of B]altil (Assur)

This cuneiform tablet is another source that I find interesting; it lists all the languages spoken at that time. Although what is written on the tablet in some cases may appear odd, it was written thousands of years ago and it does provide a glimpse of the languages known at this specific time frame.

Middle Babylonian Period (1400–1000 BC)
Provenience—Emar
Tablet collection and location—Institute of Culture, University of Tokyo, Japan
Language—Akkadian

Cuneiform Tablet Known Languages, #10c Translation

r ii 7	*tongue that is not straight*
r ii 8	*Akkadian language*
r ii 9	*Amorite language*
r ii 10	*Sutean language*
r ii 11	*Subarean language*
r ii 12	*Elamite language*
r ii 13	*Gutian language*
r ii 14	*enemy language*
r ii 15	*foreign language*
r ii 16	*enemy languages*

r ii 17	*evil language*
r ii 18	*hateful language*
r ii 19	*translator = answer*
r ii 20	*harmonic language*
r ii 21	*blocked(?) tongue*
r ii 22	*huge tongue*
r ii 23	*individual languages(?)*
r ii 24	*good tongue*
r ii 25	*tongue that is not good*
r ii 26	*tongue hanging out (of the mouth)*
r ii 27	*language of Sumer*
r ii 28	*Language of Sumer and Akkad*
r ii 29	*Sumerian*
r ii 30	*language of slavery*
r ii 31	*chosen tongue*
r ii 32	*tongues in unison*
r ii 33	*tongue twisted*
r ii 34	*language of strife*

The following tablet, currently housed at the British Museum, still needs to be translated. It reflects the Aramaic alphabet, yet it's still written in cuneiform wedge-shaped symbols. Some have suggested that the Assyrian alphabet is called Aramaic because of the new written script style they developed that went from cuneiform wedge-shaped symbols to the alphabetic twenty-two symbols; however, this tablet shows us that Aramaic was in cuneiform as well at this time.

The Assyrians changed their writing from cuneiform symbols to the alphabet because it was easier to write and remember, but they had the same meaning in their words; it evolved over time. This tablet confirms that Aramaic at this time was cuneiform symbols, and not the twenty-two–letter alphabet scripts.

Late Babylonian Period (500 BC)

Tablet collection and location—British Museum, London, UK

Language—Aramaic

Description

Clay tablet. Aramaic alphabet, 500 BC,[7] written in cuneiform signs in two columns; a third column contains professional names.

Here are some very simple examples of Akkadian words still in use today in modern Assyrian language:

Akkadian	Assyrian
Asur/Ashur	Ashur is a name and is still used
Kalhu	Kalhu or Kalu means "bride;" it also refers to the city.
Kaltu	Kaltu means "daughter-in-law."
Ahatu	Khatu or Ahatu means "sister."

---

[7] British Museum, number 25636.

Here is an example of the Assyrian language today:

Akkadian/Old Assyrian	Modern Assyrian	Meaning
Abu	Babu	their father

To simplify this further, "their father," written in modern Assyrian using the Assyrian alphabet, is as follows:

Babu would be written as follows: Bet Alap Bet Yod = Babu.

Later, the Assyrian language went through the dropping of the letter *A* in some words so often they would refer to as their language as Syriac and Syriac script, and later became *Surit*. So in essence throughout time, Asyria became Syria, or *Syriac*, and *Asurit* became *Surit*. These are all derived from *Asyria* and *Ashur*. Later in modern history their native lands were divided in multiple countires we know today as Iraq, parts of Iran, Turkey and Syria.

The Assyrian alphabet and language teachers often refer to the writing styles as either Estrangelo, or Swadaya, and these differ only in the formation of five letters of the alphabet (Alap, Daleth, Heh, Resh, and Tau). The other seventeen letters are identical.

Estrangle or Estrangelo is the alphabet script-type that Assyrians refer to as the older script writing style.

Swadaya is the modern alphabet script-type that Assyrians use today in their writing. This is an example of Swadaya writing style:

Letter Name	Letter	Translation
Alap	**ܐ**	A
Beyth	**ܒ**	B
Gamal	**ܓ**	G
Dalath	**ܕ**	D
Heh	**ܗ**	H

Waw	ఴ	W
Zayn	�	Z
Kheyth	ఴ	Kh, Ḥ
Teyth	✦	T
Yod	ఴ	Y, I
Kap	ళ	K
Lamad	ఽ	L
Meem	౧	M
Noon	౨	N
Simkath	౮	S
'Eh	౺	E
Peh	ఽ	P, F
Sadeh	౹	S
Qop	ౡ	Q
Resh	ౠ	R
Sheen	౼	Sh, Š
Taw	౸	T, Th

This ancient language is still spoken and written today by the Assyrian people, but it's endangered because the majority of Assyrians live in diaspora, and they have adopted the languages of the countries in which they currently live in. Their second language currently dominates what they speak today, and as a result, it's becoming more difficult to preserve their native language.

The Assyrian kings referred to their language as either Līšānu Akkadītu or Lisanu Asurit, meaning "language Akkadian" or "language Ashurian," so it's important to keep the integrity of this ancient language and its name, especially since the Assyrians have suffered so much to keep it.

ASSYRIAN AND BABYLONIAN ROYAL SYMBOL

The royal Assyrian and Babylonian symbol was used in the ancient cities, it appears as motifs on various items, such as the kings' bracelets, bejewelled crowns, and protective deities. Wearing it signified divinity and royalty. All Assyrian kings wore this symbol, it was later used on religious decorations such as borders around their ziggurats, palaces, including the Ishtar Gate of Babylon.

Some Assyrians have inferred the royal symbol was from the god Shamasha, the solar deity who was the power of light over darkness, and the god of justice and equality; he was judge of gods and men. It was thought wearing his symbol was an act of protection, and his blessings were placed where the chamomile flower grows; and in northern Assyria, the chamomile flower grows everywhere.

Assyrian king Ashurbanipal is displayed here wearing the sacred symbol while out hunting lions. Their crowns had a heavy ribbon on the back, here you see a bit of it carrying the same decoration as his hat or crown.

Reign 668–627 BC

King Ashurbanipal and this picture is the reverse side of the same scene you see the ribbon on the back of the hat or crown. Today, when Assyrians get married, the priest uses ribbons on their crowns that bind them. (This will be discussed more in the marriage section.)

These Assyrian deities are also known as Apkallu or angels wearing the sacred symbol. These deities with wings are a symbol of divinity and were carved in most of the Assyrian palaces and these are some of the earliest depictions of angels in ancient history.

The deities with wings could have also represented the Assyrian kings since it was thought that the kings were given from heaven and the gods. So often you will find that the features of the deities and the kings are very similar, and this is why you see the similarities in the appearance of the king and the angels; they often appear the same. Symbols of divinity are the wings, and some have crowns with horns; the wearing of the crown with horns is considered to have divine power. Here you can see the royal symbol engraved in the headpiece and the bracelet; these were made with the finest gold and precious stones. These Assyrian steles all have cuneiform writings on them, and most of them still need to be translated.

The king or deity with wings and horned crown displays a meaning of divinity with the royal sacred flower that he is holding, and it's also discplayed on his royal bracelet; you can also see the carved inscriptions in the middle of the stele.

Most of the time, the Assyrian kings were often depicted in a negative manner; however, it was quite the contrary. Here you will find in the king's own words—from the cuneiform tablet 03, 668 BC—his intentions, "In order for the strong might not harm the weak" (Ashurbanipal [reign 668–627 BC]).

In Assyrian king Ashurbanipal's (reign 668–627 BC) own words, written before his empire fell:

> *I (re-)established the privileged status of Babylon (and) appointed Šamaš<šuma>ukīn, my favorite brother, to the kingship of Babylon in order that the strong might not harm the weak.*[8]

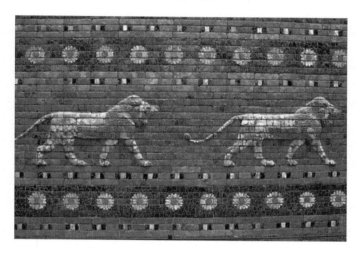

Neo-Assyrian Period (668–631 BC)
Provenance—Babylon
Tablet collection and location—British Museum, London, UK
Language—Akkadian
Cuneiform tablet Ashurabanipal Babylonian 03

Cuneiform Tablet, Ashurbanipal Babylonian, 03 Translation

> *For the god Marduk, king of all the Igīgū gods and Anunnakū gods, creator of heaven and netherworld, who*

---

[8] http://oracc.org/ribo/Q003801/.

*establishes archetypes (and) dwells in Esagil, lord of Babylon,
great lord, my lord:*

*I, Ashurbanipal, great king, strong king, king of the world,
king of Assyria, king of the four quarters (of the world); son
of Esarhaddon, great king, strongking, king of the world,
king of Assyria, viceroy of Babylon, kingof the land of
Sumer and Akkad, who (re)settled Babylon, (re)built Esagil,
renovated the sanctuaries of all the cult centers, constantly
established appropriate procedures in them, and (re)confirmed
their interrupted regular offerings, (who) restored the rites
(and) rituals accordingto the old pattern; grandson of
Sennacherib, great king, strong king, king of the world,
king of Assyria, I —*

*During my reign, the great lord, the god Marduk, entered
Babylon amidst rejoicing and took up his residence in the
eternal Esagil. I(re)confirmed the regular offerings for Esagil
and the gods of Babylon. I (re-established the privileged
status of Babylon (and) appointed Šamaššumaukīn, my
favorite brother, to the kingship of Babylon in order that the
strong might not harm the weak. I decorated Esagil ("House
whose Top is High") with silver, gold, (and) precious stones
and made Eumuša ("House of Counsel") glisten like the
stars (lit. "writing") of the firmament.*

*At that time, (with regard to) ImgurEnlil ("The God
Enlil Showed Favor"), the (city) wall of Babylon, (and)
NēmetEnlil ("Bulwark of the God Enlil"), its outer wall,
which had become old and buckled (and) collapsed, in order
to increase the security of Esagil and the (other) sanctuaries
of Babylon, with the strength of my labor forces I had
NēmetEnlil, its outer wall, built quickly anew with the work
of the god Kulla and I refitted its gates. I had (new) doors
made and fixed (them) in its gateways O (you) future prince*

during whose reign this work falls into disrepair, question skilled craftsmen! (Re)build ImgurEnlil, the (city) wall, (and) NēmetEnlil, the outer wall, according to their ancient specifications! Look atmy royal inscription, anoint (it) with oil, offer a sacrifice, (and) place (my royal inscription) with your (own) royal inscription! The god Marduk will (then) listen to your prayers.

(But) as for the one who destroys my inscribed name or the name of my favorite (brother) by some crafty device, (or) does not place my royal inscription with his (own) royal inscription, may the god Marduk King of everything glare at him angrily and make his name and his descendants disappear from the lands.

In this cuneiform tablet, called prism 106 Esarhaddon, King Esarhaddon talks about rebuilding Babylon and gathering his people.

I am the one who (re)built Babylon, (re)constructed Esagil, renewed (its) gods and goddesses, completed (its) shrines, (re) confirmed (its) sattukku offerings, (and) who gathered its (Babylon's) scattered people.[9]

Neo-Assyrian period (672–670 BC)
Provenance—Babylon
Tablet collection and location—British Museum, London, UK
Language—Akkadian

Cuneiform Tablet, Esarhaddon, 106 Translation

Esarhaddon, king of the world, king of Assyria, governor of (i 5) Babylon, king of Sumer and Akkad, pious prince who reveres the gods Nabûand Marduk

Before my time the great lord, the god Marduk, became angry, trembled (with rage), and was furious with Esagil (i 15) and Babylon; his [he]art was full of rage. Because of the wrath in his heart and his bad temper, Esagil and Babylon became a wasteland and turned into ruins.

Its (Babylon's) gods and goddesses became frightened, abandoned their cellas, and went up to the heavens. The people living in it (Babylon) were distributed among the (foreign) riffraff (and) became slaves.

At the beginning of my kingship, in my first year, when I sat in greatness on (my) royal throne (and) (ii 10) (when) they (the gods) entrusted me with the lordship of the lands, the heart of the great divine lord, the god Marduk, was

---

[9] http://oracc.org/rinap/Q003335/.

appeased, (ii 15) his mood was soothed; he became reconciled with Esagil and Babylon, (both of) which he had punished.

As for me, Esarhaddon, the servant who reveres his great divinity, it occurred to [me] (and) my heart prompted me to (re)build Esagil and Babylon, [re]novate (its) gods (ii 30) and goddesses,

[comple]te (its) shrines, (and) (re)con[firm (its) sattukku offerings]. (iii 5) I was encouraged and ordered the (re)building.

I gathered the peoples of the lands conquered by me and had them take up hoe (and) basket. I mix[ed] (the mud for) its re[v]etm[ent] with fine oil, honey, ghee, (iii 15) kurunnu-[wine], muttinnu-wine (and) pure mountain beer. (iii 20) In order to show the people his great divinity and to inspire awe (in) his lordship, (iii 25) I raised a basket onto my head and carried (it) myself.

I had its bricks made for a whole year in brickmolds of ivory, ebony, boxwood, (and) musukkannu wood.

I built a new (and) [co]mpleted Esagil, the palace of the gods, together with its shrines, from its foundations to its battlements. (iii 45) I made (it) greater than before, raised (it)up, glorified (it), (and) made (it) glisten like the stars (lit. "writing") of the firmament. I filled (it) with splendor (making it) an object of wonder for all of the people.

I refurbished the gods and goddesses who lived in it (and) (iv 1) had (them) dwell on their daises as an eternal dwelling. I (re)confirmed theirinter[rup]ted sattukku offerings. I had [whatever] furnishings (iv 10) [were ne]eded for Esagil [and] its [sh]rines made from gold, si[lver], and bronze, and I placed (them) in their midst.

I had Babylon, (which was measured by) the aslu-cubit checked by the gods, Imgur-Enlil, its wall, (and) Nēmetti-Enlil, its outer wall, built anew with the work of the god Kulla and I raised (them) like mountains.

I am the one who (re)built Babylon, (re)constructed Esagil, renewed (its) gods and goddesses, completed (its) shrines, (re)confirmed (its)sattukku offerings, (and) who gathered its (Babylon's) scattered people.

May the Enlil of the gods, the god Marduk, (v 5) and the goddess Zarpanītu, the queen, look with joy upon the work of my good deeds and order the prolongation of my days, (v 10) (and) discuss my years to be many; may they decree as my fate the protection of my offspring, the increase of (v 15) my progeny, the expansion of my family so that they branch out widely (v 20) like father and mother, may they come over to my side in battle and warfare; may they come to my aid; (and) may they make my weapons rise up (and) kill my enemies.

Let me attain whatever my heart desires (and) may they allow me to stand in victory (and) triumph over my enemies; let me squash all of my enemies (v 35) like ants; let him (the god Marduk) make the foundation of the throne of my priestly office be as secure as a great mountain; (v40) (and) let my reign endure as long as the foundations of Esagil and Babylon. May all of the great gods who sit on daises (v 45) in Babylon bless my kingship until far off days and may they order security for my reign forever.

[I had] foundation inscriptions made of silver, gold, lapis lazuli, alabaster, basalt, pendû-stone, elallu-stone (v 10) (and) white limestone, (as well as) inscribed objects of baked clay, and (vi 15) (then) I wrote the might of the great hero,

the god Marduk, (and) the deeds that I (text: "he") [had] done, my pious work. [I p]laced (these inscriptions) in the foundations (and) left (them) for far-off days.

In future days, in far-off days, may one of the kings, my descendants, whom the king of the gods, the god [Mar] duk, names to rule [the land] and people, (vi 30) [read] an inscription [written in] my name, and anoint (it) with oil, make an offering, (vi 35) (and) [re]turn (it) to its place. The god Marduk, the king of the gods, will (then) hear his prayers.

(As for) the one who changes (an inscription) written in my name, defaces my representations, destroys my handiwork, may the great divine lord, the god Marduk, (vi 50) glare at him angrily among all of the rulers, and make his name (and) his descendant(s) disappear from the land. May he have no pity on him forever.

Accession year of Esarhaddon, king of Assyria.

Ancient city of Babylon.

One of the first cities ever built in human history and one of the most prestigious cities in ancient times, the city of Ashur was the capital of Assyria and the greatest empire the world had ever seen at the time, and today these are the remnants of the ancient city of Ashur, which is over seven thousand years old.

City of Ashur

In the 1980s, the Iraq government excavated the city of Ashur, and they found an entire palace hidden underneath all the mounds of soil that throughout time had slowly buried once a great ancient past. They found a fortune of gold and artifacts, and the gold was apparently moved to Baghdad Museum, but its whereabouts is now unknown.

City of Assur in current-day Iraq.

The royal symbol still grows wild, which reminds us of her hidden glory from the ancient past to present day.

The ziggurat of Ashur in current-day Iraq is next to the Ashur palace. The ziggurats were places of worship and would normally include an image of the god or gods. They had water basins for blessings, and often the Assyrian kings would order animal sacrifices to the gods as well as offerings such as full-course meals, the finest jewels, and the finest fragrant oils and gold. Since this was the Zigguart of Ashur, it would normally be dedicated to the Ashur god.

WORLD RELIGIONS AND
THE BEGINNING

$\mathcal{G}$ods, and world religions, the Tower of Babel, and Ashurism are the first evidence that display religious symbols. These were found in Assyria, carved in stone for Ashurnasirpal II; his reign was 883–859 BC. This stele, now housed in the British Museum was found in the Assyrian king's royal palace at Kalhu, modern-day Nimrud; it displays the king pointing to the five gods as a sign of respect and as a gesture that only they are above him.

When you examine the Assyrian artifacts, you will find cuneiform writing on them, each depicting a story that the king wanted to document with a direct connection to its history and culture. Unfortunately, there are several that still need to be translated. Museums and universities helped in translating some of these complex ancient texts to decipher what is actually depicted on the images; there are still several tablets and steles that need to be translated.

The horned helmet represents divinity with the supreme god Ashur. The Shamash god is displayed as the sunstar disc; notice, in the middle, the ancient cross of Assyria. Today this is reflected in Christian symbols.

The moon god, also known as Sin, is displayed with the crescent moon and today is used for the main symbol of Islam.

The fourth symbol is the thunderbolt, which symbolizes god Adad and represents the storms with thunder and also the god of war, hunting, and the south wind. The god of thunder also became a popular symbol for the ancient Greeks, with their god Zeus; and the Tibetan Buddhists and various other religions also used the thunderbolt as their religious symbol at some point.

The fifth symbol represents the goddess Ishtar and the eight-pointed star, which, some scholars note, later becomes the symbol of Judaism.

Although all these religions have their own perspectives on how they acquired their religious symbols, you can find around the king's neck a chain with the cross in the center, along with other religious symbols. The main religious belief of the Assyrian people today is Christianity, but the use of the cross as one of their religious symbols appeared in this stele, which was created in 860 BC, long before Christianity was born.

There are several archaeological evidence that prove that the Assyrians believed in god even before Jesus came to earth or before the cross became a symbol of Christ and his crucifixion.

Although the Assyrians in ancient times were pagans, they still believed in one supreme god, who was their nation's god, Ashur.

The three main religions in society today are Christianity, Islam, and Judaism, but their symbols are clearly displayed on this stele, which predates the Bible, the Quran, and the Torah. In fact, some of the stories in these books have been found in Assyria, in King Ashurbanipal's famous library and thousands of years prior to when they were written in these holy books.

Although the majority of the Assyrian people today are Christian, some still adhere to their original religious roots of Ashurism although a much smaller number. There are also small numbers of Assyrians who practice Judaism and Islam, and some are atheists. The Assyrian people still use the same religious symbols today.

Ashurnasirpal II reigned from 883 to 859 BC. This stele is now housed in the British Museum.

This stele displays today's three main religions with the cross around the king's neck; emblems of Christianity, Judaism, and Islam are all depicted in this stele.

Further examination displays cuneiform writing on them, yet to be translated; and normally each stele had ancient writings on them, each telling a story.

The capital of the Assyrian empire the city of Ashur was considered a holy city. Ashur was the center of worship; modern and ancient terrorists destroyed a lot of it, but there is still hope that if the area is excavated, there will be information that can lead to extraordinary findings about world religions. This is one of the areas where religions first started.

The Assyrians had ziggurats, and the famous tower of Babylon was built as high as possible; these towers were built so that worshipers could go to the highest point to pray to their god so they were closer to the heavens. It was also thought that on special occasions, their god would come down to earth, so they built them high so that god could come down and people would go see him. They also had a gazebo type of structure right on the top of the ziggurat or tower. Scholars have debated the reason for these towers, and although other stories define other reasons, that is not the case; and as more artifacts are translated, it becomes more evident what the true purpose was for the tower of Babylon and the ziggurats, it was for prayer, worship, and for their gods to come down and visit from the heavens.

In reconstructed pictures, you can see a sheltered top point, which was used for prayers.

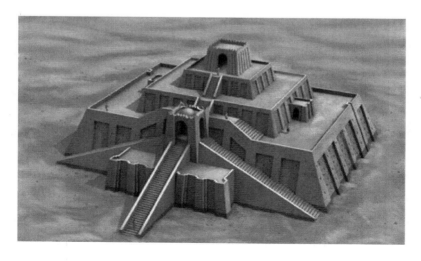

This is what the ziggurat looks like today, with the damage over time.

The Assyrians always believed in a higher power, a supreme god above other gods, which was Ashur, and the Assyrian people were named Ashuraye after their supreme god. Their main city was called Ashur, and they followed what is called the Ashurism religion. They had several deities, but only one supreme god.

It's important to note that these relics are some of the oldest in the world to display religious symbols.

Assyrians in modern times are predominantly Christian; they accepted Christianity in the AD first century. Prior to that, the Assyrians already had a belief system; they believed in a higher power and a supreme god, and this is why it was so easy for them to convert from Ashurism to Christianity when they heard of the miracles of Jesus Christ.

Although the majority of Assyrians today are Christians, in most recent years, it has come to light that there are Assyrians of all faiths, and it was recently discovered that there are an estimated 5,000 Assyrians that converted to Islam and still practice this religion today.

There are also about 500,000 who practice Judaism. There are very small numbers of Assyrians that are atheists, and there are some that still practice their ancient religion, which is Ashurism. Throughout time, some have lost touch with their roots, but slowly they are finding their way back.

The main Christian religious affiliations for the Assyrian people follow these church denominations:

Ancient Church of the East
The Holy Apostolic Catholic Assyrian Church of the East
The Syriac Catholic Church
The Syriac Orthodox Church
The Roman Catholic Church
The Assyrian Pentecostal Church
The Assyrian Evangelical Church

The Assyrians that follow the Eastern Churches and the Catholic Churches speak the Eastern Assyrian dialect of the Assyrian language.

The Assyrians who follow the Syriac, Jacobites, Armorites, or Suryoyo churches speak the Western Assyrian dialect of the Assyrian language.

During the Persian Achaemenid Empire, the name "Chaldean" lost its meaning with reference to a particular ethnicity such as the ancient Chaldeans.

Later by some earlier church clergy, Latin and Greek authors the name Chaldean referred to Catholic Assyrians.

The true Chaldean ethnicity is the people that are now called Sabeans/Mandaeans; these are the true ancient Chaldean people. One does not need to go far to determine this; just go and speak with them—they can tell you their ancient history.

A large part of the Assyrian Catholic congregation comes from the Assyrian Baz region in Iraq, known as Basnaye; some are also from the town of Alquosh (these Assyrian people are known as Alquoshnaye), and some are from the town of Zakho (known as Zakhonaye).

This is similar to Assyrians that follow Judaism being called Jewish rather than *Assyrian*.

There are various historical documents to confirm the religious historical roots of the Assyrian people, and a good place to start your research is at the Vatican.

Assyrians have faced vast persecution for their identity in their homeland, and many have tried to destroy and erase it, and this now has become a crisis because this has now followed them around the world, and they are being wiped out historically, politically, ethnically, and culturally, which is a bigger human rights issue.

These are church denominations and not labels for a people's ethnicitiy; this has caused some major confusion around the world. The only authority the church has on individuals is religion, and nothing else. In the end, each person is responsible for researching his or her own identity.

Some divisions can be attributed to certain church leaders; church leaders should maintain their focus on the Bible and the church and concentrate on preaching love and the Bible. Assyrians being wrongfully labeled strengthens the ethnic persecution they face in the Middle East and throughout the world.

Here are some designations and other names commonly used to wrongfully identify the Assyrian people by their religious affiliation:

- *Christian*: used by both the east and west church groups and also used by some people from the Middle East to differentiate them from others. This name has now followed them to the West and Europe, where the media continue to use these misnomer names to identify groups of Assyrian people. Christian is a religious affiliation and not an identity to be used to describe a people.
- *Chaldean*: used to identify the Assyrian people that follow the Catholic Church; coined when the conversion of Assyrian Catholics began. The ancient Chaldeans are ethnically Sabaeans-Mandaeans, which is why this is a misnomer.

- *Syriac*: this name developed when the Syriac language was coined by clergy to describe the Assyrian language and the church originated in the first-century CE. Syriacs follow the Syriac Orthodox Church and the Syriac Catholic Church. Syriac is derived from Asyria, but not many know this.
- *Suryoyo*: used by the Western Syriac Churches and Syriac Orthodox Churches.
- *Arameans: used by the Syriac Catholic Church of Israel.*

These errors are what writers today make when referring to Assyrians as merely religious denominations and not their true ethnicity. Calling someone by their religious affiliation totally marginalizes them, ignores their unique ethnic group, and strips them of their unique identity, culture, and traditions, which they can trace back to thousands of years before Christianity, Judaism, or Islam. So when referring to Assyrians, they need to called by their name, as Assyrians, and not by any religious denomination. Before they were Christians, they were Assyrians; they can change their religion, but they cannot change their ethnicity.

The Assyrians are a unique ethnic group and differ from all their neighbours; they are culturally, linguistically, historically, and genetically different. These groups that some people have divided into religious categories are all the same people; they all speak the same language, although they may have different dialects, but it is the same language. They share the same main beliefs, the same traditions, the same dances and ceremonies, and the same foods. Their physical features show they are of the same ethnic group; they are from the same historical religion. They are the same people.

You can't erase culture, as some have tried to do, by blowing up archaeological sites; you simply can't erase what comes directly from the earth. Those who have settled on Assyrian lands have tried over the centuries to make history disappear by blowing it up, building over it, or attempting to change it. However, there are entire countries that belong historically to Assyrians; if you peel back the earth, Assyria will still be there. The earth in native Assyrian lands has already started to reveal its history, which determines who was there before anyone else. Calling it something else will not make this go away or change historical facts. The Assyrians from modern to ancient times can trace their heritage and lineage as deeply engraved in stone, culturally and traditionally; and they still speak their ancient language, which is heavily infused by Akkadian words for centuries until today

THE ASSYRIAN TREE OF LIFE

*P*art of this stone relief of Ashurnasirpal II, 883–859 BC, that this chapter covers was sold at Christie's auction house for $31 million to a private collector in 2018. This relief belongs to the Assyrian people and should have never been sold. ISIS had control over parts of Iraq from 2014 to 2019, and the auction house had this relief listed for sale in 2018, after ISIS was taped destroying and stealing from ancient sites.

This relief was an integral part of the Assyrian people's history, heritage, and culture, which no one person can own, but Assyrian artifacts continue to be disbursed throughout the world. This contributes to their cultural genocide.

A nation's culture, heritage, and history—belonging to a people—should not be sold. These sales contribute to the terrorist organization's incentive to blow up ancient sites and sell ancient reliefs in black markets. The most recent examples of this was the city of Kalhu, modern-day Nimrud, which was blown up after they took everything they could to sell; and several sites around Mosul and the Nineveh province sites, ISIS just destroyed and looted to sell off for profit. This has continued with the erasures of the fabric of Assyrian people, and this is especially critical when there have been many documented attempts to wipe Assyrians out of history itself.

Assyrian artifacts need to be in museums for everyone to learn from, see and enjoy.

Stele of Ashurnasirpal II, 883–859 BC, sold at Christie's auction house to a private collector in 2018 for $31 million.

The sacred Assyrian Tree of Life was very significant to Assyrians; it is depicted on many archaeological artifacts, along with the Assyrian kings and deities.

The Assyrian Tree of Life signified a connection from heaven to earth that creates new life, regrowth, and rebirth; and the divinity of the god Ashur above the tree reflects that he is above all.

The Tree of Life was an integral part of their lives and rituals, and is very sacred to them. It was thought that the tree is given by the heavens and by their god. The tree gives seed so it may grow again, even when it's old, which makes it a symbol of immortality and reincarnation. The pomagrande seeds signified regrowth and incarnation. Those who eat the fruit will be immortal and will be reincarnated. These all translate to new beginning, strength, and immortality. Assyrians had beliefs with respect to life and being reincarnated after death.

The Assyrian Tree of Life is given several interpretations and has been debated for centuries by scholars. Some believe the tree is the original tree of knowledge and denotes a connection from heaven to earth; there is also the belief that after death, people go to heaven. The Assyrian Tree of Life represents a balanced life, with each side containing the exact numbers and fruits miraculously created for humans. The Assyrians honor and respect this, as this comes from the heavens.

The Tree of Life is found in many cultures around the world, including many Christian practices, and its origins can be traced to Assyria. The Tree of Life is mentioned in the biblical book of Genesis, and the knowledge that comes with it—for good versus evil, or temptation—which is also seen in Judaism and Kabbalah, where the Tree of Life is also very significant. The Tree of Life has been an important philosophical and spiritual symbol that can be seen in Christianity, Judaism, Buddhism, Hinduism, Islam, and many other places.

There has been extensive documentation on this item alone, with relation to religion. One good source to read is from Assyriologist and scholar Simo Parpola and in his paper *The Assyrian Tree of Life: Tracing the Origins of Jewish Monotheism and Greek Philosophy*; it highlights very important and analytical points.

The stele of the Assyrian Tree of Life with the Assyrian king and deities is currently housed at the British Museum (883 BC–859 BC). Some experts indicate this is the same king and the same deity on the stele carving, just a mirror image of them. While this could be right, differences in carvings on stone are not easy to detect, and this could be why these appear to be two different kings.

The differences that are noted are the following:

- The king on the left has a bracelet on this upper left arm while the king on the right does not; it appears that the clothing on that same arm is different than the king's on the reverse of the stele.

- Their crowns/hats are slightly different; the one on the right is squarer and indented.
- Their facial features are different. On the king on the right, you can see the necklace with religious emblems that confirm this is the king, while there doesn't appear to be a necklace on the king to the left. It could be the way the king is standing, but knowing Assyrian art, I don't believe these differences would exist if they were depicting the same king. Assyrian ancient art is normally presice and very detailed so I don't believe they would have missed these small factors.

I believe that on the right is King Ashurnasirpal II, and on the left is his son, Shalmaneser III. Each has an angel behind him, blessing each royal with holy water, and the sacred Tree of Life is in the middle, with the god Ashur overhead in the heavens.

The stele of the Assyrian Tree of Life with the Assyrian kings and deities is currently housed at the British Museum (883 BC–859 BC).

In this stele Shalmaneser III greets Marduk-zakir-shumi, front panel of a Throne Dais of Shalmaneser III and located at the Iraq Museum.

This is the complete dais that was found in the eastern end of the throne room in the city of Nineveh. It is currently housed in the Iraq Museum.

The upper surface and parts of the sides are inscribed with cuneiform script. The front of the relief depicts Shalmaneser III (on the right) shaking hands with Marduk-zakir-shumi (left), king of Babylon, 846–845 BC (Iraq Museum).

The kings believed they were sent from heaven, in the image of their gods, and that is why the reliefs of the kings resemble the deity. The finger pointing is a very famous gesture in various ancient relics and murals found throughout the city of Ashur, Nineveh, and

Khalu. In the carvings, the kings are pointing to god Assur in the winged disc to show that only he is above all and that there is only one higher god, god of the universe. The Assyrian belief system was having one supreme and today Assyrians still have the same belief system that there is only one god.

The deities on either side of the kings are depicted as demi-gods or angels. Assyrians believe there are angels, as do many other modern religions of today.

In the Assyrian Tree of Life stele, the deities appear with a cone in one hand and a bucket of water in the other. This is the first relief that displays a religious blessing of the king with holy water. The cone is placed in the bucket and then used to sprinkle the water on the king to bless him. These blessings were done regularly and were also done in grand events annually; they were included in elaborate monarch coronations and ceremonies.

The Assyrian angel or deity from dated 721-705 BC represents a divine being giving purifications and blessings to the king. These divine angels are sent from heaven; they are known as being divine or heavenly by their wings. It was believed they came to earth to bless the king and his royal family. It was thought that the kings were given by the heavens, so the angels would bless them on special occasions. Once the king receives these blessings, he blesses his people on special events with the annually purification rituals. There are various depicted reliefs with these scenes that display this ritual, which later was adapted by Christianity with baptisms. This is similar to how they do blessings with water and people in churches today. In ancient times, the Assyrians had high priests to perform these blessings to the king, and this tradition of blessings with water is carried through in modern times.

The usage of the pinecone and blessings in modern Christianity is located in a variety of areas, such as the Vatican museum, with the antique bronze pinecone, for various uses in the Vatican. The pinecone and water bucket has also been used in the Syriac Church to conduct blessings at the various memorials.

Water was always considered of vast importance to the Assyrians. There have been large basins located in the Ashur ziggurat—where it was used to hold water for blessings.

This is what Christians still do today in church—they are blessed using holy water; normally when they are babies or children, is when they are baptized, and the born-again Christians are baptized when they are older. This just continues to display the influence that the ancient world has on modern times. Assyrians of today still practice this ancient tradition of blessing and purifying themselves with an annual tradition called Nursadil, or Musarde. This is another tradition that is one of the oldest traditions in the world and has been carried through from ancient times until today. They celebrate this tradition by throwing water at each other to bless and purify one another. (This is discussed in more detail in a separate chapter about Musarde.)

THE HANGING GARDENS
OF NINEVEH

The Hanging Gardens have always been regarded as one of the seven wonders of the ancient world. Some historians, however, have placed the gardens in Babylon rather than in the city of Nineveh.

It was not until recently that a new idea emerged with a discovery made by the modern-day archaeologist and Oxford scholar Stephanie M. Dalley that the Hanging Gardens were actually in the city of Nineveh, and not Babylon, as previously believed by some historians. She presented archaeological evidence such as a stone relief found with the carvings of the gardens and other inscriptions that confirmed that the true owner of the Hanging Gardens was King Sennacherib.

In 2017, Dr. Dalley went to Iraq to validate her findings and to further research the matter. The reliefs she described were found in an archaeological excavation of the palace and grounds of King Sennacherib, in the ancient city of Nineveh. In King Sennacherib's inscriptions, he describes a "wonder for all peoples" and the vast canals he created to bring water to Nineveh. Stephanie Dalley also mentions a water-raising screw that was used to bring water to the higher levels of the gardens.

The Assyrian king Sennacherib (703–690 BC) built his new capital, Nineveh, and he built massive aqueducts, which are the oldest known aqueducts in the world. These impressive and massive canals started at the Kinnis River, crossing another river and bringing the water to Nineveh. The water travelled ninety-five kilometres, crossing over higher grounds and valleys. The mastermind engineering of this canal and water system was a remarkable feat on its own.

The water was also diverted from the Tigris river to these aqueducts to move water to Nineveh. This massive and impressive water system was used by the entire city. King Sennacherib's inscriptions describe them in detail, and in his own words, he mentions that the water was used by the entire city, including his gardens and animals. This water was also used for farming and for households. He also talks about how it encircled and purifies his city.

These massive aqueducts support the idea of the Hanging Gardens being in Nineveh. To add to Dr. Dalley's findings, Nineveh is situated on the east bank of the Tigris river, and the aqueducts are about 190 meters away, yet they held the water reserves to bring them back using the canals to water the city of Nineveh and its gardens. Although some have been destroyed, these massive aqueducts can still be seen today as far away as current-day Jerwan, where they still bear the Assyrian king Sennacherib's cuneiform inscriptions. This is what is left today, so many stones have been taken to be used by others for their homes, and that is the case of various aniquities of the Assyrian people, even the famous wall of Nineveh and most of the stones were stolen from the site.

To further bolster Dr. Dalley's theory, there was a picture of the Hanging Gardens carved in stone found in King Sennacherib's palace; it is currently housed in the British Museum. The Hanging Gardens were also known to have impressive symbols with exotic aromatic flowers, various plants, and trees of all kinds (several bearing fruit); and animals were brought from all around the world. It was known that the king built the Hanging Gardens for his queen.

This Assyrian relief from Nineveh displays trees and bushes, some almost suspended in air, on terraces and stone arches with walkways and a gazebo, and with what clearly appears to be water flowing up and down through the sections.

If closely examined, it appears that there is a king under the gazebo, with the famous finger pointing to God above and what appears to be a place used for prayer.

This is a close look at the Assyrian relief that attests to the Hanging Gardens being in Nineveh; it is currently housed in the British Museum.

Here is the entire Assyrian stone relief and scene.

The following cuneiform tablet was inscribed for Assyrian king Sennacherib, and it describes in detail his extraordinary gardens and canals in his own words, the canal he engineered, and how he made the water flow to Nineveh.

> *Now I, Sennacherib —king of Assyria, foremost of [all]*
> *rulers, who [march]ed about [freely] from east to we[st]*
> *thanks to the waters of the canals that I caused to be dug,*
> *[I could pl]ant around Nineveh gardens, vines, every type*

of fruit, [. . .] . . ., products of every mountain, fruit trees from all over the world, (including) spi[ces] and [olive trees]. Where water could not reach, I left waterless and [. . .] a game preserve called [. . .]all of the orchards, for entering the fields, above the city (and) below (the city),<from> the city Tarbiṣu to the city of the people of the Inner City (Aššur), I provided irrigation annually for the cultivation of grain and sesame. [10]

Neo-Assyrian period (704–681 BC)
Provenance—Nineveh
Language—Akkadian

Cuneiform Tablet, Sennacherib, 223 Translation

Deities Aššur, Anu, Enlil, Ea, Sîn, Šamaš, Adad, Marduk, Nabû, [Nerg]al, Ištar, (and) the Sebetti, the great gods, who install the lord (and)name the ruler to lead the black-headed (people) all over the inhabited world:

Sennacherib, great king, strong king, king of the world, king of Assyria, king of the four quarters (of the world), the prince who provides for them, by your firm 'yes' I marched about safely from the Upper Sea to the Lower Sea, and (then) I made rulers of the (four) quarters (of the world) bow down at my feet and they (now) pull my yoke

At that time, I greatly enlarged the site of Nineveh. I had its (inner) wall andits outer wall, which had never been constructed before, built anew and I raised (them) as high as mountain(s). Its fields, which had been turned into wastelands due to lack of water, were woven over with spiderwebs. Moreover, its people did not know artificial irrigation, but had their eyes turned for rain (and) showers from the sky

---

[10] Sennacherib palace, tablet 223, http://oracc.org/rinap/Q004028/.

I climbed high and I had eighteen canals dug from the cities Masitu, Banbarina, Šapparišu, Kār-Šamaš-nāṣir, Kār-nūri, Talmusu, Ḫatâ, Dalāyin, Rēš-ēni, Sulu, Dūr-Ištar, Šibaniba, Isparirra, Gingiliniš, Nampagātu, Tīlu, Alum-ṣusi, (and) the water that is above the city Ḫadabitu and I directed their courses into the Ḫusur River.

I had a canal dug from the border of the city Kisiru to Nineveh (and) I caused those waters to flow inside it. I named it Patti-Sennacherib. [I directed] the mass of those waters from Mount Tas, a rugged mountain near the land Urarṭu, to my land. Previously, that canal was called the[. . .] canal.

Now, I, by the command of the god Aššur, the great lord, my lord, added to it the waters on the right and left of the mountain, which are beside it, and [the waters] of the cities Mēsu, Kukkinu, (and) Piturra, cities in its environs

I d[u]g [that] canal with (only) seventy men and I named it Nār-Sennacherib. I added (its water) to the water from the wells and the canals that I had previously d[ug], and (then) I directed their courses to Nineveh, the exalted cult center, my royal residence, whose site [the king]s, my[ancestor]s, since time imme[morial] had not made large (enough), nor had they expertly carried out its artful execution.

Now I, Sennacherib—king of Assyria, foremost of [all] rulers, who [march]ed about [freely] from east to we[st] thanks to the waters of thecanals that I caused to be dug, [I could pl]ant around Nineveh gardens, vines, every type of fruit, [. . .] . . ., productsof every mountain, fruit trees from all over the world, (including) spi[ces] and [olive trees]. Where water could not reach, I left waterless and [. . .] a game preserve called [. . .]all of the orchards, for entering the fields, above the city (and) below (the city),<from> the city

Tarbiṣu to the city of the people of the InnerCity (Aššur), I provided irrigation annually for the cultivation of grain and sesame.

(To) a later ruler, one of the kings, my descendants, who deliberates (the matter) in (his) heart but is not able to believe (it), (and) s[ays] "How did he have this canal dug out wi[th] (only) these few men?" [I swear] by thegod Aššur, my great god, that I dug out this canal with (only)these [men]. Moreover, I completed the work on it within one year (and) three months; [. . .] was completed (and) I finished digging its excavation.

In order to open that canal, I sent an exorcist (and) a lamentation singer and. . . [. . .] Carnelian, lapis lazuli, muššāru-stone, ḫulālu-stone, pappardilû-stones, precious stones, turtles (and) tortoises whose likeness(es) are ca[st] insilver (and) gold, aromatics, (and) fine oil, I gave as gifts to the god Ea, the lord of underground waters, cisterns, and. . ., (and to) the god Enbilulu, the inspector of canals, (and) to the god En'e'imdu, the lord of [dike(s) and canal(s)]. I prayed to the great gods; they heeded my supplications and made my handiwork prosper.

This (sluice) gate of the watercourse opened by itself [without (the help)] of spade or shovel and let an abundance of water flow through. Its(sluice) gate was not ope[ned] through the work of human hands. According to the heart's desire of the gods, I made (it) gurgle with water. After I inspected the canal and made sure its construction was performed correctly, I offered pure sacrifices of fattened oxen (and) an abundance of sheep to the great gods, who march at my side (and) who make my reign secure. I clothed those men who dug out this canal with linen garments (and) garments with multi-colored trim, (and) I placed gold rings (and) gold pectorals on them.

In this year with the flowing (lit. "going") of this canal which I had dug, I drew up a battleline with Umman-menanu (Ḫumban-menanu), the king of the land Elam, and the king of Babylon, together with the numerous kings of the mountains and Sealand who were their allies, in the plain of the city Ḫalulê. By the command of the god Aššur, the great lord, my lord, I charged into their midst like a fierce arrow, and I repelled their troops. I dispersed their assembled host and scattered their forces.

I captured alive in the midst of battle the magnates of the king of the land Elam, including Nabû-šuma-iškun, a son of Marduk-apla-iddina (II)(Merodach-baladan), king of the land Karduniaš (Babylonia).

Terror of doing serious battle with me overwhelmed the king of the land Elam and the king of Babylon and they released their excrement inside their chariots. In order to save their lives, they fled to their (own) land(s) anddid not return ever again (saying): "Perhaps Sennacherib, king of Assyria, is so angry that he will return to the land Elam."

Fear (and) terror fell upon all of the Elamites and they abandoned their land, and (then), in order to save their lives, they betook themselves to a rugged mountain like eagle(s) and their hearts throbbed like (those of) pursued birds. Until they died, they did not make their way (back) (lit. "they did not open a path") and they no longer made war.

On my second campaign, I marched quickly to Babylon, which I planned to conquer, and (then) I blew like [the onset] of a storm and enveloped it like a (dense) fog. I besieged the city; then, by means of sapping and ladders, I [captured (it)] (and) plundered [the city]. Its people, young and old, I did not spare, and I filled the city squares with their corpses. I carriedoff alive to my land Šūzubu (Mušēzib-Marduk), the king of Babylon, together with his family (and) his [. . .]s.

I handed the property of that city —silver, gold, choice stones, possessions (and) property —over to my [people] and they kept it for themselves. My people seized and smashed the gods living inside it, and (then) they took their [possessions] (and) property. The god Adad(and) the goddess Šala, gods of the city Ekallātum whom Marduk-nādin-aḫḫē, king of Akkad, had taken and brought to Babylon during the reign of Tiglath-pileser (I), king of Assyria —I had (them) brought out of Babylon after 418 years and I returned them to the city E[kallātum], their (proper) place.

I destroyed, devastated, (and) burned with fire the city, and (its) buildings, from its foundations to its crenellations. I removed the brick(s) and earth, as much as there was, from the (inner) wall and outer wall, the temples, (and) the ziggurrat, (and) I threw (it) into the Araḫtu river. I dug canals into the center of that city and (thus) leveled their site with water. I destroyed the outline of its foundations and (thereby) made its destruction surpass that of the Deluge. So that in the future, the site of that city and (its) temples will be unrecognizable, I dissolved it(Babylon) in water and annihilated (it), (making it) like a meadow.

At the "mouth" of the canal that I caused to be dug into the mountain, [I ma]de six stele[s] (and) I fashioned image(s) of the great gods, my lords, upon them. Moreover, I had a royal image of myself expressing humility (lit. "one who strokes the nose") placed before them. I had all of my handiwork that I had undertaken in Nineveh inscribed upon them and I left (them) for ever after for the kings, my descendants.

At any time (in the future), a future ruler, one of the kings, my descendants who desecrates the work that I have done, dismantles the (canal) system that I have constructed, (or) diverts the flow of the waters of these canals from the plain of Nineveh: May the great god, as many as are named in this stele, by their holy decree, which cannot be altered, curse him with harsh [curse] and overthrow his dynasty.

Modern-day remains in Nineveh, Iraq, where the Hanging Gardens and palace of King Sennacherib remain to this day.

These are the remains of the carved stones around King Sennacherib's palace today in northern Iraq.

The Nineveh Nergal Gate (700 BC), current day in northern Iraq.

The destruction of Nineveh and the Nergal Gate, one of the oldest archaeological sites in the world, occurred on January 28, 2015, which was carried out by the terrorist group ISIS; and later again the walls of Nineveh were destroyed by the northern government in Iraq, where portions of the Nineveh wall were completely destroyed. These destructions have continued for centuries on all the ancient Assyrian cities. The ancient city of Nineveh is estimated to be over eight thousand years old.

© The Trustees of ACSYA Inc.

If these ancient sites were persevered this would help drive the tourism to Iraq, which would bolster and strengthen their enconomy. Other countries around the world have spent millions of dollars to bring pieces of these ancient sites to their country to be held in museums to preserve and create jobs, yet Iraq has these in their original areas yet they are neglected. The Iraq government should realize the importance of these ancient sites and review the preservation of these sites as one of their top priorities and they should know that the country and the people would benefit from it if they clean and protect these ancient sites.

The oldest aqueducts in the world were master-engineered by the Assyrian kings in 700–690 BC, and they emphasized the magnitude of their empire. Travelling water for thirty miles to the destination of Nineveh with cuneiform inscriptions, you can just envision the magnitude of this project.

On its ninety-five-kilometer journey from the mountains to Nineveh, the Khinis canal crossed over an aqueduct at Jerwan. Commissioned by Sennacherib and designed by Assyrian engineers, the aqueduct allowed long-distance canals to cross high ground and valleys with equal ease. The monumentality and engineering of the Jerwan aqueduct exemplifies the power of the Assyrian Empire.[11]

Dr. Dalley in her documentary also shows large logs shaped in the form of a screw to bring water to higher levels of the gardens, which was another engineering feat.

King Sennacherib's reign (704–688 BC) and his words still reach us today by describing how he built the canals. The following is seen on his cuneiform inscription, carefully carved in stone on the aqueduct in modern-day Jerwan.

---

[11] Harvard.edu (public domain) and CDLI.

Sennacherib, king of the world, king of Assyria (says): For a long distance . . . I caused a canal to be dug to the meadows of Nineveh. Over deep-cut ravines I spanned a bridge of white stone blocks. I caused those waters to flow over it.

King Sennarcherib's reign (704–688 BC) and today what remains of his water canals; this is current-day Jerwan, which is north of the ancient city of Nineveh, and what remains of the canal system today. You can still see the cuneiform writing on them today with his name.

Assyrian king Sennacherib, son of King Sargon II, was born around 740 BC. He reigned from 704 to 688 BC, and he built his capital, the city of Nineveh.

Cuneiform inscriptions found on all Assyrian palaces look similar to this, including cuneiform writing, and examples are still visible in Iraq to this day. Assyrian kings were famous for placing these types of inscriptions that detailed the actions of the king who was ruling at the time. This style was later adopted by Saddam Hussein, the president (1979–2003) of Iraq, on buildings he had built.

LAMASSU

The Assyrians had several protective deities, also known as angels. One of the main deities was the Lamassu. The Lamassu has a face of a king, the body of a bull, and the wings represented divity or heavenly so they can fly to heaven. The Lamassu has often appeared with a lion's body as well.

The Assyrian Lamassu are housed in various museums worldwide, including the British Museum, the Louvre in Paris, the Persepolis in Iran, the National Museum in Iraq, the Chicago Museum, and the Metropolitan Museum in New York.

Modern-day northern Iraq is the Lamassu's original historic place, in the city of Khalu, Nineveh, Dur-Sharrukin—originally historic Assyria. The city of Kalhu, modern-day Nimrud, was completely flattened by ISIS, the entire site. The terrorists group taped how they had main explosives placed on all the artifacts surrounding the ancient city and showed them lighting it up and bombing the entire site, completely flattening it. The Lamassu in the Mosul Museum, that were brought there from the ancient city of Khalu, were also destroyed, along with other Assyrian artifacts. Everything in the Mosul Museum were also destroyed; the terrorist group taped themselves destroying it. This deliberate destruction of Assyrian artifacts and historic sites took place from the fall of the empire to modern times in 2003 to 2019 and have continued through history.

The meaning of these mythical creatures has been debated for centuries. The Lamassu, which are protective spirits, are normally colossal in size and used mainly in main entryways at the palaces of the Assyrian kings to ward off evil. These are massive statues that were created to intimidate wrongdoers—enter with caution! The Lamassu also served as higher protection from the gods for the city and the people, and today Assyrians still have Lamassu in their homes.

The Assyrians were meticulous in designing these mythological creatures, and all aspects were considered. The Lamassu design reflects the face of a king, but most importantly, they have human heads, meaning they are the smartest beings on earth. They were created as a reflection of the king. The Lamassu has a helmet with horns, meaning it's divine—god like—and it's royal. They have wings, which means they can fly, and they have the power to control the heavens. The body is of a bull or lion, which were selected for their strength as the strongest and most powerful creatures on earth.

All aspects of the world were used to create these protective spirits: divine, royal, intelligent, strong, and controlling the earth and the sky. Lamassu have five legs. If you look at them from the front, they are standing straight at attention to intimidate those who approach; and if you look at them from the side, it appears they are walking. They were created this way to show movement when you walk past them. This has been interpreted as being as close as possible to a living, walking spiritual being.

These Lamassu were photographed after the excavations that took place in the 1840s. These excavations were ordered by the British government and conducted by Austen Henry Layard with the help of Assyrian Assyriologist and native Hormuz Rassam.

These Lamassu are in their original place, the ancient Assyrian capital city of Dur-Sharrukin (721–702 BC).

This Lamassu is photographed in 1906 in the city of Khalu (today's Nimrud) prior to excavations.

LAMASSU

The Lamassu in the ancient city of Kalhu and its original place (883–859 BC); this is prior to its destruction in 2015.

This Lamassu in Khalu 883–859 BC was photographed in modern-day Nimrud before the terrorist group destruction of the ancient site in February 2015.

This is the Assyrian king Sennacherib's palace in Nineveh, and the protective Lamassu before the ISIS destruction in 2015.

LAMASSU

This Assyrian Lamassu (883–859 BC) is housed at the British Museum. It was taken from one part of the city of Khalu during one of the first excavations that were done by Austen Henry Layard and Hormuz Rassam in 1845–1851. This Lamassu was meticulously carved by the Assyrians with the body of a lion.

THE ASSYRIAN FLAG
AND ITS ORIGIN

The Assyrian flag was created in 1971 by George Bet Atanus and reflects their ancient artifacts that are currently housed at the British Museum.

The flag was brilliantly designed to bring their ancient history to their present reflections together for the Assyrian people. Each item on the flag has vast significance and meaning, as the ancient relics do.

The top of the flag depicts the ancient Assyrian god Ashur. God Ashur was the supreme god in ancient times; he is shown with his bow and arrow to reflect the mighty Assyrian army (from ancient times) and how god Ashur was with them on their missions.

The supreme god and emblem appear on many Assyrian artifacts. They are used to decorate the Assyrian kings' palaces and places of worship. There are steles located in museums worldwide that hold this emblem—each stele tells its own story, with cuneiform inscriptions on each one. The Assyrian flag without the god Ashur on it is not truly the Assyrian flag. The original Assyrian flag has the god Ashur on the top of it.

The middle star represents the solar god Shamasha, who emerged from the heavens in the east and settled in the west; this pantheon was the power of light over darkness, life over death. He was also known for justice and equality, which inspired Hammurabi to write the first laws ever created.

Thousands of years later, the name *Shamasha* is still in use today; Assyrians use the name to describe a deacon in the church. The word *shemsha* in the Assyrian language also refers to the sun, and this word is also still in use today. The star's bright-blue colour was selected for the four points to represent the peace and tranquility that Assyrians seek.

The three wavy stripes on the flag—red, white, and blue— represent the three rivers in the heart of the Assyrian homeland. The red represents the Tigris river and reflects the Assyrian national pride; the white represents the Zab river, reflecting peace; and the blue represents the Euphrates river, which reflects abundance.

The depiction of the rivers widening and narrowing to the four corners of the solar star represent the dispersing of the Assyrian people to the four corners of the world, which is the case today. They are scattered all around the world. The narrowing of the rivers back to Shamsha at the center represents the hope that one day the Assyrians will return to their ancestral homelands.

This artifact of an Ashurbanipal II military campaign is currently housed at the British Museum. In the scene, god Ashur is shown to be with them as they prepare for battle.

The tablet of the solar god Shamasha from Sippar is currently housed at the British Museum (860–850 BC). It was found in Babylon and was excavated by Hormuz Rassam in 1881.

FOOD, DRINKS, AND TRADITIONAL CLOTHES

*A*ssyrians make butter today in the old country as they did in their ancient past by using sheepskin tied on all ends. They put milk inside of what is now a bag, hang it from a piece of wood, and two ladies would move it back and forth to help with the churning process. They did this for hours while singing and dancing to amuse themselves. It could take eight hours or more to produce the butter. When it was done, there would be fat at the top and thin milk at the bottom. They removed the fat to place it in pots to settle and solidify.

Yogurt is used in a lot of Assyrian dishes, and it is a staple in every Assyrian home. The milk water remaining from the butter-making process is used to make *daweh*, their famous drink; they add more homemade yogurt to it and water, and that becomes one of their favorite drinks, which is a mixture of yogurt and water. Salt and ice are also added, and this is a very popular drink in the Middle East.

Some of the remaining yogurt water is used to make foods such as *gurdo*, which is rice cooked with yogurt, or *kallagug*, which is a yogurt sauce with garlic—bread is eaten with the sauce. Both of these foods are eaten with melted butter on top. The rest of the yogurt water would be used to make *keshke*, which is a dry form of yogurt molded into a ball shape and dried. These balls of dry yogurt were made to keep for the winter months when milk was not as abundant. *Keshke* was known for its distinct taste and flavor.

To make *keshke*, the yogurt that remained after making butter was put in portions into cloth, more homemade yogurt is placed, and these cloth bags of yogurt were hung in a tree so that all the moisture was drawn out and dried by the sun. Once the moisture is gone, the contents turn into a doughlike substance. This concentrated yogurt would be put it into a bowl and kneaded like dough and made into fist-sized balls. The balls were then to be taken to the flat roof to be further dried by the sun. Assyrian homes in Iraq and Syria have flat roofs, so the balls were laid on a sheet, with another sheet on top, and then the sun performed its magic.

Once the *keshke* were dry, they were packed away for the winter months when milk is scarce. In the winter months, they would take one of these balls of dried yogurt and mix it with water to make yogurt again. Then the yogurt would be used in foods like *gurdo* and *kallagug*, *dekhwa*, and other yogurt-based foods.

Assyrians are famous for buried cheese and meats; this was a method of preservation in ancient times. They buried cheese and meats in large clay pots near the house, perhaps under the grapevines or large trees.

Homemade cheese is still buried this way today, and the area is watered periodically to keep the cheese cool and moist. The cheese ages for a minimum of three months before it is dug back up again; it is often enjoyed with tea and freshly baked bread. This special cheese is called *gupta tumarta*; the exact translation is "cheese buried." Buried cheese has a distinct special flavor. Until today, vast amounts of clay pots are found underground from their ancient past. These clay pots have been found in ancient Assyrian sites, and these foods were buried in the much cooler ground to act as a refrigerator since they didn't have them at that time. Today the Assyrian people in diaspora still use clay pots to drink water, its known to taste better and they still preserve buried cheese and meats in the villages of Iraq, Iran, Syria, and Turkey they mainly follow this practice to give them the distinct flavour of these foods just like their ancestors did, this practice suggests this too is one of the oldest continued traditions in the world.

Fresh bread was made daily using clay brick round domes with a wood fire in the middle. Round flat pieces of bread dough were stuck onto the side of the clay oven for even baking.

When the Assyrians roasted lamb, they called the meat *gallya*, meaning "fried meat." In the fall, they would cook large portions of meat in their clay handmade outdoor ovens. The meat was placed in a clay pot, and the top was sealed with dough; it was cooked overnight. The next day, they took out the meat, eating some of it; and in the fall, they store the rest in clay pots to bury and perserved for the winter months.

These traditions are still practiced today in some areas and even in diaspora, but sadly these ancient traditions are slowly dying.

Pastries that are famously Assyrian are *keleche*, *kade*, and *baklava*. These are all old recipes handed down from generation to generation. They are simple, but they are very old recipes enjoyed each year on special occasions like Christmas, New Year, and Easter.

Some of Assyrians' favorite drinks are tea, coffee, and *daweh*. The coffee is a thick-textured coffee. The old-fashioned tea drinkers drink their tea black, in small glass cups with sugar cubes.

Assyrians enjoy *arak*, which in the olden days was made like moonshine. Assyrians also invented beer and wine—these were luxuries enjoyed both in past and present days.

A quote from the Oriental Institute–University of Chicago:

> *The OI excavations at the site of Khorsabad which in ancient Dur-Sharrukin, or also known as "Fortress of Sargon" During the 1934–1935 excavations of the Assyrian capital city found a "wine cellar" in Residence K, one of the four residences that neighbored Sargon II's palace atop the citadel and which belonged to high court officials. The famous "wine cellar" was named as such by archaeologists because it contained 8 storage jars that were embedded halfway into mud-brick bases. While Mesopotamia might be better known for beer, wine represented an important commodity in the Neo-Assyrian period. It was an expensive luxury good that the administration controlled.[12]*

Sargon II and the palace with a wine cellar, recently found in northern Iraq.

---

[12] Oriental Institute–University of Chicago: Archives.

Traditional Assyrian foods:

- Gemar: a heavey cream that is eaten for breakfast with honey or jam
- Dolma: grape leaves, onions, other veggies stuffed with rice and meat mixer
- Biryani: rice, chicken, peas, fried potatoes—all cooked together with spices
- Gurgur: rice and yogurt mixed and cooked together
- Haresa: barley and chicken cooked together and constantly stirred
- Bushalla: yogurt broth with herbs and sometimes with Swiss chard
- Facolye: green bean stew cooked with meat and served with rice
- Bomye: okra meat stew served with rice
- Kipteh: meatballs in a tomato base sauce
- Kubba: various kubba are either fried or boiled
- Kubba Hammouth: kubba with lemon and a tomato base sauce
- Perda: in place of rice is also a favorite

All these foods can be found on social media sites; the Assyrians are real foodies, and there are some great sites with wonderful recipes.

Assyrians eat all meats normally, except those from animals that have hooves.

Some favorite foods from ancient times that are still enjoyed today are roasted lamb, stews, rice, nuts, quince, pomegranates, dates, barley, beer, and wine.

Ancient Assyrian clothes and accessories:

Ancient accessories that are also still worn today:

Assyrians have traditional clothing that they call *khomlana*, which means "fun," they wear these traditional clothes for events and weddings, and they are all handmade. They look similar to this.

These are ancient Assyrian treasures from the royal tomb of the ancient city of Khalu. In this site they found the royal tombs where the queens of Assyria were buried. When the US invaded Iraq in 2003, they discovered these treasures, which contained extensive amounts of gold jewelry, which were found in large boxes locked and in Iraq's main bank. The US military broke open the locks only to discover the ancient treasures. Austen Henry Layard and Hormuz Rassam originally excavated this ancient site from 1845 to 1847, and again from 1849 to 1851, and some artifacts uncovered in these expeditions were shipped to the British Museum.

Khalu was excavated again in April of 1989 by the Iraq government. This is when they found the royal tombs, and it contained all these treasures including more than 125 pounds of gold; about 613 pieces were discovered. In these tombs, along with their queen's crown and jewelry, they uncovered gold vases, gold water jugs with engravings, royal seals, and other items. The whereabouts of these treasures now is currently unknown. Since the discovery, this site has been plundered. This jewelry is similar to what they still wear today in the Assyrian traditional clothing in weddings and grand events.

These treasures belonged to these queens:

- Yaba, queen of Tiglathpileser III, king of Assyria, 744–727 BC
- Banitu, queen of Shalmanasser V, king of Assyria, 726–722 BC
- Atalia, queen of Sargon II, king of Assyria, 721–705 BC

The treasures include elaborate crowns with gold pomegranates, the royal symbol, and angels, which are adapted and engraved. Some also had precious stones.

The Kalhu treasure.

THE ASSYRIAN NEW YEAR
AND ASTROLOGICAL EVENTS

*A*ssyrians have been oppressed since the fall of their empire, and as a result there have been periods when Assyrians were not allowed to celebrate their special occasions, such as the Assyrian New Year. The prohibition of these celebrations was considered political—it appeared to be an attempt to reduce the strength of the ties Assyrians had to their land and to reduce Assyrians' ability to confirm their years of existence and heritage in these lands. Also, its considered that in ancient times when Assyria was at war, they did not celebrate the New Year.

In recent centuries, Assyrians were allowed to celebrate in Iraq and Syria but were restricted from celebrating in Turkey and Iran. There are several ancient traditions that Assyrians still practice today that are directly linked to what is described in cuneiform tablets; the New Year celebration is one of them. This occasion, marking the arrival of the New Year, was celebrated with grand festivals in the past, and this continues to the present day.

The observation of the full moon, blood moon, and eclipse were very significant in ancient times to Assyrians, and events were planned around these days. These events were considered as omens or signs from the heavens that something would happen; the blood moon, in particular, was seen as a sign that a war would start, or the king would die or be killed. The significance of these events, in general, was that something would happen, or there would be a celebration of new life. A lot of daily events were based on the moon, the stars, and the sky; this is also how Assyrians measured time with the twenty-four-hour clock, observing day and night and the calendar with seasons. The eclipse was considered a very bad omen, and the kings conducted special prayers to the gods on these days.

Their kings used expert astronomers, so they knew when the full and blood moons would occur; the kings used this knowledge as guidance to plan their actions and events. They used the first lenses ever created found in Kalhu current day Nimrud to view the sky and determine these celestial events.

When there was a blood moon, which was already considered a bad omen, with a star shining over it, the Assyrians had a ritual in which the people in the village would all gather outside and bang on pots and drums while chanting to make noise so that the moon would change color—and make whatever bad omen that was going to happen go away. The Assyrians still practiced this ancient ritual up to fifty years ago in the villages of Iraq, and the neighbouring Yezidis people still follow this practice up to today.

Sadly this is another tradition that Assyrians don't practice any longer, as they are scattered around the world in different countries, and there are dwindling numbers in the Assyrian homelands.

This Assyrian tradition is similar to what some native Indians do today—with banging their drums and chanting, but there is not enough research on these similarities to be able to determine whether this is significant.

The Assyrian New Year is one of the oldest traditions in the world, and it is still celebrated today, which makes it a tradition that is over seven thousand years old. The Assyrian year is calculated using the old calendar, as the Assyrian people existed prior to Christianity.

The beginning of the year was calculated based on 4750 BC + 2021 (today's year) = 6771. The 4750 BC start date that was an estimate established by the Assyrians, and with excavations continuing in the homelands, Assyrian history may go further back than this estimate implies.

In ancient Sumer, the year was divided into two seasons, based on astronomical celestial events, with the observation of the spring, which marked one celebration, and then fall, which marked another celebration of harvesting. In spring, it was marked by the spring equinox for summer; and in fall, it was marked by the autumnal equinox for winter.

The New Year was celebrated by Assyria in both Ashur and Babylon and is well documented on cuneiform tablets. This celebration quickly spread to all peoples, at the time, including Israelis and Persians.

The first calendar ever created was based on the observation of the lunar cycles. The Assyrian New Year started with the observation of new life, rebirths, new season, and renewal and was celebrated on the appearance of the first new moon after the spring equinox. We know this because of the cuneiform tablets that have been translated in modern times.

The artifact describing the first calendar ever created in the world and its current location is not clearly known, but some speculate that it's in the Turkish museum. The Akkadian/Assyrian calendar 1800 BC was found in the city of Ashur, discovered in 1910 by Walter Andrae, who led the 1908 German excavation of the ancient site of Ashur.

The Old Assyrian calendar consisted of twelve months of twenty-nine or thirty days. The months are named after seasonal events, with the end of the month determined by the day when the moon god Sin disappeared.

I	Bēlet-ekallim	VII	Ṣip'um
II	(Narmak Aššur) ša Sarrātim	VIII	Qarrātum
III	(Narmak Aššur) ša Kēnātim	IX	Kanwarta
IV	Mahhur ilī	X	Te'inātum⋆
V	Ab šarrāni	XI	Kuzallu
VI	Hubur	XII	Allānātum

This is an example of the modern-day solar Assyrian calendar that is still followed today. This calendar is called *sergada tequa*, meaning "old calendar." The Julian calendar, and later the Gregorian calendar, was also based on the solar cycle and system of 12 months and 365 days. The Jewish calendar also displays a lot of similarities to the Assyrian calendar.

This table shows the Assyrian calendar, its seasons and months.

Season	Assyrian Calendar	Gregorian Calendar
Spring/Binisanne	Nissan	April
	Yaar	May
	Khzeeran	June
Summer/Qetta	Tammuz	July
	Tabakh	August
	Eelool	September
Autumn/Chereyee	Tishrin 1 (Gamaya)	October
	Tishrin II (kharaya)	November
Winter/Sitwa	Kanoon 1 (Gamaya)	December
	Kanoon II (Kharaya)	January
	Eshwat	February
	Adaar	March

According to unpublished tablets, the Assyrian New Year in ancient times corresponds to a winter solstice on December 22, while previous interpretations of this table suggest it was after the autumn equinox on September 22; in the upper Mesopotamia, it was August. We know for certain the occasion of spring New Year festival was celebrated in grand events based on stone tables, and this tradition continues with the Assyrian people today.

Experts in the field of astrology were ultimately responsible for checking and determining the exact day of the new moon so that the celebrations could begin, and that is how the start of the New Year was identified in the ancient past.

The New Year started at the sight of the new moon after the spring equinox, and each year, the start of the year was a different day, depending on when the new moon arrived; for example, in the year 2020, the new moon was on March 24, so this was the first day of New Year for the Assyrians. The month *Nissan* was used in ancient times until today to speficiy when the New Year was celebrated and it means "April" in the Assyrian language; and in Akkadian (old Assyrian), it's called *Ninazu* or *Nisannu*, depending how the scribe spelled the word.

In modern times, when Assyrians adopted the solar calendar, they picked a standard date on which to celebrate their New Year, and April 1 was selected as the day to celebrate the New Year.

In ancient times the meaning behind the word *Akitu* refers to a temple for the gods, and there were various temples of what was called Akitu house or Akitu chapel, which displayed their ancient gods. There was one in the city of Ashur dedicated to the gods Ashur and Ishtar. The Assyrian New Year festival is often referred to as the New Year festival or the Akitu festival on stone tablets dating back to around 800 BC and today Assyrians still refer to their New Year as the Assyrian New Year, or Akitu, to signify the start of their New Year celebrations.

This ancient tablet is significant because it confirms that the first month of the Assyrian calendar is Nisannu, and today they still use the same word to signify the beginning of their year. The reference to their festival in the first month of Nisannu and the Akitu Temple is directly referred to by King Sennacherib's own words in his cuneiform tablet 168, section 22b, which is provided here in detail.

The tablets in this book are a direct translation of the scholarly works and nothing has been altered or modified. These are king Sennacheribs own words.

> Assyrian king Sennacherib cuneiform tablet 168
> Neo-Assyrian Period (911–612 BC)
> Provenience—Assur
> Tablet collection and location—Vorderasiatisches Museum, Berlin, Germany
> Language—Akkadian

Cuneiform Tablet, 704–681 BC, Sennacherib 168
(Section 22b in the Tablet)

(1)Sennacherib, great king, strong king, king of the world, king of Assyria, king of the four quarters (of the world), leader of a widespread population, the one who fashioned image(s) of (the god) Aššur and the great gods, the one who carries out to perfection the forgotten rites of Ešarra through divination, at the command of (5) the gods Šamaš and Adad, the one who makes great their purification rites, the one who returns the abandoned protective spirit of Ešarra to its place, who knows well how to revere the gods of heaven and the gods of Assyria, who exalts the great gods in their dwellings, who makes their accoutrements great,

(9b)the builder of Assyria, the one who brings his cult centers to completion, the one who makes enemy land(s) obedient, the one who destroys their settlements, the one who has canals dug, the one who opens streams, the one who makes watercourses gush, the one who establishes abundance and plenty in the wide plains of Assyria, the one who provides

irrigation water in the meadows of Assyria — (15) which from the days of yore no one in Assyria had seen or known canals and artificial irrigation and which none in bygone times had used —

(17b)the one who makes brickwork structures (lit. "the craft of the god Kulla") secure, from buildings for the living to tombs befitting the dead (made) from limestone, stone from the mountains, with which none of (20) the kings of the past (who came) before me in Assyria had used, circumspect ruler whose dominion is more praised than (that of all) kings who sit on (royal) daises, the support of his land, the one who is trustworthy in battle and combat, (and) the protection of his troops, I:

(22b)Then, after I had made the image of (the god) Aššur, the great lord, my lord, and the image(s) of the great gods, and installed them in their peaceful dwellings, in the month Nisannu (I), the first month, (the month) of father Enlil, the month of the heliacal rising of (25) the Plow-star: The festival of the feast of the king of the gods, (the god) Aššur, which from distant days, because of chaos and disruption, (and) the akītu-house of the steppe had been forgotten; the rites of the king of the gods, (the god) Aššur, had been performed inside the city. With (regard to) that work, I made up my mind to (re)build th(at) akītu-house, and (then) I found out the will of the gods Šamaš (and) Adad, and they answered me with a firm 'yes' and commanded me to (re)build (it).

(30b)In a favorable month, on a propitious day, through the craft of the purification priest (and) the wisdom of the exorcist, I laid its foundation with limestone, stone from the mountains, and I raised its superstructure. I completedit from its foundations to its crenellations with stone from the

mountains and raised it as high as a mountain. I had two canals dug around each of its sides, and (then) (35) I had it surrounded with a lush garden, an orchard with fruit, and placed a splendid plantation around it.

(36b)After I destroyed Babylon, smashed its gods, (and) put its people to the sword, I removed its earth in order to make the site of that city unrecognizable and I had (it) carried to the sea by the Euphrates River. (When) its dirt (40) reached Dilmun and the people of Dilmun saw (it), fear (and) terror of (the god) Aššur fell upon them and they brought their audience gift(s) to me. Together with their audience gift(s), they sent people mustered from their land, corvée workers, (with) bronze spades (and) bronze plowshares, tools manufactured in their land, in order to demolish Babylon.

(44b)In order to pacify (the god) Aššur, my lord, for people to sing the praises of his might, (and) for the admiration of future people, I removed dirt from Babylon and piled (it) up in heaps (and) mounds in that akītu-house.

(48)While laying the foundation of the akītu-house, the audience gift of Karib-il, king of the land Saba — pappardilû-stone, choice stones, (and) fine aromatics — [wa]s presented to me (50) and from that audience gift I laid stones (and) aromatics in its foundation. Like . . ., I . . . silver, gold, carnelian, lapis lazuli, ḫulālu-stone, muššaru-stone, pappardilû-stone, papparmīnu-stone, dāmātu-paste, (and) all of the finest aromatics in the foundation of that akītu-house. I sprinkled that foundation with perfumed oil (and) fine oil as (abundantly as) river water.

(55b)O you, foundation inscription, speak favorable things to (the god) Aššur about Sennacherib, king of Assyria, the one

who loves correct behavior, the one who fashioned the image of (the god) Aššur, (and) the one who built (this) temple, so that his offspring, his sons, (and) his grandsons may flourish together with Baltil (Aššur) and Ešarra (and) endure forever with the black-headed (people).

(60b)May any future ruler whom (the god) Aššur names for shepherding the land and people (and) during whose reign that temple becomes dilapidated renovate its dilapidated section(s). May he find my inscribed objects, anoint (them) with oil, make an offering, (and) put (them) back in their (text: "its") place. (The god) Aššur will (then) hear his prayers.

(66)(As for) the one who alters my inscribed object (and) disrespects my words, who does [un]kind things t[o] . . . and their offspring, may (the god) Aššur, king of the gods, and the great gods of heaven and netherworld curse him with a harsh, [ir]reversible curse, and may they overthrow his kingship, deprive him of his life, (and) make his name, his seed, his offspring, and his progeny disappear in all lands.[13]

This cuneiform tablet in which King Sennacherib mentions the New Year and his newly built Akitu Temple. Part of the tablet documents purifying rituals and how his city of Nineveh is encircled with water from his canals, with trees, fruits, and aromatic plants. These purification rituals were also done in the month of Tammuz, the month of July in the Assyrian calendar. Traditionally, Assyrians splash each other with water to purify one another, this is called *Nusardel* or *Musardeh*, which Assyrians still celebrate today and is documented later in this book.

[13] http://oracc.org/rinap/Q003973/.

Assyrian king Sennacherib, cuneiform tablet P336316/SAA 12 086
Neo-Assyrian Period (911–612 BC)
Provenience—Nineveh
Tablet collection and location—Vorderasiatisches Museum,
Berlin, Germany
Language—Akkadian

Cuneiform Tablet, P336316/Saa 12 086

*The se[al of] Aššur, king of the gods; the seal of God the
King, not to be contested*

*I am Sennacherib, king of the world, king of Assyria,
circumspect monarch, the perfecter of the forgotten cult of
Ešarra according to the oracular command of Šamaš and
Adad, the enlarger of their purificatory cult, the restorer of
the protective deity of Ešarra, which had ceased to function,
[to] its place.*

ruling
(Blank seal space)
ruling

*In Nisan (I), when at the New Year's Festival, on account of
chaos and anarchy, [A]ššur was going to the festival banquet
in a garden within the city; at that time, after I had made the
statue of Aššur, king of all the gods, the creator of himself,
the father of the great gods, whose figure was exalted in the
Abyss, king of heaven and earth, lord of all the gods, the
progenitor of the Igigi and the Anunnaki, the builder of the
roof of heaven and the basement of earth, the maker of all
the regions, living in the [pur]e starlit heave[ns], the foremost
god, the one who decrees the destinies, the one who lives in
Ešarra [which] is in Assur, the [great] lord, my lord, and
(after I had made) the statues of the great gods, with the clever*

understanding that Ea bestowed upon me, and with the [wis]dom that Aššur, king of the gods, had given unto me;

I pondered and on my own initiatve I performed an oracle query concerning the Akitu Temple of the steppe. Šamaš and Adad commanded me to build the Akitu Temple for the festival of Aššur, which is appropriate for his great divinity.

I took its foundations down until I reached the underground waters.

Of my [own initiat]ive I ski[lfu]lly built it from the foundation to the parapet with mountain [limestone] and raised it as high as a mountain. I opened [a canal] and called its name "That which purifies the New Year's Festival." I encircled it with [trees] of the orchard, all kinds of fruits and aromatic plants, as with a garland.

[Total x pe]rsons from Raṣappa (that) I have donated as a present to the Akitu Temple of the steppe of Nisan (I) [which] I built skilfully[according to] my own wish. I have assigned them [as the responsibility of . . .]. The prefect, the mayor or the city overseer [shall not exercise au]thority [over them]. They are [re]sponsible for the Akitu Temple.

(Break)

[. . .. . .] of heaven and earth [. . .. . .]
. . . [. . .] the great [god]s of heaven and earth [. . .. . .]
their offices, their . . ., their seed, their offspring [. . .. . .]
. . .. . . by the command of Aššur and the great gods. They are [. . .. . .].
ruling
[Witness NN], chief judge. Witness Inurta-na'id, grand [vizier].

Wi[tness NN], deputy [vizier]. Witness Nergal-šumu-lešir, [. . .] of Aššur.

Witness [NN, ... Witness] Nabû-šumu-iškun, [chari] ot dri[ver . . .].

Witness [NN, 'third] man.' Witness Aššur-bani, chief sc[ribe . . .].

Wi[tness NN, ... Witness] Aplaya, chief [. . .].

Wi[tness NN], chief physician. [Witness Ašš]ur-duri, recruitment officer.

Witness Mutaqqin-ahhe, recruitment officer. Witness [N]N, 'third man.'

Witness Aššur-dur-paniya, 'third man.' Witness . . .-damqu, cohort (commander) of [. . .].

Witness Aššur-šimanni, cohort commander of the ša šēpi guard. Witness Aššur-matu-taqqin, [. . .].

[Witness Ma]nnu-ki-Aššur, . . .[. . .].

[Witness . . .]-abu-uṣur, ditto. Witness Abi-ram, c[ity] overseer [. . .].

Wi[tness] Nabû-eṭiranni, temple scribe. Witness Šamaš-ila'i, inspector of the Aššur Gate.

Witness [. . .]su, inspector of the Šamaš Gate. Witness Mannu-ki-Ištar, ditto of the Tigris Gate.

Witness Nabû-mudammiq, city scribe.

Witness Kanunayu, chariot driver of Aššur. Witness Aššur-isse'a, 'third man' of Aššur.

Witness Kakkusu, scribe. Witness Aššur-le'i, chief gaddāyu.

Witness Sangu-Issar, commander-of-fifty of the tanners of coloured leather.

22nd year of Sennacherib, king of the world, king of Assy[ria (. . .)].[14]

---

[14] Assyrian king Sennacherib cuneiform tablet P336316/SAA 12 086, http://oracc.org/saao/P336316/.

This is a wish from the Assyrians on their New Year, found on some cuneiform tablets.

I write for your well-being on the occasion of the New Year
May you be happy

May you remain in good health
May the God who looks after you provide you with good
things

This Assyrian cuneiform relief is located at the British Museum; it is translated to, "On the sixth day of Nissan," the day and night were of equal length. This indicates the spring equinox.

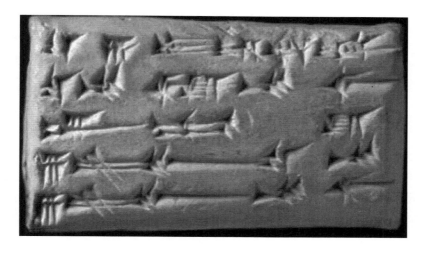

In the ancient days, the celebrations of the New Year lasted twelve days and twelve nights. They recited the epic of creation, Enuma Elish story, and each day had a planned special event.

The New Year was celebrated by grand events, and the king would invite people from different nations. There are several cuneiform stone reliefs that detail the elaborate celebrations.

King Sennacherib built an Akitu house—a temple that housed all the gods that Assyrians worshipped at the time.

During the New Year celebrations, certain days were dedicated to their main gods; each city had their main gods. God Ashur was the main pantheon in the city of Ashur, so he would be celebrated on one day, and another day would be celebrated for the god Marduk (the god Marduk was the main pantheon in Babylon) and one day for Ishtar and also the other gods. They offered animal sacrifices—lambs, goats, or oxen—and conducted prayers in the temple. They held parades, fire-lighting ceremonies, plays, and large ceremonial dinner parties for everyone. The highlight of the New Year was the procession of the gods.

This tablet documents the procession of the god Ashur and the cultic rituals associated with Assyrian New Year, SAA 20 053

Middle Assyrian Period (1400–1000 BC)
Provenience—Assur
Tablet collection and location—Vorderasiatisches Museum, Berlin, Germany
Language—Akkadian

Cuneiform Tablet, Assyrian New Year SAA 20 053

(i 1') [Ea, Belet-ili], Damkina and [Ninurta] go [to the Akit]u [House aft]er Aššur. [The Chariot, the Weapon, Amurru], Haya, Mandanu, [Nusku and K]akka go before Aššur.

(i 6') [The gods] of the Akitu House on the right and left of Aššur:

(i 7') [Aššur, Mul]lissu, *Mašmaš*, Šerua, [Sîn, Ni]kkal, Šamaš, Aya, Enlil, [Ištar of Nineveh], Kakka, Kippat-mati in the courtyard. [Hay]a and Kusu i[n] the courtyard. [Total 14] gods [o]n the right.

(i 12') Anu, Antu, Adad, Šala, Ea, Belet-ili, Damkina, Ninurta, Nergal, Nu[s]ku, and Mandanu in the courtyard. Total 11 gods on the left.

(i 16') On the second day of Nisan (I), when he (= the king) has provided cooked meat before Aššur, the chariot-driver enters. He holds the whip toward Aššur, sets [the] chariot in motion and goes to the Akitu House. The white [hors]es, the teams (and) [the . . .] s go out with the chariot. [The singer] intones, "The *former* [. . .]."

(i 23') [The . . .] of the Akitu [si]ngs: [". . ."], and goes to the House of God.

(i 25') [The . . .] holds [*the whip* toward Ašš]ur.

(i 26') [. . .. . . as] on the first day

(i 27') [. . .. . .] returns

(rest (about 4 lines) broken away)

(beginning (about 30 lines) broken away)

(ii 3') Ka[kka . . .. . .]

(ii 4') the god [. . .. . .]

(ii 5') in the *win*[*dow* . . .. . .]

(ii 6') The king [. . .s] before the *wi*[*ndow* . . .]

(ii 7') they slaughter [. . .. . .]

(ii 8') six . . . pots [. . .. . .]

(ii 9') refined oil, beer [. . .. . .]

(ii 10') he thro[ws] into it [. . .. . .]

(ii 11') he throw[s] into it [. . .. . .]

(ii 12') [He offers] hand-water t[o Aššur].

(ii 13') Aššur sets o[ut (in procession) . . .. . .].

(ii 14') As soon as he has gon[e down] to the courtyard, [. . .].

(ii 15') After he has [*reached*] the out[er] gate, [. . .]

(ii 16') Aššur [*take*] the road [*to* . . .].

(ii 17') In the evening [. . .. . .]

(ii 18') it stands [. . .. . .]

(ii 19') the chariot [. . .] in [. . .. . .]

(ii 20') (The king) goes down [*to the House of God and kisses*] the gr[ound *before Aššur*].

(ii 21') The chariot c[*omes out* . . .. . .]

(ii 22') from there [. . .. . .]

(ii 23') of *wood* [. . .. . .]

(ii 24') in the *observation post* [. . .].

(ii 25') After Aššur [has *left*] the *Ubšuk*[*kina*] house (and)

(ii 26') is on his way, he goes (and) [. . .] Aššu[r . . .]

(ii 27') goes from the gate of Aššur [. . .]

(ii 28') [en]ters with the monster(s) [. . .]

(ii 29') One who is with [. . ..].

(ii 30') an arrow [. . .. . .]

(ii 31') . . . [. . .. . .]

(rest (3–4 lines) broken away)

(totally lost)

(totally lost)

(beginning (about 6 lines) broken away)

(r v 2') the sons [of . . .. . .].

(r v 3') On the 22nd day (of Shebat) [. . . *the king goes and*] 'loads' [the brazier . . ...].
(r v 5') *in* the House of God [. . .. . .]
(r v 6') to the right of the be[d . . .. . .]

(r v 7') to the ri[ght] of the be[d . . .. Mullissu, Š]erua, [Kippat-mati, Kakka, Mandanu], Haya, Kus[u . . .]: total 7 gods of [. . .] who [go *with Aššur*] to the house of Daga[n].

(r v 12') For Mullissu [to sit] *at* the [right-side] watchtower [is favourable]. For Mullissu [to sit] *at* the [right-side] front [is favourable]. For Mullissu [to sit] *at* the [left-side] watchtower [is favourable]. For Šerua [to sit] on the right [is unfavourable]. For Šerua [to sit] on the left [is favourable. They sit thus] in the house of Dagan on the 22nd day.

(r v 18') [The . . .] cuts off the hand-water of Aššur [and *gives it*] to Mulli[ssu. He acts] as before [Aššur].

(r v 21') All the days that [. . .. . ., . . .] a calf and a spring lamb in [. . .].

(r v 23') After Aššur [has gone out] of the house of [Dagan], he is seated [at the Eastern Gate].
(r v 24') Mul[lissu . . .. . .]
(r v 25') Šerua befo[re . . .. . .].

(r v 26') The table [. . .. . .]
(r v 27') one mina [. . .. . .]
(rest (about 30 lines) broken away)

(beginning (about 4 lines) broken away)

(r vi 1') [. . .. . .] the Anzû [Gate. The *singer*] intones [. . .].

(r vi 3') [The king] performs [the sheep offering] (and) sets Aššur in motion. He performs [a sheep offering, . . . and] seats [Aššur on] the dais. [The chanters] install [the kettledrum. After the chanters have left], he provides for [the House of God].

(r vi 8') He performs the [regular off]ering, sets [Aššur] in motion and seats him [on the dais. Mullissu], Šerua, Kippat-mati, Kakk[a and Mand]anu are seated on the right, [Haya and K]usu on [the left side], oppo[site Aššur]. He pe[rforms] the shee[p offering]s before Aššur. The chanters install the kettledrum. After the chanters have left, cooked meat is provided.

(r vi 14') Haya goes to stand at the head of the boat. The gods of Subartu are made to cross over before him. Aššur sets off and is seated on the dais. He provides for the House of God.

(r vi 17') The new baths of Aššur:

(r vi 18') [The xth] of Nisan (I), the 18th of Elul (VI), [the xth] of Tishri (VII), the 4th of Kislev (IX), [the xth o]f Shebat (XI), the 7th of Adar (XII).

(r vi 21') The new [baths] of Anu:

(r vi 22') [The 4th of Iy]yar, the 3rd of Elul (VI), the 6th of Tishri (VII), [the 12th of Marchesvan (VIII)], the 18th of Shebat (XI).

(r vi 24') The new [baths] of Adad:

(r vi 25') [The 7th of Nisan (I), the 10t]h of Iyyar (II), the 16th of Elul (VI), [the 2nd of Tishri (VII), the 16th of Ma]rchesvan (VIII), the 18th of Shebat (XI).

(r vi 27') [The kettledrum (performance)s for the processions] of the gods, for the entire year:

(r vi 28') [The 8th of Nisan (I), the 17th of Elul (VI)], the 3rd of Tishri (VII), the 16th, 17th, 20th, 22nd, [23rd and 24th] of Shebat (XI).

30 lines broken away[15]

This tablet is particularly important as it mentions the New Year celebrations continued in the Hellenistic period after the fall of the Assyrian empire, and it confirms the celebrations were still conducted and the Akkadian language is still in use at this time:

---

[15] http://oracc.org/saao/P282261/.

New Year rituals on cuneiform tablet BM407 from Hellenistic period
Hellenistic Period (323–63 BC)
Provenience—Uruk
Tablet collection and location—J. Pierpoint Morgan Library;
collection—New Haven, Connecticut, USA
Language—Akkadian

Cuneiform Tablet, BM 407 Translation

1) By the command of Anu and Antu, may it (this text) go well.

(o 1)As soon as Anu has come out from the Enamena, the cella, (and) arrived at the Kamah gate, all the mašmaššu priests recites 3 times the incantation 'The king has come out'.

(o 3) The mašmaššu priests stop and after that the high priest, the mašmaššu-priests, the temple enterers and the brewers, who are yoked to the carrying pole, greet Anu, (saying) 'Great Anu, may heaven and earth greet you'.

(o 6) After the greeting, the mašmaššu priests recite 4 times the incantation 'The king has come out', up to the street Suq-ili.

(o 7) The high priest, the mašmaššu-priests, the temple-enterers and the brewers, who are yoked to the carrying pole, greet Anu, (saying) 'Great Anu, may heaven and earth greet you'.

(o 9) After the greeting, in the street Suq-ili the mašmaššu-priests recite 4 times the incantation 'The king surpassing (other) kings in heaven and earth'. They stop (reciting) the incantation and the high priest, the mašmaššu-priests, the temple-enterers and the bearers of the carrying pole greet Anu as before.

(o 12) After the greeting, the mašmaššu-priests recite 7 times each the incantation 'The king comes to the festival' and the incantation 'From the holy water-vessel', up to the quay Karkuga, the causeway of the boat Ma-Ana, the route of the gods. They stop (reciting) the incantation and the high priest, the mašmaššu-priests, the temple-enterers and the bearers of the carrying pole greet Anu.

(o 16) As soon as Anu has arrived at the causeway of the boat Ma-Ana, the mašmaššu-priests and the temple-enterers raise the incantation 'He rides the processional boat', a šu'illakku-prayer, to Anu. After that the high priest, the mašmaššu-priests, the temple-enterers and the bearers of the carrying pole greet Anu, greeting as before.

(o 20) From the the upper causeway of the quay Karkuga up to the Kagallugal gate the mašmaššu priests recite 7 times the incantation 'After (the one) surpassing (other) kings has passed by in the pure street'.

(o 22) They stop (reciting) the incantation and at the Kagallugal gate the high priest, the mašmaššu-priests, the temple-enterers and the bearers of the carrying pole greet Anu, greeting as before.

(o 24) From the Kagallugal gate up to the temple of the akītu-festival, the temple of prayer, the mašmaššu-priests recite the incantations exactly as in the street Suq-ili. They stop (reciting) the incantations and the high priest, the mašmaššu-priests, the temple enterers and the brewers, who are yoked to the carrying pole, carry out the greeting in full 7 times and so greet Anu.

(r 1) As soon as Anu has reached the temple of the akītu-festival, the mašmaššu-priests recite the incantation 'Pure

house, house of the gods', the incantation 'An, my king, to your good heart', the incantation 'The dining hall of the evening meal of heaven', the incantation 'Befitting the majestic dais', the incantation 'The temple has been purified', and the incantation 'The dwelling of the great gods'.

(r5) 'Great Anu, may heaven and earth greet you.

(r6) 'May Ellil, Ea and Belet-ili greet you joyfully.

(r7) 'May both the gods Sin and Šamaš greet you on their appearance.

(r8) 'May Nergal and the Seven greet you in the loyalty of their hearts.

(r9) 'May the Igigu (gods) of heaven and the Anunnakku (gods) of earth greet you.

(r10) 'May the gods of Apsu and the gods of Duku greet you.

(r11) 'May they greet you daily, day, month and year.'

(r12) This (is) the greeting (with) which the high priest, the mašmaššu-priests, the temple enterers and the brewers, who are yoked to the carrying pole, greet Anu 7 times, from the Reš temple up to the temple of the akītu-festival.

(r15) Incantation: 'The king has come out, the king has come out.'

(r16) (Colophon:) Written in accordance with its original and then checked and made good. Copy of an ancient writing board, the property of Anu and Antu.

(r17) Tablet of Anu-ah-ušabši, son of Kidin-Anu, descendant of Ekur-zakir, mašmaššu priest of Anu and Antu, high priest of the Reš temple, Urukean.

(r18) (Copied by) the hand of Anu-balassu-iqbi, his son.

(r18) He wrote (the tablet) for his learning, his time being long, his well-being and securing his position, and then he deposited (it) permanently in Uruk and the Reš temple, the temple of his lordship. He who reveres Anu and Antu shall not take it away by means of theft.

[r21] Uruk. (Month of) Du'uzu, *24ᵗʰ* day, year sixty 1, Antiochus, king of Uruk. (Month of) Du'uzu, *24ᵗʰ* day, year sixty 1, Antiochus, king of all the lands.[16]

This cuneiform tablet documents the daily rituals and the twelve-day celebration of the Assyrian New Year; it confirms that after the fall of the Assyrian empire, their New Year celebrations continued. It documents the traditional link from ancient to present celebrations; it also confirms the language Akkadian was still in use at this time frame and the Assyrian gods are still being worshipped.

---

[16] BM 4, 07 New Year Rituals, http://oracc.iaas.upenn.edu/cams/gkab/P296523/html.

The New Year festival rituals, TCL 06 39 (P363711)
Hellenistic Period (323–63 BC)
Provenience—Uruk
Tablet collection and location—Louvre Museum, Paris, France
Language—Akkadian

Cuneiform Tablet, P363711 Translation

1) By the command of Anu and Antu, may it (this text) gowell.

(o 1) (The month of) Tašritu, the 1st day: Ellil, Ea and (the other gods) of Uruk are clothed.

(o 2) *The silver chariot of Anu (and) the gold chariot of Anu go each day until the 8th day, at the secondary meal in the morning, to Anu's upper temple of the akītu-festival, and the musicians go in front of them.*

(o 4) *The cultic ordinances of the (divine) marriage are carried out in the Ehilikuga, the Enir of the Ehiliana, the temple of Nanaya.*

(o 6) *The 6th day: Adad, Šamaš, Lugalbanda and Ninsun are clothed. The holy water-basin is set up at dusk.*

(o 7) *The 7th day: The awakening of the temple (ceremony) by the kalû-priests and the musicians. The cook: food and singing with joy, roast meat, meat from an ox and a sacrificial sheep for the regular offerings, all kinds of finest beer together with pressed wine and milk, fine cut dates, good mixed beer and moistened mixed beer, drinking vessels, vats and pitchers (shaped like) a raven for Papsukkal and Kusibanda.*

(o 11) *For the cella: the clothing ceremony of (the statues of) Anu and Antu and the clothing ceremony of Ištar.*

(o 12) *The setting in place of the ox. Songs by the musician and the kalû-priest in the area between the curtains.*

(o 13) *A monthly offering after the clothing ceremony and the (offerings of) goats. The cleansing of the temple.*

(o 14) *The walk through the streets, the processional boats and the temple of the akītu-festival. The setting out and clearing away of the morning and evening meal, as for the 7th day of (the month of) Nisannu, ditto.*

(o 16) *The 8ᵗʰ day: The gate is opened before Anu and Antu, and Papsukkal arises and goes down to the main court and takes up his position in the EzukešHUHU opposite Anu.*

(o 18) *Nusku, Usmu and Kusu arise and stand beside Papsukkal*

(o 19) *The interior gold carrying pole is given to Anu. The weapons, sun-discs and chariots arise and take up position in the main court (facing) towards Anu. Adad, Šala, Sin, Šamaš, Ninurta, Messagunug, Palil, Lugalbanda and Ninsun arise from their temples and go down to the main court and take up position (facing) towards Anu. He (a priest) raises the water for the hands towards An and Antu and sprinkles the king and the people. He pours (from) the gold libation-vessel and presents the meal and the quickly cooked roast meat to Anu in a gold bowl. He passes the gold bowl in front of Anu on to the (other) gods who (are) in the main court.*

(o 26) *Papsukkal goes and stands on top of the (socle) Egubiduga. A temple-enterer pours (from) the gold libation-vessel, and Papsukkal and the mašmaššu-priests take the hands of Anu and he comes out among the mašmaššu-priests, with one temple-enterer around whom a sash is tied carrying the sceptre of kingship before him, and, as soon as Anu has reached the area between the curtains, he sits on the gold seat in the area between the curtains. He (a priest) raises the water for the hands.*

(o 30) *He strews on top of the place for presenting offerings and makes a merdītu-offering, an ox and a ram, in front of Anu. He places the heart of the ox and the head of the ram in front of him.*

(o 32) He turns upside down on top of the heart a gold malītu-vessel *(full)* of maṣhatu-flour. He pours the libation-vessel *(full)* of wine on top of the head of the ram. He raises the water for the hands towards Anu and [. . .] . . .. He pours *(from)* the gold libation-vessel and Papsukkal and Nusku [. . .] the mašmaššu-priests *(and)* the musicians [. . .]

(r 1') *(The 9ᵗʰ day:)* . . . [. . .] . . . [. . .] sits on his seat in the forecourt. They lift up the liver omen and place *(it)* on top of the dais of Anu.

(r 3') A member of the *(group of)* diviners and the šangû-priest of Adad take the liver omen. The main meal is cleared away and the secondary meal is presented. He *(a priest)* fills the censers and the musicians sing.

(r 5') They recite 'The temple prospers, have success . . .' but it *(the secondary meal)* is not cleared away. It is cleared away in the evening when the main meal of the evening is presented. He *(a priest)* fills the gold censer and presents an offering, an ox and a ram. The musicians sing. The main meal is cleared away and the secondary meal is presented. The musicians sing. They recite 'The temple prospers, have success . . .' but it *(the secondary meal of the evening)* is not cleared away. The nocturnal offering stays overnight. The gate is closed.

(r 10') The 10ᵗʰ day: In the night 'Authoritative lord in heaven and earth' *(is performed)* to Anu *(and)* 'The honoured one of heaven' to *(all)* the gods.

(r 11') The awakening of the temple *(ceremony)* is performed in the Ubšukkinnakku. At daybreak the gate is opened and the nocturnal offering is cleared away, and the water for the hands is raised. Oil is taken. The main meal in the morning is presented.

(r 13') The musicians sing. The main meal is cleared away and the secondary meal is presented. The secondary meal is cleared away and the main meal in the evening is presented. The musicians sing. The secondary meal in the evening is cleared away and the gate is closed.

(r 15') The 11th day: In the night 'Wild bull in his fold' (is performed) to Anu (and) 'For the honoured one roving about' to (all) the gods.

(r 16') The awakening of the temple (ceremony) is performed in the Ubšukkinnakku. At daybreak the gate is opened and the water for the hands is raised.

(r 17') Adad, Sin, Šamaš, Ninurta, Messagunug, Papsukkal, Nusku, Usmu and Kusu arise and take up position in the main court (facing) towards Anu. They sit on (their) seats in the forecourt and wait for Lugalbanda and Ninsun. The main meal in the morning is presented to Anu, Antu and all the (other) gods. As soon as Lugalbanda and Ninsun have arrived, they enter into the forecourt of Anu and take up position (facing) towards Anu. The main (meal) is cleared away and he (a priest) pours (from) the gold libation-vessel for Lugalbanda and Ninsun and those (other) gods, and they return to their seats and sit. The main and secondary meals of the (last) double-hour of the day, as for the regular offerings, ditto.

(r 25') These (are) the cultic ordinances of (the month of) Tašritu, completed.

(r 26') (Catchline: The month of) Arahsamnu, the 5th day: Mišaru arises from Ehenuna, the temple of Adad.

(r 27') Written from an old writing-board, a copy of Uruk, and then checked. Tablet of Anu-uballiṭ, the son of Nidintu-Anu

(r 28') *(and) descendant of Hunzu, mašmaššu-priest of Anu and Antu, Urukean. (Copied by) the hand of Šamaš-eṭir, the son of Ina-qibit-Anu, son of Šibqat-Anu,*

(r 29') *(and) descendant of Ekur-zakir, mašmaššu-priest of Anu and Antu, Tiranaean.*[17]

Annually, the month of Nissan (April), the first month in the Assyrian calendar, is the start of spring, and it's celebrated as the Assyrian New Year. The celebration is called Resh d'Sheta Khata, meaning "head of the new year" or "start of the new year," and is often referred to as Akitu or the Assyrian New Year. This celebration, both in ancient and present time, coincides with rebirth, new life, purification and renewal, resurrection, and spiritual cleansing. They give thanks with hopes that the new-year would be filled with a bountiful harvest, good health, happiness, and prosperity for all.

Today Assyrians often celebrate in parks, where they all gather together with singers, music, live bands, and dance. Some celebrate in church or throw parties and celebrate in banquet halls; they celebrate with food, dancing, and singing.

Assyrians of all the various church denominations celebrate the New Year. At the first sight of spring, one tradition is to collect symbols and greenery from their gardens, place them in a bunch, and hang them upside down on their front door. This bunch of greenery or flowers is called *Diqnit Nissan*, meaning, "beard of April."

Legend has it that the fall of the Assyrian empire happened during the New Year celebrations; everyone was celebrating, drinking, and did not expect the attack at their weakest and most unexpected moment.

Mostly the twelve-day celebrations have slowly faded away, but all the Assyrians around the world still celebrate the first day of the New Year on April 1.

---

[17] Cuneiform tablet on New Year's rituals: museum number AO 06459, CDLI number P363711, http://oracc.org/cams/gkab/P363711.

PRAYERS AND SACRIFICES
(SHARA/DUKHRANA)

The Assyrian prayers in church are some of the oldest in the world, and other Christian churches around the world have used them to make their own some have also recited them in the Assyrian language.

Praying is very important to Assyrians, starting from ancient times; they built vast ziggurats in order to be close to God to pray. This was the case with the tower of Babylon; the intention was to build a high tower to be closer to God so that their prayers could be heard.

Assyrians pray today as they did thousands of years ago; you can see this in any Assyrian church and this ancient relief shows how they prayed in the past.

This is a letter from Ashur-Marduk-sallim-ahhe, a scribe of the Ashur temple that contains some ancient prayers.

These are some ancient Assyrian blessings and prayers that have been taken directly from cuneiform tablets.

Neo–Assyrian Period (911–612 BC)
Provenience—Nineveh
Tablet collection and location—British Museum, UK
Language—Akkadian

Cuneiform Tablet, SAA 13 008 CDLI-P334682Translation

To the king, my lord: your servant, Marduk-šallim-ahhe, the one who blesses you. Good health to the king, my lord. May Aššur, Bel, Nabû, Sin, Šamaš, Ištar of Nineveh, and Ištar of Arbela very g]reatly bless [the king, my] lord. May they give to the king, my lord, lon[g days] and years of physical well-being.

This 5th day of Kanun (X) belongs to Talmusu. Nothing has been brought; no one came. Nevertheless for the sake of the life of the king, my lord, [I have performed and p] resented every sac[rifice] before Aššur [and the gods of] the king, my lord.[18]

(Rest destroyed)

---

[18] Cuneiform tablet P334682 / SAA 13 008, http://oracc.org/saao/P334682/.

This is another tablet found that reflects the prayers in ancient Assyria.

> Neo-Assyrian Period (911–612 BC)
> Provenience—Nineveh
> Tablet collection and location—British Museum, London, UK
> Language—Akkadian

Cuneiform Tablet, P393721 BMS 19 Translation

Prayer to god Enlil; the beginning of the tablet is destroyed.

> *Lord of lords, [. . .]*
> *Father, who be[got] the great [gods],*
> *Lord of fates (and divine) plans,*
> *Commander of the heavens and earth, lord of the lands,*
> *Who renders the verdict, whose command cannot be overturned,*
> *Who determines the fates of all [the gods]:*
> *On account of the evil of a lunar eclipse, which occurred in month (unspecified and) day (unspecified),*
> *And evil, unfavorable signs (and) portents,*
> *[Which] occurred in my palace and my land-*
> *[At] your [spe]aking, humanity was born,*
> *Of king (and) governor, you speak their names.*
> *Because creating divinity and king is within your power (lit. is with you),*
> *And (because) you make the weak equal to the strong,*
> *Among the multitude of stars of the heavens,*
> *O my lord, I trust in you!*
> *At your appearance, I have given you my attention.*
> *Determine a fate of life for me!*
> *Command a good name!*
> *Carry away evil; grant me what is good.*
> *Set over me your great protective force.*

May god and king value me,
May lord and prince do what benefits me (lit. do that of my goodness).
May my (ill-wishing) onlooker be ashamed on my account.
May my order be heard in the assembly.

May the protective spirit of ordering, hearing, and accepting
Walk along with me daily.
According to your august command that cannot be changed,
And your reliable affirmation that cannot be overturned!
It is the wording of a lifted-hand prayer to Enlil.
Incantation: Great princess, goddess of fates.[19]

This tablet is known as the covenant of Ashur tablet.

Neo-Assyrian Period (911–612 BC)
Provenience—Nineveh
Tablet collection and location—British Museum, London, UK
Language—Akkadian

Cuneiform Tablet, SAA 09 003, the Covenant
of Aššur (ABRT 1 22–23)

TRANSLATION 3.1 INTRODUCTION

(Beginning of the tablet is destroyed)
Heaven and earth are [well]; Ešarra is [wel]l; Esarhaddon,
king of Assyria, is [well].
[May the well-b]eing which Esarhaddon [has established]
gain footing!
Aššur has arranged [a feast in] Ešarra.
(missing parts of the tablet)

---

[19] https://cdli.ucla.edu/search/archival_view.php?ObjectID=P393721.

3.2 FIRST ORACLE OF SALVATION

(missing parts of the tablet)
[List]en, O Assyrians!
[The king] has vanquished his enemy. [You]r [king] has put his enemy [under] his foot, [from] sun[se]t [to] sun[ris]e, [from] sun[ris]e [to]sun[se]t!
I will destroy [Meli]d,
I will deliver the Cimmerians into his hands and set the land of Ellipi on fire.
Aššur has given the totality of the four regions to him. From sunrise to sunset there is no king equal to him; he shines as brilliantly as the sun.
This is the (oracle of) well-being placed before Bel-Tarbaṣi and the gods.

3.3 SECOND ORACLE OF SALVATION

Now then, these traitors provoked you, had you banished, and surrounded you; but you opened your mouth (and cried): "Hear me, O Aššur!"
I heard your cry. I issued forth as a fiery glow from the gate of heaven, to hurl down fire and have it devour them.
You were standing in their midst, so I removed them from your presence. I drove them up the mountain and rained (hail)stones and fire of heaven upon then.
I slaughtered your enemies and filled the river with their blood. Let them see (it) and praise me, (knowing) that I am Aššur, lord of the gods.
This is the well-being (placed) before the Image.
This covenant tablet of Aššur enters the king's presence on a cushion. Fragrant oil is sprinkled, sacrifices are made, incense is burnt, and they read it out in the king's presence.

3.4 THE MEAL OF COVENANT

The word of Ištar of Arbela to Esarhaddon, king of Assyria:
Come, gods, my fathers and brothers, [enter] into the
cove[nant . . .. . .]
(Break)
[She placed] a slice of . . . on the [ter]race and gave them
water from a cooler to drink; she filled a flagon of one seah
with water from a cooler and gave it to them with the words:
"In your hearts you say, 'Ištar is slight,' and you will go to your
cities and districts, eat (your) bread and forget this covenant.
"(But when) you drink from this water, you will remember
me and keep this covenant which I have made on behalf of
Esarhaddon."
ruling

3.5 WORD OF IŠTAR OF ARBELA

The word of Ištar of Arbela to Esarhaddon, king of Assyria:
As if I did not do or give you anything!
Did I not bend the four doorjambs of Assyria, and did I not
give them to you? Did I not vanquish your enemy? Did I
not collect your haters and foes [like but]terflies?
[As for yo]u, what have you given to me?
[There is no fo]od for my banquet, as if there were no temple;
I [am depri]ved of my food, I am d[ep]rived of my cup! I am
waiting for them, I have cast my eye upon them.
Verily, establish a seah of bowl food and a one-seah flagon
of sweet beer! Let me take and put in my mouth vegetables
and soup, let me fill the cup and drink from it, let me restore
my charms!
(Break)
and arranged [a fea]st [. . .].
[When] I was [there, they said: "We know] that you are
Ištar [of A]rbela."

*I set out [for] Assyria to see yo[ur success], to tread the
mountains [with my feet], [and to spea]k about Esarhaddon.
[No]w rejoice, Esarhaddon! [I have be]nt [the four doorjamb]
s of Assyria and given them to you; I have vanquished yo[ur
enemy. The mood of the people] who stand with you has
been turned upside down.*

[From thi]s you shall see [that] I am [Ištar of] Arbela.

*[As soon as the traitors] have been dragged forth, ['the ones at the
right and] left side' shall stand there to bear [the punishment].
(As for) those cou]rtiers and palace [personnel who] rebelled
[against] you, [I have sur]rounded them and impaled them
by their teeth.*

*[La-dagil-i]li, a prophet of [Arbela, prophesied (this)
when . . .. . .] Ištar[20] [. . .. . .].*

In ancient times, the Assyrians would offer a sacrifice of animals
or fully prepared meals; they would also offer flour, barley, wheat,
gold, and fragrance oil, which would be sprinkled with frankincense
and burned for their gods. This was done when they asked God for
something.

They offered theses sacrifices in the ziggurats or temples they
built to their gods. There are several cuneiform tablets about the
Assyrian kings' mass offerings to their gods.

They sacrificed animals—lambs, oxen, or goats—if a full moon,
blood moon, or eclipse was visible in the sky, as these were signs or
omens that something would happen to the city or to the king. They
made sacrifices to ensure that the gods did not punish them in any way.

The Assyrian people today still do these sacrifices in their ancient
lands and around the world; these events are called *Dukhrana* or *Shara*,
meaning "sacrifice" or "offering."

They sacrifice whole or partial animals, and today these are done
mainly to honor their saints; based on their Christian beliefs, there
are special months that are dedicated to celebrate the various saints.

---

[20] http://oracc.org/saao/P334927/.

In the homeland, they use animal blood to mark a cross on top of their front door so that all neighbours and passersby know they are having a *dukhrana*, so they can come in to have some food. Some people also mark a cross of animal blood on their forehead to show they are having a *dukhrana*.

Some have *dukhrana* by purchasing half a cow or a whole lamb, and the butcher cuts up all the meat. When they get home, they put meal-size pieces in bags, enough for a family meal, and hand them out to people. They normally cook large portions of the meat in water and feed all people that come by. Some *dukhrana* have several people contribute so they can buy several whole lambs that they give away to feed the homeless or the community. This serves as their sacrifice or offering to God.

There are certain families that do a *dukhrana* for each saint every year and normally this tradition has been in their family for generations. These special families collect the money all year or buy the meat on their own annually to make the *dukhrana*, and everyone is welcome to come to eat it. Anyone that wants to do a *dukhrana* can.

There are other offerings that are done: some buy food and give it to people, such as bread. Normally this is bought from local Assyrian stores, which then distribute them to other people that come in. Another type of offering involves making Assyrian pastries like Keleche or Kada, and handing them out in church. Some also make food to give to the homeless or the less fortunate.

The Assyrians that adhere to the Catholic Church have lost the tradition of *dukhrana*; but in the homelands, they still participate. Assyrians in the West adhere to the practices of the Vatican, so they don't have this specific tradition. The Ancient Church of the East, the Assyrian Church of the East, the Anglicans, and the Syriac Orthodox Churches still practice this ancient tradition.

The saints that are observed annually by Assyrians for *dukhrana* are listed here.

The date that these events are observed are taken from the perspective of the Assyrian Church of the East. The Ancient Church of the East and the Syriac Church assign their own dates.

These dates vary each year, but the month does not change. The local Assyrian church has the annual calendar, and it contains all the dates of the occasions and observations.

January 5, 2020	Dukhrana d'Mar Zaya & Mar Tawar
April 26, 2020	Dukhrana Mar Gewargis
May 15, 2020	Dukhrana d'Mart Maryam
July 5, 2020	Dukhrana d'Mar Toma
July 12, 2020	Dukhrana d'Mar Yosip Khnanisho
July 15, 2020	Dukrana d'Mar Qoryakos
August 16, 2020	Raza Quadessa Dukhrana d'Mart Maryam The Blessed Virgin
September 13, 2020	Dukhrana d'Mar Zaya and Mar Tawar
September 20, 2020	Dukhrana d'Mar Bisho
October 11, 2020	Dukhrana d'Mar Youkhana
November 1, 2020	Dukhrana d'Mar Gewargis

The Assyrian people believe in many saints. One of them is the saint Sultana Mahdokht; she was killed along with her two brothers for being Christian. An Assyrian priest built a church in the fourth century, on the location where they were killed and buried, in their honor.

The church is in Araden, which is in the Duhok region of Iraq, and this is a pilgrimage site for many Assyrians and other Christians, annually. Many miracles occurred in this church, and the villagers commemorate these saints every year.

There are several people that have seen the fruits of the devotion to this holy saint in the form of healing others from an illness that doctors could not resolve.

Legend has it that many barren women would pray to saint Sultana Mahdokht, and after their prayers to this saint, they were granted the gift of a child.

The Sultana Mahdokht church today in northern Iraq, built in the fourth century (AD 301–400).

RELIGIOUS FIGURES, SAINTS, AND BIBLICAL PROPHETS

*T*he Assyrian saints and religious figures listed here are from the Holy Apostolic Catholic Assyrian Church of the East and their traditions. Assyrian patriarchs are born from certain church families that declare their child to be part of the church. When the husband and wife make the decision to declare their child to church, they go to the church to get a formal blessing for this. When the woman becomes pregnant with a child, she becomes vegetarian for the entire duration of her pregnancy.

Assyrians call these children *nezerre*, meaning "blessed for church" or "given to church"; and once they are born, they too become vegetarian. When the child is born and while the mother breastfeeds, she is still vegetarian; and once the child is eight years old, they are turned over to the church, where they will reside from then on and devote their entire life to church. The family visits any time they want, and while the child is in church, they go to school and start learning the Assyrian prayers.

This is another tradition that has stopped because the majority of Assyrians no longer live in their homelands. The last priest to be nezerra is Mar Sargis from the Holy Apostolic Catholic Church of the East in California; before him, it was Mar Dinkha IV from the Holy Apostolic Catholic Assyrian Church of the East in Chicago, but Mar Dinkha had since passed away so now there is only one left in the entire world which was nezerra following the ancient Assyrian traditions which is Mar Sargis.

There are no others to follow after Mar Sargis as nezerre so far, so it appears this is another ancient tradition that has faded away in these most recent years.

The Assyrian patriarchs followed what is called Kanon et Sunhadous, which outlines church laws, religious events, and processes. Various non-Assyrian churches also follow their own Kanon Laws.

The saints that Assyrians believe in from the church of the east persective are listed under the section where *dukhrana* is described. Some that have personal stories that Assyrians still talk about today are mentioned here separately.

Mar Benyamin Shimun

Mar Benyamin Shimun, 1887–1918, was an Assyrian born in 1887, and he was the patriarch of the Assyrian Church of the East. He was *nezzera* and dedicated his entire life to his people and the church. He was known for being a very holy and peaceful man. In March

1918, a Kurdish man named Simko Shikak murdered the patriarch, who was only thirty-one years old.

During that time from World War I, 1913–1922, the Ottoman Empire was conducting systematic killings of the Christians in the area; it's famously known today as the Assyrian, Armenian, and Greek genocide.

Prior to Mar Benyamin Shimun's death, the Ottomans captured his brother Hormiz Shimun and threatened to kill him if the patriarch and his people did not surrender to them; after word came back to the patriarch, this is what he responded back to them.

> *It is impossible for me and my people to surrender after seeing the atrocities done to my Assyrian people by your government; therefore my brother is one, my people are many, I would rather lose my brother but not my nation.*

This saying resonates with many Assyrian people, and this is one that many cannot forget. Soon after this communication back to the Ottomans, they tortured and murdered his brother.

In 1918 Simko Shikak, the leader of Kurdish farmers sent word to the Assyrian patriarch that he wanted to discuss peace with Mar Shimun. Mar Shimun being a holy man believed in peace and love, so he set out to go meet with Simko Shikak. Many Assyrians warned against going to see him, but the patriarch insisted he would go so they could discuss peace between the two groups. About 150 Assyrians went along with the patriarch; they would not allow him to go alone—this was World War I and a very dangerous and volatile time for Christians.

When the Assyrians, with their patriarch arrived at Simko's house on March 3, 1918, they saw hundreds of Kurdish tribes surrounding the home. The Assyrians were told to leave their firearms in the yard before going near Simko's house. Yet the hundreds of Kurds surrounding the area were all heavily armed. The Assyrian men did not want to comply with their orders, but Mar Shimun insisted they leave their arms because he felt there was trust between them, and they were there to have peace talks between the two nations. So the 150 Assyrian men did as they were told, and all proceeded to go toward the house unarmed, while surrounded by armed Kurds.

It was said they talked inside the house, and once they finished, everyone proceeded to walk outside to go home. After they were outside, Simko Shikak shot the patriarch in the back. The patriarch was killed instantly, and the other Kurds began to fire on the other 150 unarmed Assyrians, killing them all. The Assyrian people know this story and are saddened when the Kurds today hold the murderer Simko Shikak as their national hero, and even named a street in his honor on Assyrian ancestral lands in northern Iraq.

A commemoration is held worldwide for the Assyrian patriarch Mar Shimun annually in the Assyrian Church of the East.

Mar Yousip Khnanisho

Mar Yousip Khnanisho was an Assyrian saint born in May 18, 1893; he was nezzera and dedicated his entire life to his people and the church. He died on July 3, 1977, at the age of eighty-four.

Most of the Assyrian people that adhere to the Assyrian Church of the East have a picture of Mar Yousip in their home. Some are privileged enough to have handwritten blessings from him on paper in their homes. This is called in Assyrian *borikta et beta*, meaning "blessing for the home." Saint Mar Yousip was very well-known for performing several miracles, and he was a very holy man. There have been several eyewitnesses to the miracles he performed, and there are multiple stories, but only a few will be written here.

Hafez al-Assad was the Syrian president from March 1915 to October 1915; he was the father of Bashar al-Assad, the president of Syria today. At that time, Syria and the surrounding areas experienced a locust infestation and plague that is very well documented. This infestation stripped their entire country of most of their vegetation during that time. This, coupled with an already depleted food supply and the 1915 Ottoman wars, made it a very difficult time.

The president was advised by his military leader, an Assyrian man by the name of Giwaryaquos(Giwargis), about Mar Yousip and his holiness. The president called Mar Yousip and told him about the situation and asked him to fly to Syria as soon as he could. A plane was sent for him, and Mar Yousip went to Syria. While they were outside, all the witnesses were there, the sky was dark by the swarming locust in the air, and Mar Yousip started to say his prayers; and when he finished, all the locust fell dead to the ground.

Other miracles that he performed were for children and people that could not walk; they were taken to him to perform his miracles. The witnesses to this said he would say his prayer, wrap a white ribbon on the legs, and when he had finished his prayers, he would remove the ribbon and say to the child, "Get up my child," and the child would get up and begin to walk. Assyrians experienced these miracles, and non-Assyrians also heard about him, and so many went to see him as well.

Mar Yousip also blessed wheat and are given to the Assyrian people so that can carry it with them wherever they go. The wheat grains that he blessed are wrapped in cloth and then sewn up this allows them to carry them in their purse or wallet, some wear them around their neck.

Mar Yousip's sister Simto dedicated her life to taking care of her brother. She would tell people that he went to his room to pray for hours, and when he came out, his face was radiant, glowing as if he had seen the face of God.

Various people talk about Mar Yousip and his miracles. Another story is that the president of Iraq at the time, Ahmad Hassan Albaker had called to bring Mar Yousip in because there were a lot of people talking about him and his miracles. The president sent people from the government to bring Mar Yousip in for questioning. When the three men went to his home, they were told, "He is in his room praying." When one of them went to open the door, all they could see was a shining light, and he was not in the room. The men were in shock and left immediately. The government never bothered Mar Yousip and his family again.

Assyrian people still visit his home, and some that are sick lie on his bed and put his headpiece on to get his blessings and to help them heal. They find comfort being where his holiness once was. This man will never be forgotten—he was a true saint that people still remember today.

These are two blessings that Mar Yousip wrote by hand at different times to be given to Assyrians to put in their home so that their home is always blessed.

Mar Eshai Shimun XXIII

Patriarch Mar Eshai Shimun XXIII (February 26, 1908–November 6, 1975) was made the patriarch of the Assyrian Church of the East in 1920.

The British, with the help of the Assyrians, had seized the territory of Mesopotamia from the Turkish Ottomans in World War I by October 3, 1932. The British promised the Assyrians that they would gain the territory back and be given their ancestral homelands back if they helped them fight the war. However, the British government never made good on that promise, and this is what the Assyrian people until today call the British Betrayal.

After WWI, the British and other foreign powers renamed the area previously known as Assyria (then named *Mesopotamia* by the Greeks) to *Iraq* in 1921. The British controlled the newly created Iraq at this point, and since so many Assyrians were displaced and uprooted from their homes and land, they were given other areas to build their new homes.

The Assyrian Levies was the first Iraq military force established by the British from 1915 to 1932; it quickly became an Assyrian-dominated battalion. Their primary role was to defend the northern frontier and the Royal Air Force. The Assyrian troops were a constant reminder to their neighbours of the unwelcome British presence in Iraq. This action would prove to have a negative impact on the Assyrian people in the future.

Mar Eshai Shimon was the patriarch of the Assyrian Church of the East at the time. He was born in the Hakkari province of current-day Turkey.

The Iraq government installed by the British had detained Mar Shimun, and he was jailed multiple times for wanting to get Assyrians their rights. They had officers outside his home watching his family constantly. In 1933, the British forces exiled the patriarch because of their growing concern on his influence on the Assyrian people and the situation in Iraq. He was forced to go to Cypress in 1933, and then in 1940, he went to the United States where he received his PhD.

The patriarch was involved in persistent advocacy to the League of Nations, the United Nations Assembly, and the United States to have the Assyrians' legitimate rights and their country returned.

On November 6, 1975, David Ismail from London, Ontario, assassinated the patriarch in cold blood at the front door of his home in San Jose, California. There are several stories about why the patriarch was killed; the trial records indicate that he was killed because David Ismail was upset that the patriarch got married; he wanted the patriarch to play a more active role in the political arena so that Assyrians could get their country back.

Other trial records say that it had to do with church rivals, but the murderer, David Ismail, was part of the Church of the East and had nothing to do with the church that Mar Eshai Shimun was patriarch of. In addition, Mar Eshai Shimun was already very politically active, some say the main reason the patriarch was murdered was because of his role in the political attempts to get Assyrians their country back.

In the month of January 1973, Mar Eshai Shimun announced his intention to retire; and this was after fifty-three years of devoted service to the Assyrian Church of the East. If you research Mar Eshia Shimun, you will see that he worked tirelessly to get the rights for the Assyrian people.

In the trail records, it was stated that in 1975, he was working diligently on something very important for a meeting he was planning to attend on November 12, 1975. In addition, it was clearly indicated that his wife saw him the day of November 6, 1975, and his desk was full of papers of what he was working on; and after he was shot, his entire desk was cleared from all his papers, which were never seen again.

There are a lot of questions surrounding the patriarch's murder case that are unclear.

Further independent research revealed that there was a United Nations general assembly, thirtieth session: 2,400[th] plenary meeting, scheduled for Monday, November 10, 1975; this was just days before he was murdered. The meeting was held in New York, and this meeting included AGENDA ITEM 77.

> Importance of the universal realization of the right of peoples to self-determination and of the speedy granting of independence to colonial countries and peoples for the effective guarantee and observance of human rights.

There is mention in the trial records that the church was having a meeting with the patriarch on November 19, 1975, which was postponed to January 5, 1976.

A lot is unclear, but it needs to be recognized that Mar Eshia Shimun dedicated his entire life and had made significant contributions and sacrifices to the church and his people—he contributed in ways that most people cannot make. Today he is remembered as a prominent member of the Assyrian community, a highly educated scholar, and a hero for Assyrian people worldwide.

It's also important to note that His Grace wrote hundreds of letters on the plight of the Assyrians. These are only a few examples mentioned in this book, and his work and documents can be located by visiting the Mar Eshia Shimum Foundation for more historical texts written by him. In appendixes 1 and 2, you will find some examples of his letters he wrote in the year 1933, before and after the Simele massacre, and on the plight of his people.

The Prophet Nahum

The biblical prophet Nahum was one prophets where his prophecies are written in the Torah and in the Old Testament. He was also known as an Elkoshite, meaning that he was from the city of Alqosh in Assyria; this is where he was born, raised, passed away, and was buried. Today it's known as Alqosh in Iraq.

Alqosh has always been an Assyrian city, and the only people that lived together in peace were the Assyrians, and some from the Jewish community.

Nahum was a Hebrew prophet, in 1948 the Jewish community was expelled from Iraq and when the last Jewish family was to leave Alqosh for Israel, they handed the iron keys for Nahum's tomb to an Assyrian man named Sami Jajouhana. They entrusted the care of the tomb to him and to this day, Nahum's tomb is safely guarded by some of the bravest Assyrian communities, known as Alqoshnaya, meaning "people from Alqosh or Elkoshite."

It is believed that Alqosh is where the prophet Nahum wrote his Old Testament book. Some also declare that Nahum's body has been hidden in a different area to protect it from harm, like that in 2014, when ISIS militants bombed the tomb of the prophet Jonah in Mosul.

Current-day Prophet Nahum's tomb in Alqosh in northern Iraq.

Over the years, people from both the Jewish and Christian faiths have visited the site as a pilgrimage, and often you will see pieces of paper tied to the fence around Saint Nahum's tomb, and these are prayers or wishes that people leave behind.

BIRTH TRADITIONS

Each culture has its own rituals for birth, marriage, and death. For Assyrians, when a child is born and the woman returns from the hospital, it's customary that the woman stays home for forty days and forty nights. Forty is a significant number for Assyrians and appears in many rituals, such as the length of a period of fasting. Forty days goes back to the Bible times, and so for forty days after giving birth, Assyrian women are not supposed to leave the home. The Assyrian saying surrounding this is that the woman has one foot in the grave after giving birth, and it's not good for the woman to go out, except for doctor visits. If new mothers go out before the forty days are up, it's generally frowned upon by Assyrian elders, normally friends and family go to visit the new mother and the baby.

Most Assyrians like to baptize their children soon after birth so that if something happens to the baby, they will go to heaven, according to their Christian faith.

Prior to their Christian conversion, the Assyrians already believed in holy water and blessings by water, and this is evident by several steles that have been excavated and preserved in the British Museum. The deity with the bucket of water and the cone was used for blessings; this is discussed in more detail in a previous chapter.

When Assyrian children are born, the family places a small cross and blessed wheat, if they have them, on a safety pin and pins them to the child's clothing, which helps to protect the child. The blessed wheat is from his holiness and Saint Mar Yousip.

Normally the new parents choose godparents, and when it time to have the child baptized, it is arranged with the church. There is also a celebration after the baptism. When the child is changed from their white baptismal clothes, it is customary that those clothes are washed only in a river or by hand in a small tub; the water is not supposed to be poured down the drain because it's blessed. Instead, the traditions are that the water is poured in a place where feet will not touch it, such as flowerbeds or rivers. The same tradition is followed for the water that is used to bathe the child right after their baptism.

Another tradition for babies is to put a silver piece, all silver, with a piece of bread, some wheat, and some salt into a cloth; then the cloth is placed under the mattress where the baby lays its head. This is meant to protect the child, and this tradition goes back to ancient times. The silver piece is meant to ward off evil, the bread or wheat is for blessings (*bourikhta*) to the child, and the salt is to protect the baby.

When the child's umbilical cord falls off, it is customary to keep it in the house to serve as the child's connection with their home—it is never discarded. The native Indians have a similar tradition with the umbilical cord; they, too, don't discard it but place it somewhere in their land to connect the child with their land.

It's customary that the children leave the house when they marry, but tradition is that the son of the house stays in his childhood home with his wife to take care of his aging parents.

Assyrian women wrap their baby in a swaddling blanket; this helps the newborn feel secure and sleep better. Another practice since the ancient times is that after giving birth, the mother wraps her stomach very tightly in white cotton cloth, similar to the use of corsets and waist trainers today. This helps all the organs to move back into place faster than normal and reshape the woman's body back to what it was prior to having her child. Today, a lot of women still use this method of waist trainers after birth.

Another customary tradition is when the new mother visits her parents' home for the first time after having her baby; her parents put money and candy inside the child's clothes before he or she enters the home. This is meant to serve as good luck; the money is for the child's prosperity, and the candy is to make him or her a sweet child.

When Assyrian couples are having trouble conceiving, it's customary for them to pray to a saint, asking for a child. Each person is connected to a saint, or they have a favorite one that they pray to; others pray to Saint Sultan Mahdokht. This saint is known to help women and men in conceiving a child.

When this saint blesses parents with a child a the woman is finally pregnant, it's normally always a boy, and it's customary not to cut the boy's hair until he is six or seven years old. The boy is dressed in colourful dresses until his hair is cut; this display shows people that this child was a gift from the saints. When it's time to cut the child's hair, it's done through prayers in church, and the priest cuts the hair. The parents save the hair and pass it on to his family when he is older. The boy is dressed in boy's clothing after this.

MARRIAGE TRADITIONS

*A*ssyrians have a lot of beautiful marriage traditions. Many Assyrian girls come from strict families who prefer that they marry Assyrian men, and vice versa, to ensure that they preserve their culture and traditions. However, in recent years it, these customs are changing.

Assyrian children are normally very close to their family members and are family oriented; family is a very big part and an integral part of their lives, so it's rare that Assyrian children go against their family's wishes.

It's customary that Assyrian children, for the most part, stay home until they are married. The boy of the house would normally stay with his parents to care for his aging parents. There was no option for old-age homes in the homeland, now since couples need to work there is no time to care for their aging parents so there are old-age homes, and each family chooses what is best for them.

The traditional marriage custom when a man wants to get married is to send his family to the girl's house to ask her parents' permission. If they accept, this is called a promise to marry; in Assyrian, it's called *mashmetta*, meaning "hearing." In the older days, the man did not go with his family to the girl's house, but in modern times, they do accompany the family. This gives the families an opportunity to get to know each other, and because the Assyrians are a close-knit community, they normally all know each other.

When the man's family is at the girl's home, it's customary not to eat or drink anything until they get the blessings and approval of the father. Normally, the sons family will ask the permission from the girl's family; and after they receive the approval, the man's family starts the celebrations by putting a gold cross around the girl's neck as a promise to marry. Some girls receive a promise ring, but usually it's a cross. There have been cases where the parents have said no, and the man's family can go back up to three times to ask. This rule is according to church custom, and if the girl's family still says no, the couple does not get married. Some have eloped; this is called *majnewe* in Assyrian and is not considered a good thing in Assyrian culture.

After the family says yes, that is when the happiness begins and the wedding process starts. Not too long ago, in my parents' time, some couples never even talked together prior to the *mashmetta*, and if the girls' family liked the family and the man, they would ask their daughter her feelings. Sometimes the couple talked for the first time at the *mashmetta* and decide whether to marry or not.

If they decide they like each other, the families ask other people about the other family to see what they are like before their children get married. Then if everything turns out well, the man would send his parents a second time, this time to formally ask her parents for her hand in marriage. It's the parents or an elder of the man that would ask the girl's parents for permission for their son to marry their daughter.

Today, a lot of these customs are skipped—the couples have already gone out together, and they know each other—but they still follow the ancient traditions of asking the girl's parents' permission to marry their daughter.

It's customary for the man's family to take the girl to buy her gold, and she can select whatever she wants. In modern times, they buy the engagement ring, and some still also buy gold bangles, earrings, necklaces, or whatever the bride chooses, but in older times, the man's family would take her to the jeweller and buy her whatever she selects at the store. Some close family members buy the bride gold as gifts for her engagement or wedding present but mainly today they are given money as a gift.

Assyrian communities normally have big weddings, which displays how close they are as a group. Another tradition is for the families to gather before the wedding to sew a quilt to be presented to the bride and groom as a symbolic gift. Each woman brings a piece of fabric to sew into the quilt. They make the quilt, and they make a big party of it, with lots of food, drinks, and dancing.

Some Assyrians from the Baz tribe celebrated weddings for seven days and seven nights prior to the wedding, and this tradition has lasted for centuries.

The day before the wedding, the groom's family gathers together and participates in shaving the groom and washing and cutting his hair. This ritual is meant to clean him so to speak from any evil. The Assyrians make a party of this, and celebrations continue after the ritual.

There are several wedding day traditions; one of these traditions is that the groom's family goes to the girl's house to pick her up. This is when the bride to say farewell to her parents and her home, because after the wedding, she will live with her husband and his family. The groom and his ushers will go to the church, as he is not supposed to see the bride before she walks down the aisle.

Before the groom's family enters the bride's home, one of the bride's family members will hold the front door and not allow them to come in until they pay a dowry to the girl's family. Whatever the bride's family asks for must be paid before the door is opened. The groom's family traditionally sings and dances at the bride's house. While at the bride's house, they put corsages on each family member and take pictures before they are ready to leave for the church. Usually the music of *zorna* (small horns) and *dawolla* (drums) accompanies the family, as they all sing and dance in front of the bride as she walks out of her parents' home.

On the groom's suit jacket, while in church, they place pins on each shoulder to form a cross; some even gently pierce the groom with the pin, and this is meant for good luck and to ward off evil.

In the homeland, and even up to about forty years ago, the wedding ceremony was done in two parts, first half of the marriage ceremony was the blessings part and was done when the bride and groom got engaged, and the second part was done in church which finalizes the marriage.

In the olden days and in their homelands, the second part of wedding ceremony would take place at four o'clock in the morning, before the sunrise. Only close family would come that early and while at the church, when the ceremony started, one person from each side of the family would go around the church while moving a pair of scissors in a cutting motion around the entire church; this was done to ward off any evil. Sadly, this tradition is no longer practiced, and the entire ceremony is done on the day of the marriage.

The marriage blessings are a special ceremony in church, with many blessings given to the bride and groom. Crowns are put on them; they also tie red and white ribbon around their left arms. This tradition is specific to the Church of the East, the Assyrian Church, and the Syriac Church. These ribbons are blessed with the couple on their wedding day, and the same ribbons are used again when the couple has a baby.

When the couple has a baby and it's time for the baptism, they present the same ribbons that were used when the parents were married and blessed so they can be blessed again with the baby's baptism. After the baptism, these ribbons, along with the silver piece, the bread/wheat, and salt—in the same cloth—are put under the mattress where the baby lays his/her head.

The Chaldean (Catholic) Assyrians use a white bow on the arm and not the red/white ribbons, as they follow the Vatican marriage traditions.

When the couple comes out of church, they are showered with rice, candies, and sometimes coins.

The reception is started with the bridesmaids and groomsmen coming into the hall one at a time, after they are introduced. They often have a handkerchief (*yalikhta*) that they wave in the air to

Assyrian music. Then the bride and groom make a grand entrance, and almost everyone in the hall dances in front of them as they walk in. The guests dance with yalikhta that are decorated with beads and sequins, and the person leading the dancing holds a bead-encrusted cane called a *kopalla*.

There is a tradition in the wedding where a guest will hold the chairs of the bride and groom until someone pays them to move.

After the wedding and prior to entering the groom's home, the family puts a ceramic vase full of walnuts wrapped in cloth on the floor; and before the bride and groom walk in, the groom will smash the vase with his foot to break it. This ensures good luck and prosperity for the couple. The walnuts are shared with everyone, and then they walk into the home; sadly this is another tradition that we have not seen while living in diaspora.

DEATH RITUALS

$\mathcal{T}$he death rituals in the homeland are very different than those in diaspora. One main difference is that, in the homeland, there is a special house where the dead are bathed from head to toe with holy water and dressed in their best clothes. This tradition has died out in diaspora.

At the mourner's home, family and friends often bring coffee, tea, and rice with them when they come to pay their respects. They are served bitter coffee and bitter tea with no sugar to symbolize the state of the household. Viewing the dead usually takes place for one or two days after the death, and almost the entire community comes to pay their respects. The participation of the community shows the mourners that they are not alone.

By the third day, the dead are taken to church, and special prayers are said. They must be buried by the third day. After the church, the men go to the burial site. There are also special prayers for the ritual at the burial site. On the third day, they believe the soul will rise to go to heaven, as Jesus did. Some women now go to the burial site, but the elders do not, as the tradition is that women do not normally go to the burial site on the third day.

Several special prayers are said for the dead, and it's customary to be buried in the ground, and nowhere else. The belief is "dust to dust"; we came from the ground so we must go back into the ground.

After the burial, everyone goes to a hall or a church where they all eat together. Some friends bring food, and the mourners may cater food for everyone. The community pays their respects to the family again, and then they go home.

The family will often visit the dead, and they pay their respects by burning frankincense at the burial site while some light candles. Assyrians like to be buried close to one another and their community so when they rise, they will see their family, friends, and community.

The family mourns by wearing traditional black clothing for forty days and at the end of forty days, they go to church again to say prayers for the dead and pay their respects, and the remembrance of that person is done again. In respect for the dead, their names are said in church; and in their honor, the family buys breakfast for the entire congregation at church. They all eat together, and the congregation pays their respects to the family. This remembrance is done again in one year.

BIBLICAL ROGATION OF THE NINEVITES / BAWOTA ET YOUNAN ENWEYA

The great city of Nineveh was the capital of the ancient kingdom and empire of Assyria. The people of Nineveh were called Ninevites in ancient times, as they referred to people by their geographical location. It was not until later that the Assyrian kings named them *Ashuraye min matta Ashur,* meaning "Ashurians from the city of Ashur." Later, the Greeks called them *Assyrians from the city of Assyria.*

The Ninevites tradition that is well-documented in the Bible is a fast called *Bawota Et Younan Enweya,* or *Ba'wtá d-Ninwáyé,* which translates to "fasting per Jonah" or "fasting of the Ninevites." This is the fast conducted by the people from the biblical city of Nineveh. This tradition is still adhered to from biblical times to now and is held annually with the start of it on the third Monday of February and lasts for three days; this tradition is over two thousand years old. Assyrians use this fast to remind them of the biblical story and to allow them to purify the mind and soul.

This tradition goes back to the biblical story of Jonah as he was asked by God to go see the people of Nineveh and to ask them for atonement. Jonah was hesitant to go, but God insisted that he go to preach to them. Jonah went on a ship, and there was a storm at sea that threw him overboard; and while a whale swallowed him, he remained alive for three days and three nights.

There are various stories and books about the Nineveh fast, such as Moby Dick and various other church stories, and the most famous one is the biblical story of the Nineveh fast.

The main points of the biblical story are listed here, but you can read the entire story directly from the Bible.

> *"Arise, go unto Nineveh, that great city, and preach unto it the preaching that I bid thee.*

> *So Jonah arose, and went unto Nineveh, according to the word of the Lord. Now Nineveh was an exceeding great city of three days' journey.*

> *And Jonah began to enter into the city a day's journey, and he cried, and said, "yet forty days, and Nineveh shall be overthrown."*

> *So the people of Nineveh believed God, and proclaimed a fast, and put on sackcloth, from the greatest of them even to the least of them.*

> *For word came unto the king of Nineveh, and he arose from his throne, and he laid his robe from him, and covered him with sackcloth, and sat in ashes.*

> *And he caused it to be proclaimed and published through Nineveh by the decree of the king and his nobles, saying, Let neither man nor beast, herd nor flock, taste any thing: let them not feed, nor drink water:"*

> *But let man and beast be covered with sackcloth, and cry mightily unto God: yea, let them turn every one from his evil way, and from the violence that is in their hands.*

> *Who can tell if God will turn and repent, and turn away from his fierce anger, that we perish not?*

*And God saw their works, that they turned from their evil
ways; and God repented of the evil, that he had said that he
would do unto them; and he did it not.*

*When Jonah reached Nineveh he asked to speak with the
King and once Jonah spoke with the King he told him
God's wishes and the King believed. The King told his
entire nation that it would be time for atonement so he put
on sackcloth to humble himself, and they would fast together
as a nation and even their animals were put on a fast. The
fast was with no food or water for three days.*[21]

All the Ninevites today fast together annually as they did
thousands of years ago, based on the story of Jonah. This fast occurs
on selected dates by the various churches that observe this fast, such as
the Ancient Church of the East, the Assyrian Church of the East, the
Orthodox Churches, the Syriac Churches, and the Assyrian Catholic
Churches. The fast normally occurs in the month of February and
lasts for three days.

In the three-day fast, some abstain from eating meat and all dairy
products, or some may eat only after sundown. They pray daily,
and on the third day, they mix seven grains together to make what
Assyrians call *pokhin*, and one of items in the mixture needs to be salt.

On the third day, they drink a minimal amount of water, and
with the thumb, they scoop out seven times of the mixture to put it
in a bowl, and then they eat the completely dry mixture. After they
eat the mixture, they should not drink water or talk; they pray and
then go to sleep.

Legend has it that on this day if you see a dream, the dream comes
true. Often, people see their future spouse in these dreams.

The biblical prophet Jonah was buried in an Assyrian church
located in Mosul, the ancient Assyrian city of Nineveh. This ancient
church was later converted to a mosque, which ISIS blew up in July

---

[21] King James Bible (Jonah).

2014. In 2017, when Nineveh was liberated, the site was visited by various archaeologists to assess the damage; they uncovered the palace of the Assyrian king Sennacherib and found remnants of the king's palace dated back to 704–681 BC. At the time of his son Esarhaddon's reign, the palace was renovated (672 BC). No one knows how many artifacts were stolen and removed from the site.

When archaeologists inspected the area, they discovered a marble cuneiform inscription of King Esarhaddon from the Assyrian empire in 672 BC.

Throughout the centuries, Christian churches, mosques, or synagogues have been built on Assyrian archaeological sites. They have also suffered further damage by other governmental buildings being built over top of them.

The Peshmerga Kurdish group that are stationed in Khorsabad, the ancient Assyrian capital of Dur-Sharrukin, had severely damaged the ancient archaeological site by digging offensive trenches in the area in October 2016. This caused irrevocable damage to relief sculptures, cuneiforms inscriptions, and various decorative objects.

Most recently in 2021, the ancient Nineveh walls that have been standing for over seven thousand years were further destroyed, completely wiping out large sections of the citadel wall by the northern government.

Thousands of artifacts containing important information about Assyrian culture and history have been taken or stolen throughout the ages or completely wiped out until today.

Often historians and the Bible have painted the Assyrians in a different light; however, its important to note these biblical prophets, Jonah, Nahum and Ezekiel choose to live among them and to be buried there.

EASTER/EDA (SURA)

rior to Christianity, the celebration of Ishar was for the Assyrian and Babylonian goddess Ishar. She was the goddess of love and fertility and this is where eggs and bunnies originate. The fertility symbols are of pagan origins; later, Christianity adopted these traditional symbols that have nothing to do with resurrection. Several scholars have referred to Assyrian mythology as the basis of Christian traditions; this has been debated for centuries.

Assyrians celebrate Easter along with the rest of the Christian world using the Gregorian calendar while others use the Julian calendar to have their celebration days. In the Julian calendar, Easter is celebrated later; it is referred to in Assyrian as *Eta Tiktha, Eta Tiktha* refers to the old calendar and this calendar is normally used in the ancient Church of the East and the Orthodox Church to establish the dates to celebrate Easter, Christmas etc.

The Holy Apostolic Catholic Assyrian Church of the East and the Assyrian Catholic Churches celebrate Easter on the standard calendar.

Some Assyrians fast for forty days before Easter, and most fast on the Good Friday by abstaining from eating meat, this is a day of mourning because this is when Jesus died.

On Easter Sunday, the celebrations begin because this is when Jesus has risen. It starts with going to church; and after church, the congregation have breakfast at church, and it's tradition to break hard-boiled eggs with one another. The meaning behind this is when the egg is broken; it means that Jesus has risen and went to heaven.

At home they have colorful eggs and more traditional foods. Usually they prepare elaborate meals for this day, like roasted whole lambs, or their famous dishes such as *dolma* or *pacha*. Each family has whatever their favourite family meal is.

Twelve days after Easter, when Assyrians go to church, they receive holy water to be taken home for blessings.

BRIDE ASCENSION /
KALU SULAQA

*A*ssyrians celebrate a tradition called *Kalu Sulaqa*, which is a
mock wedding, and its origins can be traced back to ancient
times and on Ishtar's day as part of New Year events when several
people would be married at the same time. In different parts of the
homeland, some Assyrians still celebrate the Assyrian New Year by
several couples being married on the Assyrian New Year's Day.

Later, Christianity adopted this tradition, and *Kalu Sulaqa* became
"bride ascension." There are a few variations of the origins on this
celebration, and one of these is that it is the celebration of Jesus and
his ascension day from earth to heaven, which is forty days from
Easter Sunday to May; this is celebrated as the ascension of Jesus into
heaven, and the Holy Spirit comes as a symbolic bride. The bride
wearing white reflects purity and innocence.

Another legend for this tradition is that starting in the fifteenth
century during the battle between the Mongol invaders and Assyrian
fighters, the wife of Malik Shalita, the governor of Mosul, gathered
all the Assyrian women; they were all organized to wear white, and
they went to the nearby villages to collect provisions to feed the men
that were fighting their attackers.

Although word came that a lot of their people in Tikrit and
Mardin had lost their lives, the women still joined the men to fight
against the Mongols until their end. To honor this day, it is said that

it became tradition that young girls dressed in white and go door-to-door to collect provisions.

Today, this annual Assyrian tradition of *Kalu Sulaqa* is a tradition they have observed for thousands of years. They dress their little girls as little brides or as bridesmaids, and they go door-to-door, mainly to Assyrian homes, to collect treats such as walnuts, raisins, candies, or money. Then the girls share all their treats with one another.

This tradition is celebrated in the homeland, but this is yet another tradition that is slowly disappearing. In Europe and the Western countries, there are often parties or picnics that include live singers and lots of food and dancing to celebrate *Kalu Sulaqa*.

In diaspora, the Assyrian churches and organizations have played a pivotal role in keeping Assyrian traditions and language alive, especially the Ancient Church of the East, the Assyrian Church of the East, and the Syriac Orthodox Churches. The church reminds people of the special events, while in other countries, like the US, Canada, and Australia, there are large numbers of Assyrian organizations that plan these events and celebrations.

ANNUAL WATER PURIFICATION/
MUSARDEH/NUSARDEL

A vital and renewable resource that has been tied to civilization since the beginning of time is water, and with water comes purification, used for cleansing of sins and renewal, which plays an important role in spiritually. The Assyrian people call this day *Musardeh* or *Nusardel,* depending on the Assyrian dialect. This ritual is still celebrated by Assyrians annually and is similar to the renewal process of the New Year celebrations, which, in ancient times, also had a purification day when the Assyrian king would sprinkle water on the people and the crops to act as blessings for the entire year.

Musardeh/Nusardel was another day in which purification and renewal were celebrated. This celebration is depicted on various artifacts and inscriptions—the most famous one being with the Assyrian Tree of Life and using the cone, the bucket, and water.

Musardeh/Nusardel in ancient times was traditionally celebrated in the month of Tammuz (July). The tradition was that the king would sprinkle water on them to purify them and wash away "bad things," and in preparation for the month of Tammuz. Water was also used to bless their crops in order to ensure a good harvest.

Water was considered sacred; they used large basins to hold the water, which is still evident today around the ancient city of Ashur; you can see these large water basins in their original location from thousands of years ago. They used these water basins for annual water purification rituals, which contained sacred water brought from freshwater springs around the empire. They also used water from the Tigris and Euphrates rivers because these waters were also considered scared.

They used fire as part of their cleansing ceremonies as well; fire was an important element used to be rid of bad intentions or "bad things." It was believed that if Assyrians had bad dreams, they would tell the dream to a piece of wood or reed and than burn it until it was completely consumed. Similarly today, when Assyrians tell their bad dreams to flowing water, it is considered as having made the bad dream go away. Today this practice is done in their homes normally, where they run tap water and say the bad dream to the flowing water to make it go away.

Later, Christians adopted this water purification ritual for their baptisms. Many people had adopted the water and fire purification traditions; mainly with the Persians and Israelis of today, you see traces of these rituals still being practiced, whether it's part of the New Year rituals where fire is used by either the Assyrians in the homeland and Yezidis as they dance around it, or when the Persians light a fire and jump over it as part of their ritual for purification. The Jewish people still have a custom that uses the water purification process as part of their rituals.

In modern times, tracing their roots from ancient traditions to present day, Assyrians still practice these rituals annually in the month of July or August; they throw water on each other in the homeland and diaspora.

Some Assyrians in the homeland will go in the Tigris or Euphrates rivers and jump in the water to purify on this annual water purification practice. This signifies blessings, purification, and renewal. Assyrians in the homeland would also go out into their neighbourhoods with their buckets and splash water on each other. In diaspora, groups organize and put together events to celebrate together, which normally are held in parks.

Today, in certain parts of diaspora, Assyrians celebrate this day by having singers, dancing, food, and celebrations in parks, where they throw water at each other.

In the homelands, all Assyrian church denominations celebrate *Musardeh*, and when people go outside after their church service, the priests sprinkle water on the people as they go out; this acts as a blessing to all of them.

In diaspora, the Ancient Church of the East, the Assyrian Church of the East, and the Syriac Orthodox Churches still practice this ancient tradition; and when service is finished, the priests bless the people by sprinkling water on them to celebrate *Musardeh*.

We have sadly seen a decline in the Assyrian fire-lighting ceremony, and it's becoming another tradition that has since diminished through the ages. The annual water purification ritual is still celebrated, but not as much as it was in the homeland.

This artifact is currently located in the Brooklyn Museum and came from the Assyrian king Ashur-nair-pal II's palace and reflects the water purification image.

> The geographical location of the artifact:
> Place made: Assyria, ancient Kalhu
> Dates: circa 883–859 BC
> Period: Neo-Assyrian Period

The Assyrian kings sometimes depicted themselves as gods by the addition of wings. It was considered that kingship was an instruction from the heavens or that God made them kings as they were the chosen ones.

The Assyrian deities are often carved in the king's own reflection or image, and the deity has a bucket so that he can start the purification ritual. At purification rituals like the *Musardeh* festival, the king would bless all the people with water spinkling water using a pinecone.

The water basin was discovered in the courtyard of the Ashur temple. It was severely damaged, but it was restored and moved to the Pergamon Museum in Berlin. The basin reflects all the water gods—these are the ones with the fish-decorated attire—and they are all holding buckets of water. Some have a cone and bucket, and if you look closely, you can see the water flowing from above to the ground; the gods collected this blessed water to bless the earth and people.

In the middle of the relief, you will find the Assyrian king, and the purification and cleansing is shown by the water flowing to him from above and from both sides. This could be the basin that was used to purify the Assyrian kings in their royal ceremonies, and it also could have been used as part of the New Year celebrations, as the king also blessed all the people on this day.

From the city of Ashur in northern Assyria (also known as Mesopotamia, and modern-day Iraq). The Neo-Assyrian period, the reign of Sennacherib, was 704–681 BC. This artifact is currently housed in the Pergamon Museum, Berlin.

This artifact is part of a larger scene that displays the angel and the purification of the famous Assyrian Tree of Life. It is currently housed in the Metropolitan Museum.

ASSYRIAN MARTYR'S DAY

The Assyrian people hold August 7 (Shawa bet Tadabbakh) as the National Day of Mourning. This day serves as a memorial day for all the Assyrian people who lost their lives in government-sponsored conflicts, with its collaborators to systematically massacre the Assyrian people. This day also serves as a reminder for all the Assyrian people that have been murdered or assassinated simply for who they were.

Although Assyrians hold August 7 as the Assyrian Martyr's Day in recognition of the 1933 Simele massacres, they also remember and hold memorials on April 24, which is known as the Day of Seyfo, or the Day of the Sword. This day is in remembrance of the massacres that took place in attempt to wipe out the Assyrians along with the Greeks and Armenians in the Middle East between the years of 1914 and 1924 at the hands of the Ottoman Empire. One and a half million Armenians, 750 thousand Assyrians, and 400 thousand Greeks were murdered because they were Christians.

August 7 was selected by Assyrians to commemorate a day of mourning because, in the town of Simele, between August 7 and 11, 1933, the Iraq Army entered the town in northern Iraq, specifically targeting the Assyrian people and killing and terrorizing them. This led to the death of more than three thousand innocent people, including men, women, and children—they were killed for absolutely no reason.

The Assyrian people have faced multiple massacres in the past, with each one being more horrendous than the last. August 7 was selected specifically, as the bones of their ancestors that were killed still remain on display in the dirt hills of the town of Simele today in northern Iraq. The lack of respect for this sacred ground by the governments in Iraq is simply despicable and repulsive.

The statement below was written and delivered by an Iraq parliament member named Sayed Chabali Haji Thabit, on June 28, 1933. Not only does this speech display the ignorance of some people and governments, but also confirms what Assyrians have endured for centuries.

This was the exact speech that initiated, and later delivered the Simele massacre to the Assyrian people.

This is the statement made by Sayed Chabali Haji Thabit in the Iraq parliament meeting held on the twenty-eighth of June 1933 (Vide Al Istiqlal. No. 1929, of the twenty-ninth of June 1933 and currently located in the League of Nations and the official journal). This is the exact translation of his speech:

> *I have to throw light on the public opinion, especially on that of our press, regarding this misleading name "Assyrians," which is in common use. As you are aware, this term is only recently coming into being. There is nobody who reasonably deserves this name; if there is any, we are the first to grasp it, as we are the original inhabitants of this country. I take this from the physical and not the political point of view. The same question arises in Egypt, it is called Pharoahs, but really Mosul is Arab even before the Islam. I regret to note that our press still sticks to this mysterious name. The group which calls itself Assyrians, should be named Tyaris, they intermingle with the Syrianis and Chaldeans; this is confirmed by their being bilingual. If for example, there is any of them who can decipher the tablets maintained in our museum, he can make us believe that they are descendants of the Great Assyria Proverb, "if he passed the examination set, he deserves honour; if he fails he is liable to spit into his face and kick him out."*

The Tyaris can be divided in the following sub-sections: (1) Tyari Bila, (2) Tyari Zair, (3) Tyari Jilu, (4) Tyari Bazi, and (5) Tyari Dizi—they all go under the name "Tyari."

In the pre-war days, they inhabited (1) Hikkari, Julamark, Bashqala, and Van in the Turkish territories, with their religious headquarters in Qudshanus and (2) Persia, their headquarters in Urmia, (3) Russia and (4) part of them lived in the Barwari villages in the outskirts of a mountain which is named after them, viz, Tyari Mountain in the vicinity of Madia, and their headquarters being in Ashita, where their religious leader resides who puts his untimely claims before the government. These villages are within the Turkish border, but some of them are happily situated in the Iraqi side, they are genuine Iraqis; they are entitled to share the benefit of our country; ours is theirs and theirs ours.

The above mentioned Tyaris are therefore aliens, and not former inhabitants of this country. They are nearly 20,000 who fled from Persia, Russia and Turkey, with the strong desire the colonial office. When they poured into Mosul and began living by illegal means, the inhabitants there were somewhat indisposed and cried to get rid of them but, unfortunately, their pleadings were not listened to until some unhappy event took place in Mosul. The Mosulawis cried loudly and insisted on their being removed to their former homes or at least scattered in the villages, to avoid further accidents. It was prophesied at that time that, their settling together would jeopardize the general security, and disturb peaceful citizens. The government migrated them to Kirkuk; as though Kirkuk was not Iraq! They caused there the most bloody accident Kirkuk has ever seen, and made hundreds of our myrters (sic) to lose their dear lives. This happened during the celebration of the "Id al Fatir."

I cannot help weeping when I remember that doomed event; still, some mysterious hand plays havoc, and moves them to and fro. Recently one of their priests (Rev. Bedari) who resides in Mosul, published the most notorious article against the poor government.

The police authorities in the spot confiscated his cursed pamphlets, but his honour the priest, was able to dispose some fifty copies and distribute them among the prominent people. May I ask his excellency as to the steps taken against such behaviours?

This wretched and corrupt people was housed and fed in Iraq, and were expected to be loyal and dutiful subjects, but on the contrary, after being surfeited and ungrateful to the hospitality shown by their hosts claim humorous rights. Experience, however, shows that these are armed to the teeth and are in a position to inflict the severest blow on the government. We are not so coward, but we wait to see what steps will be taken against those interlopers - what is the government's attitude towards them in this respect, and why she keeps quiet and postpones their punishment? To make it known from what source they obtained their arms. We therefore request and recommend their being stripped of their arms forthwith, or at least, arm their neighbors for defensive measures.

We cannot clearly understand the (sic) program of their settling together in the Zibar area. The government further sanctioned 13,000 Dinars for their settlement, and the settlement office intends to settle some of them in the Barzan area; as though we dislodged the Barzanis to make room for those, and to breed the poisonous germ in the head of the government.

These will, at any time, be an obstacle in the way of the government, we therefore, should scatter them in all the liwas to be able to rule them peacefully. We understand that they imagine special status, out these cannot be attained to, and cannot at our will, create a difficult situation similar to that already created in Palestine (Zionists).

Further, what is the British Consulate at Diaaaa [Diana]? and what are the intelligence officers scattered in the country? and what is this mythical hand that which turns this unseen machine? We were under the impression that this game would come to an end with the mandate, but they wish to restart it in an Independent State. We can wait no longer, everything is ripe, we request the government to take punitive measures against them.

Gentlemen, the most important problem to solve is to remedy this bleeding wound, to do this; we shall cry and cry loudly. The soil of this country is formed of the bones and blood of our ancestors, how can we close our eyes and be indifferent in defending our sacred fatherland? (Applause). Our ally wants many things, in this country of their adoption; we must guard it against any intruders.

Right after this speech, and in early August 1933, the Iraq government ordered the Assyrians to surrender, disarm, and give their weapons to the authorities or face severe punishment. Here is the text of that order as translated:

To the Assyrian Rebels

By this notice, the government declares:

You have sixty hours starting at 12:00, midday Saturday of August 12, to show your good intentions to your surrender all your weaponry to the closest government offices, military camps or police stations.

All disciplinary actions by government armed forces will be put on hold until the grace period.

If you do not give in and surrender your weapons by the above mentioned authorities during this grace period, the government armed forces will resume its operations against you with the worst possible outcomes.

Take advantage of this valuable opportunity and accept the advice to avert your bloodshed.

For the government Lieutenant Governor Mosul State Khalil Azmi[22]

On June 1933, the speech to initiate the massacre, which was followed with the governmental letter to disarm the Assyrians, started early on August 1933 when the authorities went door-to-door to collect their weapons; they were promised protection by the government, similar to what happened in the 2014 ISIS invasion—that promise of protection became mass murders.

Once all the weapons were collected from the Assyrian people, the Iraq army encouraged nearby Arabs and Kurds to start looting and raiding Assyrian villages and homes. More than sixty villages were violated and raided, and the Assyrians attempted to flee from one village to another, only to be followed by more looters and terrorists. Their neighbours stole their livestock, raided and stole their possessions, and stole their freshly cut wheat and barley. The atrocities committed against the Assyrians during this time were unspeakable, but this was only one event, with more to follow.

By the order of the Iraq government, thousands of native people of Iraq were terrorized and murdered. This is the actual site today; it shows the lack of respect and the atrocities committed against the Assyrians. Today, the site is surrounded by garbage, with no proper burials or memorials for the exposed bones.

---

[22] http://www.aina.org/releases/20040805022140.htm.

This is the Simele site today with exposed bones.

Mar Shimun wrote about the massacre as follows:

> *Girls and women were raped and made to march naked before Iraq's commanders. Pregnant women were bayonetted while children were flung in the air and pierced by bayonets, while others were smashed against brick walls. Children were run over by military cars. Bibles were used for the burning of people and homes.*

Simele today.

Colonel Stafford of the British army was in Iraq at the time and was required to report on current events in Iraq. Here is his report on the Simele massacre. This is the text from his letter:

Simmel is on the main road to Zakho, about eight miles from Dohuk, under the administration of which qodha it came. It was the largest village in the neighborhood and consisted of over one hundred Assyrians and ten Arab houses. The total population would have been about 700, most of the Assyrians belonging to the Baz tribe, with others of the Upper Tiyari and the Diz. The headman was a strong supporter of the Mar Shimun and with fifty others had followed Yacu into Syria. These fifty were almost entirely Tiyari, hardly any of the Baz being among them. The feeling of unrest in the village increased. On August 8th the Qaimaqam of Zakho appeared with a lorry full of soldiers. No satisfactory answer has yet been given to the question why he should have come with troops into a district that was outside his administration. He entered the village and told the Assyrians to surrender their rifles, as he feared that fighting might occur between the rebel Assyrians and the Government forces, in which case the people of Simmel would be less likely to be involved if they had no rifles. Plausibly, but with lies in his heart, he assured them that they would be safe under the protection of the Iraqi flag which flew over the police post for Simmel, being a large village, had a police post of one sergeant and four men. The Assyrians then handed in their arms, which were taken away by the troops.

Next day, more troops returned, this time without the Qaimaqam, and disarmed further Assyrians who in the meantime had come in from the surrounding villages. The following day, the 10th, passed comparatively quietly.

Nothing happened except that Arabs and Kurds could be seen looting neighboring villages. They even came in and stripped the communal threshing floors on the outskirts of Simmel, where the cut barley and wheat was stacked in piles, for it was full time of harvest and the villagers were engaged in threshing and winnowing. The unarmed Assyrians could do nothing and the police did not intervene; they explained that they had no orders and that in any case their numbers were insufficient.

It was becoming quite clear now to the Assyrians what was likely to happen. Not only had they seen this looting going on, but they suddenly found they were forbidden to draw water from the village spring, being permitted only to go to the main stream, which was dirty. They knew that the Army had already shot many Assyrians.

They had seen their head priest, Sada, taken out of Simmel. All day they watched the looting Arabs and Kurds. Not one of them dared to move from the neighborhood of the police post, except one or two whose houses were nearby, and who went to and fro on pathetic household tasks such as the making of bread, the last meal that many of them were destined to eat. They were now in a state of deadly fear, and they spend that night in and around the police post, which is built on a small hill. They now knew only too well the sentiments which the Arabs, and particularly the Arab Army, harboured towards them, and in the small hours of the 11th, when the moon had risen, the watching Assyrians began to observe their Arab neighbours of the village starting away driving their flocks before them. This opened their eyes beyond possibility of error. They realized the trap they had been led into and they knew that they were entirely helpless.

187

These letters have never been easy to read, no matter how many times I have read them, yet these are only a few examples that have been used here, and it has taught the Assyrians some very tough lessons. Even though time goes by, it might be a different century and a different time; history will continue to repeat itself, and it's very important that we must learn from our past.

HALLOWEEN/SOMMIKA

*T*raditionally in October, Assyrians would go door-to-door to remind their fellow Assyrians of the upcoming Christmas holiday and when fasting would begin, and this is what they used to call *sommika* at that time. Assyrians typically fast on the holidays such as Easter and Christmas, and some fast during specific saints' days. The fast for Christmas can be as long as fifty or forty days. *Somma* means, "fasting" in Assyrian.

Later *sommika* became a rather different tradition and became the Halloween tradition that is known today. Everyone around the world is familiar with the celebration by dressing up and handing out candy. Today *sommika* means "Halloween" to Assyrians, and they celebrate by dressing up and getting candies, like the rest of the world. This is another tradition that has changed in recent years.

CHRISTMAS/EDA GURA

Christmas is a big holiday for most Assyrians with the majority that celebrate on December 25; and the congregation that follows Shawa Be Yarkha celebrate Christmas at the same time as the Orthodox Christmas.

For the December celebrations, they start by going to church at midnight mass on the twenty-fourth or first thing in the morning on the twenty-fifth. They normally wear new clothes or their best clothes for Christmas. Some may have been fasting for forty or fifty days, where they abstain from eating specific foods or eat only vegetarian foods for the duration of the fast.

After church, the congregation has breakfast together, and when they get home, they start the preparation for the big feast. While most make their traditional special foods on this day, they typically make foods that take the most effort, like *pacha*, which is cow stomach, or *dolma*, or roasted lamb. They have desserts like *Kada*, *keleche*, and *baklava*. They follow the evening with tea and coffee and presents. Some of them open their gifts as soon as they get home from church.

Christmas is a time for family, and they use this time, like everyone else in the world, to gather together. Those that don't stay home may choose to go to a community Christmas party, and they have live singers and bands. They have food, drinks, and lots of dancing. In the city of Mosul in northern Iraq, which is on the outskirts of the ancient city of Nineveh, the church bells had rung for thousands of years on Christmas; however, the year 2014 was the first Christmas in history that those church bells did not ring, because the city was invaded by ISIS, the terrorist group.

ASSYRIAN TRADITIONS

Bourikta

*A*ssyrians have various ancient traditions, superstitions, and culture that they still practice today. One ancient tradition that appears to have almost been lost is putting wheat and barley in a bunch on the top of the doorsill so that anyone who walks in will walk in with blessings. In Assyrian, it's called *Bourikta*.

Blessing homes

Assyrian homes are normally blessed by saying prayers and lighting frankincense throughout the home before the family moves in. When Assyrians move to a new home, they either have a priest come to bless the house, or they perform the purification themselves. They burn frankincense—similar to the way it's done in church—while saying a prayer. They walk around the entire house, corner to corner saying the Lord's Prayer. They normally will not sleep in the house unless the house has been blessed.

Cupping

Assyrians have used cupping to relieve sore muscles and pain for thousands of years. This is a fairly recent discovery in the West and Europe, but Assyrians have used this method for a long time. They use small glass cups with cotton balls inside, the cotton balls are lit on fire, and then the glass is placed on the back to produce suction on the skin to help relieve back pain or muscle pain. This ancient tradition has been practiced for centuries to help relieve any type of muscle pain.

Cramp relief

This tradition goes back to when they cured illnesses the natural way. To stop the pain of stomach cramps or menstruation, they would pinch the nerves in the back beside the shoulder bone. This supposedly stops the menstrual pain.

Setting bones

This is another old method of healing bones that have been broken. They had special people that the community relied on when they were injured. These special families passed down these abilities from generation to generation and used a wide variety of remedies that would cure people while only using natural methods. As recent as fifty years ago, there were still people doing this, and in their homelands, Assyrians that didn't have access to a hospital nearby had a man that fixed broken bones the natural way—he would set the bone and wrap it with raw fish. The smell was atrocious, but it worked; within thirty days, the break was healed, and although it's not certain that perhaps the setting of the bone just healed itself or whether the fish minerals had something to do with it, this will never be clear. Since ancient times until fifty years ago, sadly it's another ancient practice that has disappeared.

Special healing gifts

The Assyrians have special people with unique gifts; these gifts are passed down from generation to generation, and only one person in the family is blessed with these gifts. This is a true story from seventeen years ago: there was a lady who could take fear away from people by conducting a special prayer. There was a little girl, two years old at the time; she was scared of bees and would cry and try to swat bees even when they were not around. The little girl was taken to this lady to help cure her, and this special lady, using a handkerchief near the child, would say a special prayer. The child was brought to her three times, and after the third time, the little girl was miraculously cured, and she was no longer afraid of bees. Sadly, another ancient Assyrian tradition that will eventually cease to exist in my lifetime.

Cure for bad dreams

The Assyrian people have some unique beliefs, including this very old one: a cure for bad dreams is that legend has it to put a piece of steel or slver under your mattress, and this will ward off any bad dreams.

Good luck for travellers

Assyrians follow this tradition until today when they leave for a long trip and as they drive off, the person that stays behind will throw water behind the ones that drive away to serve as good luck. Water again from ancient times until today plays an important role in Assyrian lives. This is another ancient tradition that slowly and sadly is starting to vanish.

Rooftop naps

The Assyrians in the homeland love to sleep on their rooftops, so in addition to their normal beds in their homes, they also have rooftop beds in Iraq, Syria, Turkey, and Iran. Most of the roofs in these countries are flat, and many people sleep on the roof for afternoon naps. Many people have vivid memories of sleeping on the roof every day. They have sheets suspended above the beds to keep the sun and bugs out, and some say these rooftop naps were some of their best memories.

Old sayings

This is a very old saying, and because Assyrians are very culturally inclined, they have saved their traditions for centuries. These are passed on from generation to generation.

When there is a crescent moon in the sky, Assyrians believe this saying will help them prosper:

Assyrian language:

- Sarah Khata
- Brekha el mata
- Akhnan teake
- Aten Khata

*Now you need to look at *dawa*.

English translation:

- Moon new
- Welcome to town/village
- We are old (ancient)

- You are new

*Now you are supposed to look at gold so you can have a prosperous year.

CONCLUSION

The joys of reading what Assyrian kings said thousands of years ago in their own words is remarkable, and I am so thankful to all the scholars around the world that helped translate the old Assyrian cuneiform texts, which allows us to have a glimpse of their world back then.

The Assyrians were the first empire builders and one of the first superpowers. They were no different from the superpowers of today—some tactics may have been different, but in essence, they are very similar.

Since the beginning of the 2003 US-led invasion of Iraq, they have faced considerable persecution from extremists. Some thought they would find newfound freedom with the US regime; however, it certainly proved to be the contrary. Either protect yourself or be persecuted. The Middle East needed a strong hand to govern and protect people from mayhem; the Assyrians in the past were the protectors, the ones that governed using the first laws ever created. They have always had to protect themselves—you can see it from their stone carvings—and although some portray them as villains, it is clear throughout time they were not.

This recent example of the ISIS terrorist group is what the Assyrians were protecting against back then, and this gave the world a brief glimpse of the atrocities they faced—just imagine how horrific the invaders were in the ancient times. Ninety percent of Assyrian people live in diaspora; this fact is very telling at the reality they face. They prefer to live in their homelands if they can live in peace, however it's clear peace has not been possible. When ISIS took over northern Iraq in 2014, this clearly displayed the lack of governmental strength to stop this terrorist group and the lack of protection that the citizens faced. The terrorist group did everything possible to destroy Assyrian ancient sites, including the destruction of ancient sites that have been around longer than the beginning of time. They destroyed the city of Kalhu, the Nineveh wall; they burned the oldest and most rare books in the world; they burned down homes and ancient churches; and most importantly, they violated and murdered many people. This was all done on the watch of the two governments that have been installed by the US regime in Iraq and while the US army was still in Iraq.

The systemic erasure of Assyrian history and the Assyrian people is real; some people in the local governments conspire on historical revisionment, and although the Assyrians are the indigenous people, their history is not even learned in school. If you walk around Iraq today, you can clearly see the attempts to distort Assyrian history. Some place themselves as the creators of the citadels and artifacts when they have no history in the region until modern times.

For those that try to erase the Assyrian name it will simply not work in the academic world, this false information that is given will not go far in the real world. The world embraces world history, and its accuracy, and historians and academics know who the indigenous people are. I would also encourage them to read this book; it traces their modern culture rituals to ancient times. They can also check the analysis done on Assyrian DNA, which traces them back to ancient times. And most importantly, the language they still speak today—most of it can be traced to cuneiform stone tablets and the use of the same exact words.

Although the Assyrian people still live in their native lands, which they have inhabited for thousands of years, the reality is they have become the minority; and now as a result, they are at the verge of extinction. Their ancient culture and traditions will disappear without a strong presence in their homeland—without the ability to go back and preserve their culture. It's been evident in this book how many ancient traditions have just stopped, and this was only in my mother and my lifetime. This is a grave concern, especially to the Assyrian language, one of the oldest languages in the world. Assyrians are gradually speaking the language of their adoptive countries and not their own at home, and slowly, as a result, they are losing their native language.

It is with hope and perseverance that keeps them going in restarting their lives, rebuilding their homes, which they have done for centuries. History will continue to repeat itself if this endangered group is not protected and given their rights in their native lands. Assyrians need their own state, governing and protecting themselves, with international protection. Various groups have been given these basic rights; even groups that don't even belong to an area historically have been given rights to someone else's lands so why are the indigenous people ignored? This is imperative and vital to their survival, and as every other person in the world have rights and have their own country, so do Assyrians need to have their rights.

It is estimated that 40 million Assyrian people thrived in the ancient world, and they have survived with a recorded history of over seven thousand years, and now only 4.5 million still survive today. The 80 percent of Assyrians that are living in diaspora are living in the melting pot, trying desperately to hand on the remnants of their culture and traditions that have still survived through the ages.

Cuneiform tablets have been provided here and referred to as creditable sources and examples, as they were written thousands of years ago—carved in stone by scribes, written for the Assyrian kings. These texts are provided here to ensure accuracy and to ensure that integrity is maintained in the recounting of the Assyrian history. It is important that it is not limited to one's own perspective—the point is in telling the Assyrian story without being restricted to a limited point of view.

The Assyrian people have inhabited their ancestral lands for thousands of years, and they are one of the oldest nations in the Middle East, where their foundations still lie beneath the earth today. It is said, "Put a shovel in the ground, and you shall find Assyria waiting to be unveiled." Their history is deeply engraved in stone and scattered throughout the Middle East and located in museums worldwide, and although several attempts have been made to wipe out their existence, it's their artifacts and land that speaks for them, and will do so for generations to come.

It was sad to document some of these historical occurrences, along with the treasured cultural traditions, it is important that people know their history, both good and bad. This process, and the retelling of these historical references, was only to document what has actually happened so that it doesn't get distorted throughout time. These are historical references, and I am not the first one to write about them. The intention was to document them because they are part of the Assyrian story, and it certainly was not meant to offend anyone.

It's important for people to know some of the nicest people in the world come from the Middle East; they are some of the kindest, most good-hearted, and most hospitable people you could ever meet. Extremists come in all forms; they come from all countries, and most importantly, they are not limited to one country or group. Extremists are often indoctrinated and injected in certain areas or certain countries only to cause havoc and chaos and only to serve someone's interests.

There are several people around the world that are persecuted. We all need to come together in the aid of world peace, doing what is right, and that is what everyone's mission should be every day. Life is way too short and it's way too hard, so we all need to do what we can to make this world a better place for all of us. Seeing the world in a positive perspective changes your point of view in life, and soon it changes your destiny. The positive energy generates positivity all around you, and it automatically makes things much better. We all need to stop and smell the roses, literally, and find the beauty in everything and everyone. Once we all do this and appreciate the little things in life, that is when we all can live in peace, and I am positive we will one day.

ADDENDUM

$\mathcal{H}$ ere at the end, I leave you with one of my ancient king's legacy:

- Library collection: World's Greatest Literature
- Published work: *Babylonian and Assyrian Literature*
- Translator: Sir H. Rawlinson, KCB, DCL, etc.
- Publisher: P. F. Collier & Son, New York
- Copyright: Colonial Press, 1901

Notes from page 212:

This inscription of Tiglath Pileser I is found on an octagonal prism and on some other clay fragments discovered at Kalah-Shergat and at present in the British Museum. The text is published in the "Cuneiform Inscriptions of Western Asia," Vol. I, pp. ix-xvi. Four translations of this inscription, made simultaneously in 1857 by Sir H. Rawlinson, Mr. Fox Talbot, Dr. Hincks, and Dr. Oppert, were published in that year under the title of "Inscription of Tiglath Pileser I, King of Assyria, B.C. 1150." Dr. Oppert has also given a revised translation in his *Histoire de l'Empire de Chaldée et d'Assyrie*," 8vo, Versailles, 1865, extracted from the *Annales de la Philosophie chretienne*" of the same year, 5e Series, p. 44 and foll. The translations simultaneously published were submitted to the Asiatic Society in that year as a test of the advance made in Assyrian interpretations and the close approximation made by scholars in their interpretation of Assyrian texts. The notes contain some of the different readings of the other Assyrian scholars at that time and give a few of the principal varieties of reading some of the words. It was generally considered a very triumphant demonstration of the sound basis on which the then comparatively recent Assyrian researches were placed and a confutation of certain opinions then prevalent, that no certain or accurate advance had been made in the decipherment of Assyrian inscriptions. On the whole for its extent and historical information relating to the early history of Assyria this inscription is one of the most important of the series showing the gradual advance and rise of Assyria, while as one of the first interpreted it presents considerable literary interest in respect to the details of the progress of Assyrian interpretation. It is also nearly the oldest Assyrian text of any length which has been hitherto discovered and is very interesting from its account of the construction of the temples and palaces made by the King in the early part of his reign. S.B.

Inscription of King Tiglath Pileser I

[1] *Ashur*, the great Lord, ruling supreme over the gods; the giver of sceptres and crowns; the appointer of sovereignty. Bel, the Lord; *King of the circle of constellations*; Father of the gods; Lord of the world. Sin; the leader the *Lord of Empire* the *powerful* the *auspiciolus* god; *Shamas*; the establisher of the heavens and the earth; . . . ; the vanquisher of enemies; the dissolver of cold. *Vu1*; he who causes the tempest to rage over hostile lands and *wicked* countries. *Abnil* Hercules; the champion who subdues heretics and enemies, and who strengthens the heart. *Ishtar*, the eldest of the gods; the Queen of *Victory*; she who arranges battles.

[2] The great gods, ruling over the heavens and the earth, whose attributes I have recorded and whom I have *named*; the guardians of the kingdom of Tiglath Pileser, the Prince inspiring your hearts with *joy*; the proud Chief whom in the strength of your hearts ye have made firm, (to whom) ye have confided the supreme crown, (whom) ye have appointed in might to the sovereignty of the country of Bel,

to whom ye have granted pre-eminence, exaltation, and warlike power. May the duration of his empire continue forever to his royal posterity, lasting as the great temple of Bel!

[3] Tiglath Pileser the powerful king; supreme King of Lashanan; King of the four regions; King of all Kings; Lord of Lords; the *supreme*; Monarch of Monarchs; the illustrious Chief who under the auspices of the Sun god, being armed with the sceptre and girt with the girdle of power over mankind, rules over all the people of Bel; the mighty Prince whose praise is blazoned forth among the Kings: the exalted sovereign, whose servants Ashur has appointed to the government of the country of the four regions (and) has made his name celebrated to posterity; the conqueror of many plains and mountains of the Upper and Lower Country; the conquering hero, the terror of whose name has overwhelmed all regions; the bright constellation who, according to his power has warred against foreign countries (and) under the auspices of Bel, there being no equal to him, has subdued the enemies of Ashur.

[4] Ashur (and) the great gods, the guardians of my kingdom, who gave government and laws to my dominions, and ordered an enlarged frontier to their territory, having committed to (my) hand their valiant and warlike servants, I have subdued the lands and the peoples and the strong places, and the Kings who were hostile to Ashur; and I have reduced all that was contained in them. With a host of kings I have fought . . . and have imposed on them the bond of *servitude*. There is not to me a second in war, nor an equal in battle. I have added territory to Assyria and peoples to her people. I have enlarged the frontier of my territories, and subdued all the lands contained in them.

[5] In the beginning of my reign 20,000 of the *Muskayans* and their 5 kings, who for 50 years had held the countries of Alza and Perukhuz, without paying tribute and offerings to Ashur my Lord, and whom a King of Assyria had never ventured to meet in battle betook themselves to their strength, and went and seized the country

of Comukha. In the service of Ashur my Lord my chariots and warriors I assembled after me . . . the country of *Kasiyaia*, a difficult country, I passed through. With their 20,000 fighting men and their 5 kings in the country of Comukha I engaged. I defeated them. The ranks of their warriors in fighting the battle were beaten down as if by the tempest. Their carcasses covered the valleys and the tops of the mountains. I cut off their heads. The battlements of their cities I made heaps of, like mounds of earth, their movables, their wealth, and their valuables I plundered to a countless amount. 6,000 of their common soldiers who fled before my servants and accepted my yoke, I took them, and gave them over to the men of my own territory.

[6] Then I went into the country of *Comukha*, which was disobedient and withheld the tribute and offerings due to Ashur my Lord: I conquered the whole country of Comukha. I plundered their movables, their wealth, and their valuables. Their cities I burnt with fire, I destroyed and ruined. The common people of Comukha, who fled before the face of my servants, crossed over to the city of *Sherisha*, which was on the further banks of the Tigris, and made this city into their stronghold. I assembled my chariots and warriors. I betook myself to *carts of iron* in order to overcome the rough mountains and their difficult marches. I made the wilderness (thus) practicable for the passage of my chariots and warriors. I crossed the Tigris and took the city of Sherisha their stronghold. Their fighting men, in the middle of the forests, like wild beasts, I smote. Their carcasses filled the Tigris, and the tops of the mountains. At this time the troops of the *Akhe*, who came to the deliverance and assistance of Comukha, together with the troops of Comukha, like chaff I scattered. The carcasses of their fighting men I piled up like heaps on the tops of the mountains. The bodies of their warriors, the *roaring* waters carried down to the Tigris. Kili Teru son of Kali Teru, son of Zarupin Zihusun, their King, in the course of their fighting fell into my power. His wives and his children, the delight of his heart I dispossessed him of. One hundred and eighty iron vessels and 5 trays of copper, together with the gods of the people in gold and silver,

and their beds and furniture I brought away. Their movables and their wealth I plundered. This city and its palace I burnt with fire, I destroyed and ruined.

[7] The city of *Urrakluiras* their stronghold which was in the country of Panari, I went toward. The exceeding fear of the power of Ashur, my Lord, overwhelmed them. To save their lives they took their gods, and fled like birds to the tops of the lofty mountains. I collected my chariots and warriors, and crossed the Tigris. *Shedi Teru* the son of Khasutkh, King of *Urrakluiras* on my arriving in his country submitted to my yoke. His sons, the delight of his heart, and his favorites, I condemned to the service of the gods: 60 vessels of iron; *trays* and *bars* of copper . . . with 120 cattle, and flock he brought as tribute and offerings. I accepted (them) and spared him. I gave him his life, but imposed upon him the yoke of my empire heavily forever. The wide spreading country of Comukha I entirely conquered, and subjected to my yoke. At this time one tray of copper and one bar of copper from among the service offerings and tribute of Comukha I dedicated to Ashur my Lord, and 60 iron vessels with their gods I offered to my guardian god, *Vul.*

[8] From among my valiant servants, to whom Ashur the Lord gave strength and power, in 30 of my chariots, select companies of my troops and bands of my warriors who were expert in battle, I gathered together. I proceeded to the extensive country of *Miltis*, which did not obey me; it consisted of strong mountains and a difficult land. Where it was easy I traversed it in my chariots: where it was difficult I went on foot. In the country of Aruma, which was a difficult land and impracticable to the passage of my chariots, I left the chariots and marched in front of my troops. Like . . . on the peak of the rugged mountains, I marched victoriously. The country of *Miltis*, like heaps of stubble, I swept. Their fighting men in the course of the battle like chaff I scattered. Their movables, their wealth and their valuables I plundered. Many of their cities I burned with fire. I imposed on them *religious service*, and offerings and tribute.

[9] Tiglath Pileser, the illustrious warrior, the opener of the roads of the countries, the subjugator of the rebellious . . . he who has overrun the whole Magian world.

[10] I subdued the extensive country of Subair, which was in rebellion. The countries of Alza and Purukhuz, which deferred their tribute and offerings, the yoke of my empire heavily upon them I imposed, decreeing that they should bring their tribute and offerings into my presence in the city of Ashur. While I was on this expedition, which the Lord Ashur, committing to my hand a powerful rebel subduing army, ordered for the enlargement of the frontiers of his territory, there were 4,000 of the *Kaskaya* and *Hurunaya* rebellious tribes of the Kheti who had brought under their power the cities of Subarta, attached to the worship of Ashur, my Lord (so that) they did not acknowledge dependence on Subarta. The terror of my warlike expedition overwhelmed them. They would not fight, but submitted to my yoke. Then I took their valuables, and 120 of their chariots fitted to the yoke, and I gave them to the men of my own country.

[11] In the course of this my expedition, a second time I proceeded to the country of Comukha. I took many of their cities. Their movables, their wealth, and their valuables I plundered. Their cities I burnt with fire, I destroyed and overthrew. The soldiers of their armies, who from before the face of my valiant servants fled away, they would not engage with me in the fierce battle: to save their lives they took to the stony heights of the mountains, an inaccessible region: to the recesses of the deep forests and the peaks of the difficult mountains which had never been trodden by the feet of men, I ascended after them: they fought with me; I defeated them: the ranks of their warriors on the tops of the mountains fell like rain: their carcasses filled the ravines and the high places of the mountains: their movables, their wealth, and their valuables I carried off from the stony heights of the mountains. I subdued the country of Comukha throughout its whole extent, and I attached it to the frontiers of my own territory.

[12] Tiglath Pileser, the powerful King, the vanquisher of the disobedient, he who has swept the face of the earth.

[13] In profound reverence to Ashur my Lord, to the country of Kharia, and the far-spreading tribes of the Akhe, deep forests, which no former King (of Assyria) had ever reached, the Lord Ashur invited me to proceed. My chariots and forces I assembled, and I went to an inaccessible region beyond the countries of Itni and Aya. As the steep mountains stood up like metal posts, and were impracticable to the passage of my chariots, I placed my chariots in wagons, and (thus) I traversed the difficult ranges of hills. All the lands of the Akhe and their wide-spreading tribes having assembled, arose to do battle in the country of *Azutapis*. In an inaccessible region I fought with them and defeated them. The ranks of their (slain) warriors on the peaks of the mountains were piled up in heaps; the carcasses of their warriors filled the ravines and high places of the mountains. To the cities which were placed on the tops of the mountains I *penetrated* victoriously: 27 cities of Kharia, which were situated in the districts of Aya, Suira, Itni, Shetzu, Shelgu, Arzanibru, Varutsu, and Anitku, I took; their movables, their wealth, and their valuables I plundered; their cities I burnt with fire, I destroyed and overthrew.

[14] The people of Adavas feared to engage in battle with me; they left their habitations, and fled like birds to the peaks of the lofty mountains. The terror of Ashur my Lord overwhelmed them; they came and submitted to my yoke; I imposed on them tribute and offerings.

[15] The countries of Tsaravas and Ammavas, which from the olden time had never submitted, I swept like heaps of stubble; with their forces in the country of Aruma I fought, and I defeated them. The ranks of their fighting men I levelled like grass. I bore away their gods; their movables, their wealth, and their valuables I carried off. Their cities I burnt with fire, I destroyed and overthrew, and converted into heaps and mounds. The heavy yoke of my empire I imposed on them. I attached them to the worship of Ashur my Lord.

[16] I took the countries of Itsua and Daria, which were turbulent and disobedient. Tribute and offerings I imposed on them. I attached them to the worship of Ashur.

[17] In my triumphant progress over my enemies, my chariots and troops I assembled; I crossed the lower Zab. The countries of Muraddan and Tsaradavas, which were near Atsaniu and Atuva, difficult regions, I captured; their warriors I cut down *like weeds*. The city of Muraddan, their capital city, and the regions toward the rising sun, I took possession of. Their gods, their wealth, and their valuables, one *soss* bars of iron, 30 talents of iron, the abundant wealth of the Lords, of their palaces, and their movables, I carried off. This city I burnt with fire, I destroyed and overthrew. At this time this iron to the god Vul, my great Lord and guardian, I dedicated.

[18] In the might and power of Ashur my Lord, I went to the country of Tsugi, belonging to Gilkhi, which did not acknowledge Ashur my Lord. With 4,000 of their troops, belonging to the countries Khimi, Lukhi, Arirgi, Alamun, Nuni, and all the far-spread land of the *Akhi*, in the country of Khirikhi, a difficult region, which rose up like metal posts, with all their people I fought *on foot*. I defeated them; the bodies of their fighting men on the tops of the mountains I heaped in masses. The carcasses of their warriors I strewed over the country of Khirikhi like chaff. I took the entire country of Tsugi. Twenty-five of their gods, their movables, their wealth, and their valuables I carried off. Many of their cities I burnt with fire, I destroyed and overthrew. The men of their armies submitted to my yoke. I had mercy on them. I imposed on them tribute and offerings. With attachment to the worship of Ashur, my Lord, I intrusted them.

[19] At this time 25 of the gods belonging to those countries, subject to my government, which I had taken, I dedicated for the honor of the temple of the Queen of glory, the great ancestress of Ashur my Lord, of Anu, and of Vul, the goddess who is the guardian of all the public temples of my city of Ashur, and of all the goddesses of my country.

[20] Tiglath-Pileser, the powerful King; the subduer of hostile races; the conqueror of the whole circle of kings.

[21] At this time, in exalted reverence to Ashur, my Lord, by the godlike support of the heroic "Sun," having in the service of the great gods, ruled over the four regions imperially; there being found (to me) no equal in war, and no second in battle, to the countries of the powerful Kings who dwelt upon the upper ocean and had never made their submission, the Lord Ashur having urged me, I went. Difficult mountain chains, and distant (or inaccessible) hills, which none of our Kings had ever previously reached, tedious paths and unopened roads I traversed. The countries of Elama, of Amadana, of Eltis, of Sherabili, of *Likhuna*, of Tirkakhuli, of Kisra, of Likhanubi, of Elula, of Khastare, of Sakhisara, of Hubira, of Miliatruni, of *Sulianzi*, of Nubanashe, and of Sheshe, 16 strong countries, the easy parts in my chariots, and the difficult parts in wagons of iron, I passed through; the thickets of the mountains I cut down; bridges for the passage of my troops I prepared; I crossed over the Euphrates; the King of Elammi, the King of Tunubi, the King of Tuhali, the King of Kindari, the King of Huzula, the King of Vanzamuni, the King of Andiabi, the King of Pilakinna, the King of Aturgina, the King of Kulibartzini, the King of Pinibirni, the King of Khimua, the King of Paiteri, the King of Vairam, the King of Sururia, the King of Abaeni, the King of Adaeni, the King of Kirini, the King of Albaya, the King of Vagina, the King of Nazabia, the King of *Amalziu*, the King of Dayeni, in all 23 Kings of the countries of Nairi, in their own provinces having assembled their chariots and troops, they came to fight with me. By means of my powerful servants I straitened them. I caused the destruction of their far-spreading troops, as if with the destroying tempest of Vul. I levelled the ranks of their warriors, both on the tops of the mountains and on the battlements of the cities, like *grass*. Two soss of their chariots I held as a trophy from the midst of the fight; one soss of the kings of the countries of Nairi, and of those who had come to their assistance, in my victory as far as the upper ocean I pursued them; I took their great castles; I plundered

their movables, their wealth and their valuables; their cities I burnt with fire, I destroyed and overthrew, and converted into heaps and mounds. Droves of many horses and mules, of calves and of lambs, their property, in countless numbers I carried off. Many of the kings of the countries of Nairi fell alive into my hands; to these kings I granted pardon; their lives I spared; their abundance and wealth I poured out before my Lord, the sun-god. In reverence to my great gods, to after-times, to the last day, I condemned them to do homage. The young men, the pride of their royalty, I gave over to the service of the gods; 1,200 horses and 2,000 cattle I imposed on them as tribute, and I allowed them to remain in their own countries.

[22] Tseni, the King of Dayani, who was not submissive to Ashur my Lord, his abundance and wealth I brought it to my city of Ashur. I had mercy on him. I left him in life to learn the worship of the great gods from my city of Ashur. I reduced the far-spreading countries of Nairi throughout their whole extent, and many of their kings I subjected to my yoke.

[23] In the course of this expedition, I went to the city of Milidia, belonging to the country of Khanni–rabbi, which was independent and did not obey me. They abstained from engaging in the rude fight with me; they submitted to my yoke, and I had mercy on them. This city I did not occupy, but I gave the people over to religious service, and I imposed on them as a token of their allegiance a fixed tribute of . . .

[24] Tiglath-Pileser, the ruling constellation; the powerful; the lover of battle.

[25] In the service of my Lord Ashur, my chariots and warriors I assembled; I set out on my march. In front of my strong men I went to the country of the Aramaeans, the enemies of my Lord Ashur. From before Tsukha, as far as the city of Qarqamis belonging to the country of Khatte, I smote with *one blow*. Their fighting men I slew;

their movables, their wealth, and their valuables in countless numbers I carried off. The men of their armies who fled from before the face of the valiant servants of my Lord Ashur, crossed over the Euphrates; in boats covered with bitumen skins I crossed the Euphrates after them; I took six of their cities which were below the country of Bisri; I burnt them with fire, and I destroyed and overthrew; and I brought their movables, their wealth, and their valuables to my city of Ashur.

[26] Tiglath-Pileser, he who tramples upon the Magian world; he who subdues the disobedient; he who has overrun the whole earth.

[27] My Lord Ashur having urged me on, I took my way to the vast country of Muzri, lying beyond Elammi, Tala, and Kharutsa; I took the country of Muzri throughout its whole extent; I subdued their warriors; I burnt their cities with fire, I destroyed and overthrew; the troops of the country of Comani hastened to the assistance of the country of Muzri: in the mountains I fought with them and defeated them. In the metropolis, the city of Arin, which was under the country of Ayatsa, I besieged them; they submitted to my yoke; I spared this city; but I imposed on them religious service and tribute and offerings.

[28] At this time the whole country of Comani which was in alliance with the country of Muzri, all their people assembled and arose to do battle and make war. By means of my valiant servants I fought with 20,000 of their numerous troops in the country of Tala, and I defeated them; their mighty mass broke in pieces; as far as the country of Kharutsa, belonging to Muzri, I smote them and pursued; the ranks of their troops on the heights of the mountains I cut down *like grass*; their carcasses covered the valleys and the tops of the mountains; their great castles I took, I burnt with fire, I destroyed, and overthrew into heaps and mounds.

[29] The city of Khunutsa, their stronghold, I overthrew like a heap of stubble. With their mighty troops in the city and on the hills I

fought *fiercely*. I defeated them; their fighting men in the middle of the forests I scattered like *chaff*. I cut off their heads as if they were *carrion*; their carcasses filled the valleys and (covered) the heights of the mountains. I captured this city; their gods, their wealth, and their valuables I carried off, and burnt with fire. Three of their great castles, which were built of brick, and the entire city I destroyed and overthrew, and converted into heaps and mounds, and upon the site I laid down large stones; and I made tablets of copper, and I wrote on them an account of the countries which I had taken by the help of my Lord Ashur, and about the taking of this city, and the building of its castle; and upon it I built a house of brick, and I set up within it these copper tablets.

[30] In the service of Ashur my Lord, my chariots and warriors I assembled, and I approached Kapshuna, their capital city; the tribes of Comani would not engage in battle with me; they submitted to my yoke, and I spared their lives. The great castle of the city and its brick buildings I trampled under foot; from its foundations to its roofs I destroyed it and converted it into heaps and mounds, and a band of 300 fugitive heretics who did not acknowledge my Lord Ashur, and who were expelled from inside this *castle*, I took this band and condemned to the service of the gods, and I imposed upon the people tribute and offerings in excess of their former tribute; and the far-spreading country of Comani throughout its whole extent I reduced under my yoke.

[31] There fell into my hands altogether between the commencement of my reign and my fifth year 42 countries, with their kings, from beyond the river Zab, plain, forest, and mountain, to beyond the river Euphrates, the country of the Khatte and the upper ocean of the setting sun. I brought them under one government; I placed them under the Magian religion, and I imposed on them tribute and offerings.

[32] I have omitted many hunting expeditions which were not connected with my warlike achievements. In pursuing after the game

I traversed the easy tracts in my chariots, and the difficult tracts on foot. I demolished the wild animals throughout my territories.

[33] Tiglath-Pileser, the illustrious warrior, he who holds the sceptre of Lashanan; he who has extirpated all wild animals.

[34] The gods Hercules and Nergal gave their valiant servants and their *arrows* as a glory to support my empire. Under the auspices of Hercules, my guardian deity, four wild bulls, strong and fierce, in the desert, in the country of Mitan, and in the city Arazik, belonging to the country of the Khatte, with my long *arrows* tipped with iron, and with heavy blows I took their lives. Their skins and their horns I brought to my city of Ashur.

[35] Ten large wild buffaloes in the country of Kharran, and the plains of the river Khabur, I slew. Four buffaloes I took alive; their skins and their horns, with the live buffaloes, I brought to my city of Ashur.

[36] Under the auspices of my guardian deity Hercules, two *soss* of lions fell before me. In the course of my progress on foot I slew them, and 800 lions in my chariots in my exploratory journeys I laid low. All the beasts of the field and the flying birds of heaven I made the victims of my shafts.

[37] From all the enemies of Ashur, the whole of them, I exacted *labor*. I made, and finished the repairs of, the temple of the goddess Astarte, my lady, and of the temple of Martu, and of Bel, and Il, and of the sacred buildings and *shrines* of the gods belonging to my city of Ashur. I *purified* their shrines, and set up inside the images of the great gods, my Lords. The royal palaces of all the great fortified cities throughout my dominions, which from the olden time our kings had neglected through long years, had become ruined. I repaired and finished them. The castles of my country, I filled up their *breaches*. I founded many new buildings throughout Assyria, and I opened out

irrigation for corn in excess of what my fathers had done. I carried off the droves of the horses, cattle, and asses that I obtained, in the service of my Lord Ashur, from the subjugated countries which I rendered tributary, and the droves of the wild goats and ibexes, the wild sheep and the wild cattle which Ashur and Hercules, my guardian gods, incited me to chase in the depths of the forests, having taken them I drove them off, and I led away their young ones like the tame young goats. These little *wild animals*, the delight of their parents' hearts, in the fulness of my own heart, together with my own victims, I sacrificed to my Lord Ashur.

[38] The pine, the, . . ., and the *algum tree*, these trees which under the former kings my ancestors, they had never planted, I took them from the countries which I had rendered tributary, and I planted them in the groves of my own territories, and I *bought* fruit trees; whatever I did not find in my own country, I took and placed in the groves of Assyria.

[39] I built chariots fitted to the yoke for the use of my people in excess of those which had existed before. I added territories to Assyria, and I added populations to her population. I improved the condition of the people, and I obtained for them abundance and security.

[40] Tiglath-Pileser, the illustrious prince, whom Ashur and Hercules have exalted to the utmost wishes of his heart; who has pursued after the enemies of Ashur, and has subjugated all the earth.

[41] The son of Ashur-ris-ili, the powerful King, the subduer of foreign countries, he who has reduced all the lands of the Magian world.

[42] The grandson of Mutaggil-Nabu, whom Ashur, the great Lord, aided according to the wishes of his *heart* and established in strength in the government of Assyria.

[43] The glorious offspring of Ashur-dapur-Il, who held the sceptre of dominion, and ruled over the people of Bel; who in all the works of his hand and the deeds of his life placed his reliance on the great gods, and thus obtained a prosperous and *long life*.

[44] The beloved child of Barzan-pala-kura, the king who first organized the country of Assyria, who purged his territories of the wicked as if they had been . . ., and established the troops of Assyria in authority.

[45] At this time the temple of Anu and Vul, the great gods, my Lords, which, in former times, Shansi-Vul, High-priest of Ashur, son of Ismi Dagan, High-priest of Ashur, had founded, having lasted for 641 years, it fell into ruin. Ashur-dapur-Il, King of Assyria, son of Barzan-pala-kura, King of Assyria, took down this temple and did not rebuild it. For 60 years the foundations of it were not laid.

[46] In the beginning of my reign, Anu and Vul, the great gods, my Lords, guardians of my steps, they invited me to repair this their shrine. So I made bricks; I levelled the earth, I took its *dimensions*; I laid down its foundations upon a mass of strong rock. This place throughout its whole extent I paved with bricks in *set order*, 50 feet deep I prepared the ground, and upon this substructure I laid the lower foundations of the temple of Anu and Vul. From its foundations to its roofs I built it up, better than it was before. I also built two lofty cupolas in honor of their noble godships, and the holy place, a spacious hall, I consecrated for the convenience of their worshippers, and to accommodate their votaries, who were numerous as the stars of heaven, and in quantity poured forth like flights of arrows. I repaired, and built, and completed my work. Outside the temple I fashioned (everything with the same care) as inside. The mound of earth (on which it was built) I enlarged like the firmament of the rising stars, and I beautified the entire building. Its cupolas I raised up to heaven, and its roofs I built entirely of brick. An inviolable shrine for their noble godships I laid down near at hand. Anu and Vul, the

great gods, I glorified inside, I set them up on their honored purity, and the hearts of their noble godships I delighted.

[47] Bit-Khamri, the temple of my Lord Vul, which Shansi-Vul, High-priest of Ashur, son of Ismi-Dagan, High-priest of Ashur, had founded, became ruined. I levelled its site, and from its foundation to its roofs I built it up of brick, I enlarged it beyond its former state, and I adorned it. Inside of it I sacrificed precious victims to my Lord Vul.

[48] At this time I found various sorts of stone in the countries of Nairi, which I had taken by the help of Ashur, my Lord, and I placed them in the temple of Bit-Khamri, belonging to my Lord, Vul, to remain there forever.

[49] Since a holy place, a noble hall, I have thus consecrated for the use of the great gods, my Lords Anu and Vul, and have laid down an adytum for their special worship, and have finished it successfully, and have delighted the hearts of their noble godships, may Anu and Vul preserve me in power. May they support the men of my Government. May they establish the authority of my officers. May they bring the rain, the joy of the year, on the cultivated land and the desert during my time. In war and in battle may they preserve me victorious. Many foreign countries, turbulent nations, and hostile Kings I have reduced under my yoke; to my children and descendants may they keep them in firm allegiance. I will lead my steps, firm as the mountains, to the last days before Ashur and their noble godships.

[50] The list of my victories and the catalogue of my triumphs over foreigners hostile to Ashur, which Anu and Vul have granted to my arms, I have inscribed on my tablets and cylinders, and I have placed them to the last days in the temple of my Lords Anu and Vul, and the tablets of Shamsi-Vul, my ancestor, I have raised altars and sacrificed victims (before them), and set them up in their places.

[51] In after-times, and in the latter days . . ., if the temple of the great gods, my Lords Anu and Vul, and these shrines should become old and fall into decay, may the prince who comes after me repair the ruins. May he raise altars and sacrifice victims before my tablets and cylinders, and may he set them up again in their places, and may he inscribe his name on them together with my name. As Anu and Vul, the great gods, have ordained, may he worship honestly with a good heart and full trust.

[52] Whoever shall abrade or injure my tablets and cylinders, or shall moisten them with water, or scorch them with fire, or expose them to the air, or in the holy place of god shall assign them a position where they cannot be seen or understood, or who shall erase the writing and inscribe his own name, or who shall divide the sculptures, and break them off from my tablets,

[53] Anu and Vul, the great gods, my Lords, let them consign his name to perdition; let them curse him with an irrevocable curse; let them cause his sovereignty to perish; let them pluck out the stability of the throne of his empire; let not offspring survive him in the kingdom; let his servants be broken; let his troops be defeated; let him fly vanquished before his enemies. May Vul in his fury tear up the produce of his land. May a scarcity of food and of the necessaries of life afflict his country. For one day may he not be called happy. May his name and his race perish in the land.

In the month of *Kuzallu*, on the 29th day, in the High-Priesthood of *Ina-iliya-hallik*, (entitled) *Rabbi-turi*.

End of translation.

BOOKS FOR FURTHER READING

Mazin Zara, *Akkadian: Assyrian Words Still Used in Qarakosh Today*

Fred Aprim, *Assyrians: The Continuous Saga, Indigenous People in Distress*, and various books on the subject of Assyrians

Dr. Efrem Yildiz, *Grammar of Modern Assyrian Language*

Dr. Zakkay Cherry, *Aramaic Loans Words in Neo-Assyrian*

Rosie Malek-Yonan, *The Crimson Field*

The Assyrian Tragedy, 1934, written and published anonymously for Mar Eshai Shimun

Simo Parpola, various books on the subject of Assyrians

H. W. F. Saggs, *Everyday Life in Babylonia & Assyria*, 1965

Henry Layard, various books on the subject of Assyrians

G. R. Driver, *Semitic Writing from Pictograph to Alphabet*, 1954

Thorkild Jacobsen, *Toward the Image of Tammuz and Other Essays on Mesopotamian History and Culture* (Harvard University Press, 1970)

S. Langdon, *Tammuz, and Ishtar: A Monograph upon Babylonian Religion and Theology* (Oxford Clarendon Press, 1914)

The Assyrian Dictionary of the Oriental Institute of the University of Chicago (CAD), twenty-one volumes, 1956–2010

APPENDIX 1[23]

*L*etters to the League of Nations by Mar Eshai Shimun, August 1933, about the plight of the Assyrians.

---

[23] Original document credit to the Mar Eshai Shimun Foundation

ANNEX 1478 b.

Official No.: C. 538???. 1933. I.

PROTECTION OF MINORITIES IN IRAQ.

_____

I. PETITIONS, DATED AUGUST 16TH AND 30TH AND SEPTEMBER 12TH, 1933, FROM THE MAR SHIMUN, CATHOLICOS PATRIARCH OF THE ASSYRIANS CONCERNING THE SITUATION OF THE ASSYRIAN MINORITY IN IRAQ

Note by the Secretary-General:

At the request of the representatives of Mexico, the Irish Free State and Norway, the question forming the subject of these petitions has been included in the agenda of the Council on the basis of two previous petitions from the same petitioner (see document C.504.1933.I).

The Secretary-General has now the honour to circulate, for the examination of the Council, three new petitions, with annexes, from the Mar Shimun, dated, respectively: Baghdad, August 16th, and Nicosia (Cyprus), August 30th and September 12th, 1933.

Any observations the Iraqi Government may wish to present thereon will be communicated to the Council as soon as they reach the Secretariat.

_____

List of Documents.

_____

I. Report of August 4th, 1933.

As from Patriarchate, Mosul,
c/o Y.M.C.A., Baghdad,
August 16th, 1933.

To the Secretary-General,
League of Nations,
Geneva.

LEAGUE OF NATIONS.

Communicated to the Council.　　　　　　　　C. 556.1933.I.

Geneva, October 3rd, 1933.

PROTECTION OF MINORITIES IN IRAQ.

Supplementary petition of the Mar Shimun, "Catholicos"

Patriarch of the Assyrians, concerning the situation of

the Assyrian Minority in Iraq.

(See documents C.504, 519, 535 and 545.1933I.)

Note by the Secretary-General.

By document C.519.1933.I., the Secretary-General communicated to the Council a telegram, dated September 16th, 1933, from the Mar Shimun, "Catholicos" Patriarch of the Assyrians, concerning the situation of the Assyrian Minority in Iraq.

The Secretary-General now has the honour to circulate, for the examination of the Council, a letter from the same source, with annexes, dated September 24th, 1933, and concerning the same question.

The text of this communication is being sent at the same time to the Iraqi Government, for its observations. The Secretary-General will not fail to forward to the Council any observations that Government may present thereon.

September 24th, 1933.

To the Secretary-General.

Excellency,

In confirmation of my telegram dated 16th September 1933,* which ran as follows:-

"Twenty eight more known Assyrians including women massacred between twentieth August and third September. Large number individual murders continue. Detailed report follows"

In confirmation of the above statement, I forward herewith:

(a) a statement (marked A) showing names of the Assyrians killed between the dates stated in the telegram. It should be remembered that the orders to stop massacre wars alleged to have been given by the Minister of Interior who, during the massacre operations between the 11th and 14th August, was at Mosul. I am endeavouring to obtain a complete list of persons killed which I will submit to the League of Nations as early as possible.

Would you please not that, despite official denial, the Iraq postal service is under strict postal censorship.

(b) a statement (marked B) made by an Assyrian woman, Victoria Yokhannan. After these atrocities, forced conversion to Mohammadanism is not unnatural in Iraq where Holy War was made public property.

---

* See C.519.1933.I. (Note by the Secretary-General).

(c) a statement (marked C) made by an Assyrian woman, Rabi Armunta. Her statement tallies with that of Nimo Abo in regard to the Quaimaqam of Dohuk with whose knowledge the massacre took place. The statement of Nimo Abo was forwarded to you under the cover of my letter dated September 12th 1933.**

(d) a statement (marked D) made by Miryam, wife of David Jindo. You will see that the Assyrians, whether with Iraqi nationality papers or not, suffered likewise without discrimination. The statement of the Iraqi Government that they took punitive action against the alleged disloyal Assyrians falls to the ground.

(e) a statement made by Youshia Dinkha. A further statement to confirm the fact that military as well as civil Iraqi authorities participated likewise in the massacre.

(f) a statement made by an impartial observer who witnessed the attacks made on the Assyrian civil employees at Baiji, in the service of the Iraqi Petroleum Co.

Mawlud Mukhlis, the Arab senator, was the man who instigated the Arabs to attack the Assyrians. This man whose past history leaves much to be desired is originally from Takrit and still enjoys a certain amount of influence in that district. The Arab killed by the police is one of his relatives. The Arab demonstrators actually telegraphed to Mawlud for help and it was Mawlud together with three other Arab senators who, six weeks before the general massacre, had posed questions to the Iraqi Prime Minister on the Assyrian settlement and asked that "an exceedingly careful reply should be given".

If the contents of the statement regarding the Baiji affair are carefully checked with the dates of events in the Mosul ???iwa, it will be clearly seen that the general attack was prearranged.

** ???

225

I have the honour to be,
Excellency,
Your obedient servant,

(signed) Eshai SHIMUN

By the Grace of God,
Catholicos Patriarch of
the Assyrians.

A.

———

The following Assyrians were killed between August 20th and
September 3rd, 1933.

———

District	Name of person killed.
Barwari Zairi	1. Dinkha Samano
	2. Khoshaha Adam
	3. Yokhannan Yonan
	4. Odishu Pithyu
	5. Shim'un Iyyar
	6. Tamar Maroguil
	7. Shim'un Makko
	8. Yaqu Makko
	9. Benyamin Mamo
	10. Jiwo Yaqu
	11. Elia Adam
	12. Chaba Shlaimun
	13. Chaba Yokhannan
	14. Yokhannan Giwargis
	15. Shim'un Odishu
	16. Sliwu Majji
	17. Dinkha Hormizd
	18. Zia Yawila
	19. Yokhannan Yonan
	20. Giwargis Dinkha
	21. Chikku Dadishu
	22. Chaya Ruwal
	23. Lawandu Yonathan
	24. Qasha Mansur

Aqra	25. Guzzi wife of Shmiwal Majji
	26. Bibi wife of Dinkah Hormizd
Dohuk	27. Qasha Toma (priest)*
	28. Wife of Qasha Toma* (No. 27 above).

---

* Killed on 3/9/33.

Statement made by Victoria Yokhannan, a young girl of 12 years of age of the tribe of Diz.

On the 13th August, I was in the village of Badi, district of Dohuk. On that day we saw about 40 policemen and Kurds with police uniform coming to Badi. They went from house to house arresting men, and I saw with my own eyes that they selected 4 young men and shot them down there and then. They took other men to the mosque and the Mullah of the village. These were all old men and at the mosque they were asked whether they would embrace Mohammadinism. As the first man refused to do so, one of the policemen knocked him down with the butt of his rifle and then shot him dead. They asked the others who, having seen the fate of the first man, were terrified and did not dare to say "No".

Their names were later on written down and given by the Police to the Mullah of Badi. The Mullah from that time took charge of them in instructing them the Mohammadan religion and the way of prayers in the Mosque and also in the Chaikhana of the village.

The policemen remained in the village for 5 hours sending away on mules the loot which they took from the Assyrians, in the village.

About evening, they arrested young women and took them to the village of Kuzoo (?) whilst other remaining men were sent by these policemen to Dohuk during the day time. I remained 5 days in Badi and on the 6th day I was secretly taken out of the village by an Assyrian policeman, and was then sent to Mosul.

(C)

Statement made by Rabi Armunta, an Assyrian woman.

On the 11th August, 1933, whilst I was living in the American Mission house at Dohuk, I happened to see two Assyrian young men of Diz tribe named Baba of Makhtan and Gambul of Bait Shamasha (both known personally to me). They were tied together and their hands handcuffed. They were being taken under escort of 5 policemen and I saw them passing towards Qishla (Government House). Five minutes later I heard 3 shots and a short while after that I saw the five policemen coming back laughing whilst one of them was carrying with him the handcuffs.

(2) On the second day (12/8), I went to Qasha Shmiwal's house to tell the story of the two young men. Whilst I was in Qasha Shmiwal's house, two policemen came and took him to the Qaimaqam. Before leaving the house, Qasha Shmiwal took ten dinars with him saying that he may want this money in after time. The policemen, as soon as they took the priest out of his house, started pushing and kicking him and for that reason his wife and children and myself followed him to Qishla but when we arrived there Qasha Shmiwal had already been put in a car and they drove him away. We only heard him saying to the Qaimaqam "For God's mercy be good", and we saw him departing with tears in his eyes. His wife then approached the Qaimaqam telling him "O Qaimaqam, why did you do this to my husband? What shall I do with these children?" And she cried in the presence of the Qaimaqam. The Qaimaqam told her "Don't be afraid. I have only sent your husband to Mosul;" but she kept crying before the Qaimaqam, and he at last told the police: "Draw this bitch away". Two policemen pushed her away from the Qaimaqam's presence.

(3) Just before leaving Qishla, I saw a party of policemen arriving in a car and with them another Assyrian of Diz, bleeding from a

230

gun shot wound in his body. They threw the young man in front of Qishla's gate. He was crying and begging the police to take him to doctor. The Qaimaqam came out and seeing him in that condition, ordered the policemen: "Drag this dog away from this place", whereupon two policemen caught him with his hands and legs and dragged him to the stream side about 150 yards from Qishla and left him there, There was a huge gathering of Muslims in front of the Government house at that time, and this cruel scene enjoyed them very much. The name of the said man was Ishu Gilyana.

(4) Whilst this scene was going on and I was about to leave the Qishla with Qasha Shmiwal's family, our eyes again caught him being taken in the car with another Assyrian whom I did not know, across the bridge under escort of four policemen. The car went and passed behind a place which is known as the shrine of Mar Dala (a Christian Church), and then the car went out of the way towards the hill of Mar Dala. We saw Qasha Shmiwal being brought down from the car and the policemen taking off his clothes. When they had done this, they took him behind the cover of the hill and suddenly we heard the gun shots and then we saw the policemen coming back to Qishla. I then returned to the American Mission house, and Qasha's family to her own house. I remained 3 days in the Mission House and then I was taken with the other refugees to Mosul.

(D)

Statement made by Miryam, wife of David Jindo, a corporal in the Iraq levies.

I am wife of David Jindo of upper Tiyari. My husband is serving on the levies and myself was living in the village of Simel.

On Tuesday the 8th August 1933 as I remember, a strong party of the Iraq army returned from Zakho to the village. They collected all the rifles and ammunition in possession of the Assyrian men. A few hours after they had done this, they again returned the rifles to the owners, but not the ammunition. Next day which was Wednesday, all the Assyrian families and men who were in the village in the neighborhood of Simel came to Simel to take refuge with the police force there. On the same day the Quimaqam of Dohuk came with the Iraqa soldiers and the armoured cars and collected all the rifles and any other weapons from the Assyrians and sent them to Dohuk. He (The Quimaqam) summoned to himself priest Sada of Liwon tribe, Rais Tailo of Baz tribe and another named Badal of the village of Kharabkuli. He arrested them and took them towards Dohuk in the armoured cars. But on reaching near a village Aloka which is between Simel, they were murdered by the order of the Qaimaqam of Dohuk. Eye-witnesses say that they had seen the dead bodies of all 3 and that the body of the priest Sada had been outrageously mutilated, i.e., his male organ having been cut was placed in his mouth, his head had been severed from his body; most probably he had met his death by beheading.

On Thursday, August 10th, the armoured cars filled with soldiers again came from Dohuk; they arrested 2 men of the Albaq tribe and 1 of Nodiz tribe (The Albaq men, one was of the village of Mansuriyah and the other of Kharab Kuli, who were in Simel on that day and the man of Nodiz was a resident of Simel). They were taken in the armoured cars in the direction of Zakho but before going very far on their way we saw them from the roofs being murdered with sharp weapons. I saw this because I myself saw them falling like dead bodies on the ground and their bodies were later seen.

On Friday, August 11th, the policemen came and drove us out of the fort where their post was. They say that we had no longer any fear of life and that we could go out and live in the houses of the village. No sooner we were out of the fort then all the round of the village was surrounded by armoured cars and soldiers, when another column of the Iraq army arrived from Zakho direction. Now the fear for life and panic ruled every body Some run from their houses (mostly of Baz tribe) and took refuge with one Rais Goriyil of Baz who boasted that he being loyal to the Iraq Government, no harm would happen to anyone who took refuge in his house, where he had erected a white flag as a sign of submission. He had received a letter from Malik Khamo of Baz, his chieftain, telling him to be at ease and not fear any harm since he was his follower who had remained 'loyal' to the Government. Others hide themselves in the houses of the village. Those in the house of Rais Goriyil numbered 82 men only of Baz tribe with their families and there were others with them from other Assyrian tribes. The soldiers first opened machine gun and gun fire on the village, their objective being every house. Then they assaulted the village killing every one who came in their way. When they knew of the great number having taken refuge in Goriyil's house, they brought a machine gun at close range and opened a terrific fire in the courtyard, first killing Goriyil and his son, who came to meet them, and then directing the fire into the windows and doors of the rooms where the remaining men were and shot them all down.

The soldiers then remained in the village remaining about to find any male person and shoot him down. About evening they entered the places (i.e., the Fort and other houses where the women and children had gathered together). Amongst the women and children there were nearly about hundred men and grown-up boys, who being without arms to save themselves had put on woman's clothes; they were all discovered by the soldiers and police (as every woman and other person in female dress was examined by the soldiers and the police) and they were all killed.

Also male children of about 6 years of age were not spared. Amongst the man who, in order to save themselves had disguised in women's clothes, was one Qasha Ishmail (priest). The policemen in charge of the post put up for the protection, discovered him also. I saw the police sergeant kicking and dragging the priest outside the fort. I saw the police sergeant also dashing the priest's two children of 4 and 6 years of age against the wall because they were clinging to their father and screaming after him as he was being taken away. Qasha Ishmail was taken outside where he joined another priest, Qasha Irsanis, whom the police had found in another house. They were both murdered just below the fort in front of a house known as of Khishaba. Their beards were cut off and their hair was dashed in their mouths.

On Sunday the 12th August, another column of the Iraq army came from Zakho direction. They hurriedly collected all the dead bodies and covered them, the majority in a pit situated below a house of one Yodan where Goriel of Baz had been living since he had come to Simel and where the massacre of all the people of Baz tribe under Goriel had taken place the previous day. I can mark out several of the places (pits and heaps of rubbish) where the dead bodies had been covered. I cannot exactly say, how many people were massacred on Friday 11th August but the number was in hundreds including men, women and children. I know 12 women by their names and several of them with their children who were killed. I also know of a woman named Kuti, who after being beheaded, the soldiers took off her clothes and a set of artificial golden teeth from her mouth. The children were mostly stabbed to death as they were throwing themselves on their mothers when being shot.

On Saturday the 12th, five British aeroplanes came, four of which landed at the aerodrome and one was flying over Simel; no one of the British officers in the four landed planes came to see us and we were confined by the police and could not go to them. Otherwise we would have gone to bring them to see the newly buried dead bodies by hundreds of men, women and children. After the soldiers had finished their work of killing and hiding the bodies, the Bedouin tribesmen and Kurds swarmed into the village of Simel pillaging everything that they wanted to take. We who were still remaining alive, i.e., women and children only, mostly girls, as all male children had been massacred, were very strictly confined to the Fort. We were not allowed even to go to fetch water to drink and the police did not give us any water to drink. After two days from Saturday 12th August, we were allowed outside for the purpose of drinking water and sanitation. But as all our clothes and belongings had been taken from us by soldiers, police, Arab Bedouin and Kurds, we passed the most miserable life. Most of the women and children were left only with one shirt with which they had to to cover themselves day and night.

A few days later we were removed from Simel, some to Dohuk, some to Mosul. I was brought to Hinaidi as my husband is in the levies there.

Statement made by Yushiya Dinka, of
Malik Ismail of Upper Tiyari.

After living in Diana, Rowanduz, during its occupation by the Assyrian levies for four and a half years, our family moved to Simrl, near Dohuk, on account of the evacuation of Diana by Assyrian levies. We had been at Simel for a period of 3 months.

On 30th July, the police sergeant in charge of the police post at Simel came to my house and said 'The Qaimaqam of Dohuk is waiting for you on the road and wants to see you there.' I went to the Qaimaqam and, after saluting him, he told me 'I give you one day's warning, you must either go to Mosul tomorrow or give a security for of one thousand dinar guaranteed by a person who is known to the Government. Or otherwise, you will have to undergo imprisonment for seven years.' I replied 'Yes, Beg, but I want to know for what reason.' He said that I had only to obey, and that he would let me know the reason when he returns from Faishkhabour, where he was going then.

I proceeded to Mosul as I was ordered and stayed there until 10th August, when I received a message from my aunt who was living at Kur Gawana (a village in Dohuk district), saying that she was ill and wanted me to go and bring her to hospital at Mosul. I started for Kur Gawana on the 7th August and on arrival at a spring near the village, I saw 3 armed Assyrians in the midst of a party of 40 armed Kurds. The Kurds wanted to disarm the Assyrians. I also was taken with the 3 Assyrians by the Kurds and I asked them why they wanted to take our rifles. They said 'It is the order of the government to us, the Muslims, to kill any Assyrian whom we see outside the village; the government will then present us with the Assyrian rifles, and one dinar for every head we produce to the government. But now you see, those swine they will not give up their rifles to us and if we shoot them down they will also shoot us, and to avoid this we will take them to the police post at Kur Gawana.' So they took us to Kur

Gawana and from there together with 2 other Assyrians to Dohuk, under an escort of 4 Kurds and 2 policemen.

At Dohuk our hands were handcuffed.

On 9/8 Wednesday, about 12 o'clock, another party of eleven Assyrians were brought to us. At about 6 p.m. on that day, they were all bound together with ropes, among them a priest named Qasha Sada and they were taken in armoured cars by a party of Iraqi soldiers of blue uniform to Zakho valley and slaughtered there.

At 10/8, another party of 8 Assyrians was brought into the prison. This party had no priest with them, whilst the previous one and all the others whom I am going to mention were all with a priest each of them. About 6 p.m. they were tied together as the first party and taken near the village of Maltayi and killed there.

On Friday 11/8 I saw a third party of 15 other Assyrians brought in and at 6 p.m. of that day the soldiers in blue uniform came and tied them 8 of them together, also a priest and took them out of the prison swearing at their religion and pulling the priest with his beard. This party was taken near the village of Aloka and slaughtered there.

On Saturday the 12th August, a 4th party of 8 Assyrians were brought in. The soldiers with blue uniform took these 8 and the other 7 who had remained from the previous party together with another priest named Qasha Shmiwal in the armoured cars outside Dohuk and massacred them.

On Sunday, the 13th August, a police inspector came into the prison in the morning and informed us who were still in the prison to get ready for death as it was our turn now. About evening, whilst we were trembling and awaiting our death, we saw no soldiers with uniform of blue coming to take us away. On Monday a priest named Qasha Etnayil was brought to us; then we thought out death had been delayed only because there had been no priest to accompany us to death the previous day, and it was so. But on that day a Minister came from Baghdad and he stopped further massacre. About 6 p.m., the slaughtering party came to take us. The Qaimaqam told them the massacre has now been stopped.

We remained in Dohuk until Wednesday the 16th August, and on Thursday we were sent to Mosul where we were released by Mutasarrif. Qasna Ithnayil was detained in Dohuk and I afterwards understood that he was compelled by tortures to write a letter to Yaqu Ismail telling him of the ill-treatment of the Assyrians who were suffering at the hands of the government, and that when he had written this document it had been produced as an evidence as treachery against the government, and he was arrested and sent to Mosul. What has since happened to him I do not know, as I left Mosul and came to Baghdad.

When I was proceeding from Dohuk to Mosul, on Thursday the 17th August, I saw the bodies of 3 of the persons mentioned by me above. The first party of the 3 which I saw were lying outside the Dohuk gardens, about 10 yards from the road, the second, near the bridge of Aloka by the stream side on the right of the bridge, whilst the dead bodies of the third party had fallen at a spot between the village of Aloka and Faidi, ten yards from the road.

(F)

Attack on the Assyrians employed by the Iraq Petroleum Co. Baiji.

On the evening of August 9th, 1933, the Arab employees of the Iraq Petroleum Co. attacked the Assyrians and used chairs and sticks. Six Assyrians were wounded and the remainder ran away. The police intervened and arrested two Arabs and three Assyrian wounded. They were taken to the court at Tukrit (in the Baghdad liwa) when the Arabs were acquitted and an Assyrian sentenced to 10 days' imprisonment.

The following day it was strongly rumoured that a second attack by armed Arabs would follow, as their instructions were that they should leave no Assyrian alive. The Iraq Petroleum Co. was compelled to collect all the Assyrians in one place for protection and brought also to this place the Assyrians employed at point K.2, a distance of 5 miles from Baiji. The number of Assyrians thus collected was some 150.

Rumours of impending attacks by Arabs became rife. There was no attack on August 10th, but on the 11th news received indicated that the Arabs in the employ of the Iraq Petroleum Co. themselves would carry out the attack. The Assyrians who were not prepared for such an eventuality ran to the British bungalows for protection. It should be remembered that there was a number of policemen and guards of the Iraq Petroleum Co. for protection purposes, but as soon as the lights were out these deserted their posts and went away. Simultaneously with this the Assyrians were attacked. 14 were wounded and 1 was killed. An Arab employee of the Iraq Petroleum Co. made a demand that the body of the Assyrian who was killed should be burnt, but the British did not agree.

The rumours that the Arab tribesmen would also attack did not die away. 20 Arab horsemen demonstrated the following day before the camp of the company, and before the British officers.

239

After the attack of August 11th, 1933, and at the request of the Iraq Petroleum Co., 40 policemen and 2 machine-guns were sent for purposes of protection.

On August 13th, the rumours of the impending attack died away but the Arab employees went on strike. They demanded the dismissal of all the Assyrian employees. Those who went on strike were about 200. They were joined by 200 Arab tribesmen. On the evening of that day, the Arab employees carrying Iraqi flags went to attack the camp. The police intervened. The ring-leader was summoned and as the British officer would not consent to the contemplated attack, the latter was insulted by the ring-leader. The strikers then returned to the Station and on their way back they burnt down a car belonging to the Iraq Petroleum Co.

At 9 in the evening, the Assistant Commandant of Police, with a car loaded with a machine-gun, proceeded to the Station and asked the strikers to be dispersed. This they refused to do. An enthusiastic – but excessively enthusiastic – Arab rose and said:

"The religion that dominates is that of Muhammed and death means nothing to us."

The strikers thereupon attacked the police officer, who responded, with the result that 2 Arabs were wounded and 1 was killed.

On the 14th, the Iraq Petroleum Co. despatched its aeroplanes to Baghdad and returned to Baiji carrying the Mutasarrif and the Commandant of Police, Baghdad. These interviewed the strikers, with the result that all the Assyrian employees were discharged with the exception of a few Assyrian clerks.

A Chaldean (Catholic) was also wounded during these disturbances.

APPENDIX 2[24]

[Communicated to the Council.]   *Official No.:* **C. 535**, 1933. I.

Geneva, October 2nd, 1933.

LEAGUE OF NATIONS

PROTECTION OF MINORITIES IN IRAQ

PETITIONS OF THE MAR SHIMUN, "CATHOLICOS" PATRIARCH OF THE ASSYRIANS, CONCERNING THE SITUATION OF THE ASSYRIAN MINORITY IN IRAQ

Note by the Secretary-General:

At the request of the representatives of Mexico, the Irish Free State and Norway, the question forming the subject of these petitions has been included in the agenda of the Council on the basis of two previous petitions from the same petitioner (see document C.504.1933.I).

The Secretary-General has now the honour to circulate, for the examination of the Council, three new petitions, with annexes, from

---

[24] Original document credit to the Mar Eshai Shimun Foundation.

the Mar Shimun, dated, respectively: Baghdad, August 16th, and Nicosia (Cyprus), August 30th and September 12th, 1933.

Any observations the Iraqi Government may wish to present thereon will be communicated to the Council as soon as they reach the Secretariat.

LIST OF DOCUMENTS.

Page

I. REPORT OF AUGUST 4TH, 1933.

As from Patriarchate, Mosul,
c/o Y.M.C.A., Baghdad,
August 16th, 1933.

To the Secretary-General,
League of Nations,
Geneva.

I humbly beg leave to send you a copy of my report, with copies attached of the official documents, and translations of various speeches, and a copy of a report made by an eyewitness of many years' experience of this country and its people. I have made my report in this way not to express bitter feelings, but that the League and the world may make unbiased judgments.

Since writing this report so much has, and is taking place, such as massacre of the women, children and old men which were left in the villages, the robbing and burning of the latter, as revenge taken by the police and Arab army, and certain Kurdish and Arab tribes, because of their defeat and failure to subdue the spirit of the Assyrians who resisted the Government's policy, first by leaving the country to prepare for the exit of all, according to the alternative policy which the Government officials told them (see report of meeting held in Mosul July 14th, 1933).[25]

The Government received this decision from the leaders and a copy was sent to me (copy attached to my report).

The circumstances of my forced detention in Baghdad made it difficult to tell the outside world, but I have been able to send out letters and cablegrams through various friends as in this case, with the hope that they reach their destination. So far I have received no acknowledgments.

I beg your help in that an International Commission will be sent out to investigate both sides of this question at the earliest possible moment.

I fully realise that this communication is not coming to you through the proper channels as laid down in the League's regulations, but under the circumstances I have no other alternative.

> *(Signed)* ESHAI SHIMUN,
> *By the Grace of God, Catholicos*
> *Patriarch of the Assyrians.*

---

[25] According to the annexes to the report, this meeting took place on July 10th, 1933.— *Note by the Secretary-General.*

THE PRESENT ASSYRIAN SITUATION. AUGUST 4ᵀᴴ, 1933. THE OFFICIAL REPORT BY MAR SHIMUN, PATRIARCH OF THE ASSYRIANS.

INTRODUCTION.

It is not an easy matter for me as Patriarch of the Assyrian Church to make a report under the present circumstances.

I am held in Baghdad under Government detention, my residence watched day and night by plain-clothes police and my mail censored and confiscated.

The reason given through the *Iraq Times* and local Press by the Government, is that I have refused to give the guarantees required by the Government.

Attached is the translation copy of the guarantees which I refused to sign, and a copy of my reasons. I must say that a very brave effort was made by Sir Kinnahan Cornwallis and Major Edmunds, the British Advisers to the Minister of Interior, to produce a document which both the Minister on behalf of the Government, and I on behalf of my people, could agree to sign. This was helped by the Acting British Ambassador, Mr. Ogilvie Forbes, the British Air Vice-Marshal Burnett, and his intelligence officers.

These efforts beginning on May 21ˢᵗ and continuing to June 25ᵗʰ (much of which is in writing) ended in the Arab Government threatening to resign and my being detained as a prisoner in Baghdad. My reply to the Minister detaining me in Baghdad, copies of which were sent to the various legations in the city, is also attached to this report.

Mr. Ogilvie Forbes, the British diplomat who was sympathetic to me, informed me that I was to be detained in Baghdad and again a few days later told me that His Majesty, King Faisal, had cabled to the Prime Minister from England to release me from detention. No word of such was sent to me by the Government in any shape or form, in fact neither the Arab nor the British officials have had any communication with me since June 25ᵗʰ. Since then I have been separated from my people and home in Mosul, and have been obliged to maintain a double establishment at my own expense.

Before giving my conclusions on the cause of the present situation it is necessary to report at least some of the Assyrian side of the question. I therefore wish to make a summary of such under four periods:

1. From June 1932 the time when it was broadcasted that the mandatory Power in Iraq would cease, till the time when I was delegated by my people to proceed to Geneva to plead their cause before the League of Nations.
2. From the time of proceeding to Geneva, to my return to Mosul on January 11th, 1933.
3. From January 16th to my coming to Baghdad on May 26th.
4. From May 26th to June 25th when I received my detention order in Baghdad (1933).

FIRST PERIOD.

In June 1932 on the eve of the termination of the British mandate in Iraq, the Assyrians, still refugees, after a long and bitter experience of broken promises, from the time they gave and lost practically their all for the Allied cause, until the hour of writing, decided to make a determined effort to get their question settled before Iraq entered the League of Nations.

Those Assyrians who were enlisted under contract with the British Government in the levies, gave the authorities a month's notice to terminate their contracts, stating very definitely their reasons. Those scattered in the various Kurdish districts asked their leaders to make a final petition which was submitted to the League of Nations via the mandatory Power. Sir Francis Humphrys, the then British High Commissioner, in his anxiety to prevent the levies resignation taking effect, requested my help.

Having been dangerously ill, I was ignorant of the levies action until this time. The many definite and helpful promises made by Sir Francis in his letters through me (see copies attached) satisfied the Assyrians that we could expect much, and so trusting his word, the levies withdrew their notice, and continued to carry out their duties; and my people in the villages to wait patiently for the fulfilment of his promises.

I was asked by my people and encouraged by Sir Francis to go to Geneva to represent the cause of my people, the necessary expenses being subscribed by the refugees.

Before concluding this period, I want it to be known that the levies action on the one hand, and my going to Geneva on the other, was considered to be the unforgivable crime of the so-called "Patriarchal Temporal Power" and was the reason for the beginning of the Iraqi Government's present policy –– viz., breaking the power of the people's chosen leaders, and attempting to scatter the people; a very definite breach of the fundamental law.

SECOND PERIOD.

At Geneva, the question of the Assyrians was sidetracked until after the entry of Iraq into the League of Nations although the Permanent Mandates Commission did examine the Assyrian Petition on November 14th, 1932, and endorsed its Rapporteur's conclusions,[26] with unbiased judgment, it became no longer legal as the mandate no longer existed. The essential point to which it drew the Council's attention was the Assyrians need to be settled in a *"homogeneous group"*. The Rapporteur further stated:

> "They (the Assyrians) are encamped there in conditions which in most cases are precarious and miserable. They are refugees. We find an expression of insecurity inspired in the Assyrians, not only by climate . . . but especially by the scattering of this community among populations of other races . . . The root cause of the state of unrest revealed by the

---

[26] See Annex 1418 to the Minutes of the Sixty ninth Session of the Council (*Official Journal*, December 1932, pages 2290-2296).–– *Note by the Secretary-General.*

petition resides in the fact that it has not been possible to collect the Assyrians of Iraq into a 'homogeneous group'. It has not been proved to the satisfaction of impartial observers that lands combining the requisite conditions for settlement of the Assyrians in a *homogeneous group* do not exist in Iraq."

Sir Henry Dobbs in his *"Statement of Proposals" for the settlement of the Assyrian people in Iraq* copy to Lady Surma dated May 1924 states:

"His Excellency the High Commissioner has ascertained that there are more than sufficient deserted lands, the property of the Iraqi Government to the north of Dohuk in Amadia and the northern hills upon which the latter class of persons could be permanently settled."

In the appendix to the Iraqi Prime Minister's letter dated August 2nd, 1932, which was presented to the League of Nations, the following facts appear: In the Mosul Liwa Settlement Scheme 1927 the Council of Ministers had made provision to settle in various places of the Mosul Liwa, various tribes of the Assyrians, numbering altogether 7,500 people, but those actually settled there now are only 686 families. As pointed out in my notes on this report, which I presented to the Council of the League on November 3rd, 1932, there is still room for another 4,500 persons in this district of Mosul, if the report of the Iraqi Government on past settlement for 1927 is correct. But the administrative inspector who undertook settlement in 1930 said "there was no suitable area in the Mosul Liwa where Ashutis (= Lower Tiari) could be settled together".

Thus from all this it will be realised that a "homogeneous group" was the finding of the Permanent Mandates recommendation after fully examining the Assyrian petition. The committee who were authorised by the Council to produce a solution to the problem, seems to have overlooked this in the resolution which it presented and which was passed by the Council on December 11th, 1932,[27] especially in the declaration by the Iraqi representatives which I quoted:

> "Notes with satisfaction the declaration by the representative of Iraq of the intention of the Iraqi Government to select from outside Iraq, a foreign expert to assist them for a limited period in settlement of all landless inhabitants of Iraq, including Assyrians; and in the carrying-out of their scheme for the settlement of the Assyrians of Iraq under suitable conditions and so far as may be possible, in *homogeneous units*, it being understood that the existing rights of the present population shall not be prejudiced."

I appeal to those who see the difference between the words of the Mandates Commissioner's endorsement, and that produced by this resolution –– viz., "homogeneous group" and "homogeneous units". That alteration of group into units was just sufficient to destroy the whole spirit of the League's intention, for it enables the Arab Government to scatter the people into units, instead of settling a group. Thus I returned to my people from the League of Nations (who had in the past assigned our old homes to Turkey, in the settlement of the Iraq and Turkish boundary dispute) empty handed, still refugees and at the mercy of an Arab Government.

I had to inform the League that the third (Assyrian) petition (which Iraq's representative referred to) in which certain Assyrians professed their satisfaction with their present status under the Iraqi Government that the signatures were partly forged, and partly obtained under improper pressure exerted by Government officials, and that I was prepared to substantiate these statements. To-day I discover that 65 per cent are forged and the rest signatures of men who have no following. The fact is, that the Iraqi Government is unable to

---

[27] See Minutes of the Council meeting held on December 15th (not 11th), 1932 (*Official Journal*, December 1932, pages 2285-2290). –– *Note by the Secretary-General.*

carry out its policy towards the Assyrians and the present situation is evidence of this. Before leaving Geneva I, as the representative head of the Assyrians, submitted a protest to the Permanent Mandates Commission in writing, and asked them to reconsider their decision otherwise disaster was bound to occur to my unfortunate people (see my petition of December 16th, 1932). Just before my departure from Geneva I received a letter from the Prime Minister of Iraq, Nuri Pasha, informing me that I should not return direct to my home in Mosul, but via Baghdad to see the Acting Prime Minister. I took this invitation at its face value. On the frontier of Iraq I was treated with the utmost vigilance by the authorities, and made to sign a statement that on arrival in Baghdad I would report to the police. I have since realised that this was an expression of the Government's disapproval of my going to the League of Nations. However, whilst in Baghdad I had an audience with His Majesty King Faisal, who as always, graciously expressed his goodwill towards my people and myself, as did the Acting Prime Minister.

As was customary in the past, on my return to Mosul, I called together the Assyrian leaders to report to them all that had taken place at Geneva. For this, I was informed by the Government's representative in Mosul that I had no power to do so without his sanction. The meeting was finally permitted and took place on January 16th, 1933. I explained to the chiefs the decision of the League, asking them to remain loyal to the Iraqi Government and to wait and see what the settlement would be.

Third Period.

The following period was a real foretaste of the type of rule we had expected, and I was surprised to find that it had already begun during my absence in Geneva. Those of us conversant with "the minorities guarantees" not only wonder why they were so easily broken, but why the Arab Government appointed over the people as leaders, certain Assyrians as their representatives who were paid to carry out a policy of sowing dissension among the people, and a settlement scheme which was bound to fail: it was in the spirit of units or a scattering, and a settlement covering only a very small proportion of the refugees. The people's real leaders were not only ignored, but were ordered to give guarantee that they would not interfere, failing which they were to be imprisoned. No business could be done with the Government's settlement or otherwise, except through those paid Assyrians appointed by Government to force on the people its will.

For nearly seven months this state of affairs has been going on, and my people through their leaders sought my advice. I protested where possible, and asked the people to again wait patiently for the coming of the new Foreign Settlement Expert, as per the Iraqi Government's promise to the League of Nations. In the meantime pressure was being brought to bear on the people and their leaders to profess that they were happily settled and force was being exhibited to make them sign documents accordingly. In fact we now realise that the great idea was to stage a sham settlement scheme to influence the Foreign Settlement Expert to carry on with the Government's settlement policy, which had already failed. When I asked the officials to substantiate their accusations blaming me for the failure, they failed to do so: but adopted the same methods with me as with the people's leaders, and tried in every possible way to destroy the Patriarchal influence over the people, giving out the old falsehood that I was fighting for my own family and its position (see the conversation recorded by Sir K. Cornwallis's note attached, in which I refused to be treated apart from the people's settlement).

FOUR PERIOD.

On May 22nd I was called to the Mutassarif's office in Mosul and told by him that the Minister of the Interior wished me to go to Baghdad to discuss the Assyrian Settlement with him and the Foreign Expert, Major Thomson. Because of the Baghdad heat and my health, I asked that I would not be detained more than four days. On reaching Baghdad I informed the Minister of the Interior of

250

my arrival, and was kept six days waiting before an interview with him. In the meantime, the Foreign Expert had arrived in Mosul at the time I was called to Baghdad. Now I realise, I was brought to Baghdad on false pretences. I therefore sent a special letter to His Majesty King Faisal (see attached copy) but received no reply as His Majesty left for Europe next day. During my interview with the Minister, Assyrian settlement and the Foreign Expert were not mentioned in the conversation that took place. I was informed of the unfavourable attitude of the Iraqi Government towards me, and that I should receive a letter accordingly in which I should be asked to sign guarantees (see copies of the Minister's letter and my answer). To this day no definite accusation of any wrong I have done has ever been told to me. The only possible thing the Government can say against me is that I refused to be a party to the present policy which had incensed the people before I got back from Geneva. It was officially stated in the Press that Major Thomson was in Iraq "purely in an advisory capacity and he will have no executive powers". My one meeting with Major Thomson only confirmed the Government's attitude towards the Assyrian settlement scheme. I did my utmost to change this policy. Advisers did their best, but as will be seen from copies of the official documents, nothing happened except my continued detention in Baghdad.

The threat of the Government to resign brought things to a standstill, as far as I was concerned, and no official, Arab or British, has been to see me or transacted business with me since. The exception being that I took a copy of my protest against detention to the British Ambassador, as I did to the other diplomatic representatives.

CONCLUSION.

From this time on the Government officials in Mosul did their utmost to force the Assyrians to submit to their policy which ignored the sacred minorities guarantees given to the League of Nations. On the other hand, the idea that we were refugees, wanting to be subjects and not serfs, did not occur to them. They forgot that we were tribal people and had traditional customs going back for at least 1,900 years. They demanded guarantees from us before they satisfied us that we would be settled (in a homogeneous group?), where we could live and not starve. We had already had experience of land settlement which had been altered three times. We had no guarantees from the Arab Government of land settlement except broken ones; in fact we had no chance to accept or reject settlement, but were imprisoned if we refused to give guarantees accepting their policy.

By the attached reports it will be seen what has been happening. The Arab Press has published articles full of hatred towards the Assyrians and myself. The reports of speeches made in the Parliament are most bloodthirsty and inflammatory. The Army Commander in Mosul threatened to exterminate the Patriarchal House and the Assyrians in that city, and made the Arabs very hostile towards the Assyrians there. The police arrested my private chaplain and some other Assyrians. Why? It eventually transpired that one of his officers living in the same block of houses as myself, was very annoyed by the mysterious throwing of stones into his courtyard on several nights. His Moslem servant was giving the customary warning of an immoral woman in the house. Even the *Iraq Times* published the Government reports which were full of untruths, ridiculous fabrications and contradictions. I attach the speeches of the Mosul officials which were given at the meetings on July 10th and 11th. Can anyone wonder why the Assyrians chose to leave Iraq, when they were told to go if they were not satisfied? My people were led to believe that their final settlement would be at least in homogeneous groups or units and that their lost lands and homes would be replaced in Iraq, and they would be enabled to settle down again in peace after nearly twenty years of refugee life. This was not to be:

1.   They had either to accept the Government policy of being as now scattered as serfs to Kurdish Aghas as their landlords, and with a Government tax to pay as well in most cases, or if they settle on

Government land, it would be liable to be taken away any time, at the whim of some local official, as past experience has shown. The British officials left in the country having no executive power, are even an incentive to the local officials doing whatever they like, and being ignorant of the law of the land and also the fundamental law. Politics being their only qualification for office.

2.   They must fight for their rights, or,

3.   Leave the country.

The first meant starvation and persecution. The second spelt disaster. The third was the only possible alternative to those Assyrians unable to agree to the Government's policy.

Attached is a letter which those who crossed the frontier into Syria sent to the Minister of the Interior of Iraq.

No British official now left to deal with the Assyrian case, has any real first-hand knowledge of my people, or what they have suffered during the past nineteen years.

The League of Nations betrayed us

(1) By giving our old lands and homes to Turkey;
(2) By handing us over to an Arab Government.

At the moment of closing this report I have knowledge of the burning of an Assyrian village, the local papers are full of news of fighting between Assyrians and Arabs on the frontier, the deporting of some of my relations and Assyrian notables from Mosul, and carrying away of cattle and other properties from the villagers.

(Signed) ESHAI SHIMUN,
By the Grace of God, Catholicos
Patriarch of the East.

Annexes.

No. U. 1104 Baghdad,
28/5/1933.

Honourable Mar Shimun,

During my last visit to Mosul, I informed you of the Government's attitude with regard to your personal position.

I wish now to confirm in writing what you heard from me verbally. The Government desires to recognise your Spiritual See (leadership) over the Assyrian people, and is promising that you will maintain the honour due to your above-mentioned position for always, and as previously the Mutassarif of Mosul has already informed you that the Government desires to obtain your assistance in establishing a Community Law, on the same basis of the rules at present in force with regard to other peoples.

In order that you may maintain your spiritual leadership, in a fitting manner, the Government is at present discussing the means of finding a permanent income towards your support, and it is not the intention of the Government to decrease the monthly allowance which at present is paid to you, until such time when the Government is satisfied that you are in receipt of sufficient income from other sources.

I must however inform you that the Government cannot agree to transfer to you the temporal power and your position will be the same as that of other spiritual heads of other people in Iraq, and that all the Assyrians should conform to all the administration rules and regulations which are enforced on all other Iraqis.

It is needless to assure you of the Government's sincere desire to fulfil whatever is possible to see the Assyrian people satisfied and happy, and that your people may become one of the most faithful subject peoples to His Majesty the Great King; the Government by its declaration before the League of Nations has fully declared itself to this effect, and this policy has been accepted and approved. I am to state that the Government, according to the agreement of last autumn, has been making efforts to secure the services of a foreign expert, to advise in the important question of settlement, and this foreign expert who is Major Thomson will very likely arrive at Mosul at the end of this month, the most important and greatest part of his work will be for the Assyrian peoples. I very strongly hope that he will get full assistance from all those who wish good of this people.

I very much regret to say that according to certain reports which have reached us, your honourableness have up to the present adopted a non-assisting and obstructive attitude towards this important question. I therefore deem it very essential to ask you to give a written guarantee that you will never take an action, which may be an obstacle to the work of Major Thomson, and cause difficulty to the Government.

If there are any points which are not mentioned in this letter, I shall be glad if you draw my attention to them. The Government's official recognition of your above-mentioned position is subject to your desire to accept it, and your giving a definite promise that you will always and in every way be as one of the most faithful subjects of His Majesty the Great King. I shall be very glad to receive your written reply to this letter as per attached text.

(*Signed*) Hikmat SLIMAN,
Minister of Interior.

The text referred to is as follows:

"I Mar Shimun have studied the letter from Your Excellency No.U.1104 dated May 28th, 1933, and have accepted all it contains.

"I do hereby promise that I will never do anything which may be an obstacle to the duties of Major Thomson and the Government of Iraq, namely in whatever it concerns the settlement scheme: that

I will always and in every way remain as one of the most faithful subjects of His Majesty the Great King."

————————

No. AP/S/35.

Baghdad,
as from Assyrian Patriarchate,
Mosul, dated June 3rd, 1933.

Dear Minister,

I beg to acknowledge the receipt of Your Excellency's letter No.U.1104, dated May 28th, 1933, and I am with due respects replying to its essential points as follows:

1.   With regard to my interview with Your Excellency on April 12th, 1933, at Mosul, may I request Your Excellency's recollection to the conversation which then took place. Your Excellency said that a new co-operative policy with regard to the Assyrian Settlement Scheme would be introduced by you, and that the orders would be issued to the Mutassarif to that effect, and that he would also be asked to consult me on all matters affecting the Assyrians.

2.   The Community Law mentioned in Your Excellency's letter however a useful factor it may be, at this stage of affairs would appear to be an immatured measure, owing to the fact that such a law is necessarily applicable to a settled community. Moreover, in order to formulate this law, time would be required to consult with the Canons of the Church.

3.   With regard to the term "temporal power" alluded to by Your Excellency when you say "the Government cannot agree to transfer to you any 'temporal power'. I would be glad to know how this term is interpreted by you.

Although I do not desire to dwell on this point in length I think it is necessary for me to try and elucidate the term "spiritual and temporal" power united together in this special case of the Patriarch Catholicos of the East, since it seems to me that Your Excellency and the Government have taken a grave view of it. This Patriarchal authority is a great historical and traditional usage of the Assyrian people and Church, and it has been one of the established and most important customs. The temporal power has not been assumed by me but it has descended to me from centuries past as a legalised delegation of the people to the Patriarch. It was not only tolerated but also officially recognised in past by the old Sassanite Kings, Islamic Caliphs, Moghul Khans and Ottoman Sultans. No proof of any misuse of this power as far as any King or Government whose subjects the Assyrian people have been, can be traced in history, whilst on the other hand besides being in no way preventive to the application of the law of the country, it has proved to be the best method of dealing with a people living under the circumstances as the Assyrians are.

Under the above circumstances I very much regret to say that it is impossible for me to comply with your order —— viz., to sign the written promise outlined by Your Excellency —— since such an action would only mean that I am willingly withdrawing myself from the duty to my people; the duty which as mentioned above is a legal delegation of the people to me and it is only to them to take it away. In this connection, I would further like to point out that I am very much surprised by the step Your Excellency has proposed to take, more so under the present circumstances, since such an action is only applicable in case of a rebel. This being so, may I ask Your Excellency whether my honour and the honour of my people has not been insulted.

I fail to trace any precedent to this action of Your Excellency unless I am to blame because I most candidly have represented the case of my Assyrian people in a legal manner before the late mandatory Power, the League of Nations and His Majesty's Government with a view of securing a solution to it which I believe it is in the interests of all concerned.

4.   With regard to the allegation that I have hitherto adopted an unfavourable and rather obstructive attitude towards the Assyrian Settlement Scheme. This point was also verbally raised by Your Excellency during my interview with you on May 31st when I more than once asked for facts of this allegation. This is more discouraging to me when I think of my incessant endeavours in persuading my Assyrian people to settle and become a useful element in this country as also they have been hitherto.

I close this my letter with offering my respects to Your Excellency and with apology for having to write it in a foreign language as at present I have not a suitable writer in Arabic at my disposal.

If there are any points which Your Excellency wishes to learn from me I shall be only too glad to answer them, as I propose to leave Baghdad on Monday evening, June 4th.

I remain,
Yours most respectfully,
Mar SHIMUN.

To His Excellency Hikmat Sliman Beg,
    The Minister of Interior, Baghdad.

Copy to His Majesty the Great King Faisal the First.

Ministry of the Interior,
    Iraq Baghdad.   June 6th, 1933.
[*Urgent.*]   D. O. No. C/288.

Beatitude,

I send you a copy of a note which I have written to His Excellency the Minister of Interior on our conversation of this morning.

I shall be grateful if you will confirm that it correctly represents what passed between us.

Yours sincerely,
(Signed) K. CORNWALLIS.

His Beatitude Eshai Shimun,
　　Assyrian Patriarch,
　　　Baghdad.

His Excellency the Minister of Interior.

I saw His Beatitude Mar Shimun this morning and discussed with him his letter of June 3rd to Your Excellency. I pointed out to him that certain passages in his letter were liable to misconstruction and said that I wished to clear up the misunderstanding which would inevitably arise.

The result of our discussion was as follows:

1.　It became clear to me that His Beatitude feels that he has been misrepresented by ill wishers and that the assurances which he was asked to give implied a slur on his loyalty and honour which is not justified. This feeling undoubtedly influenced him when replying to Your Excellency.

2.　His Beatitude expressed his gratitude and thanks to Your Excellency for your kindness in saying that the Government has under consideration the creation of a source of income to assist him in a permanent manner. He places the needs of his community above his own and considered that if the intention is to allocate lands to himself personally or in the name of the community, such allocation should be made during the course of the Settlement and with due regard to the needs of individuals.

3.　As regards his personal position, His Beatitude fully recognises that in all matters of administration the members of the

Assyrian community must conform to the laws, regulations and manner of procedure which applies to all other Iraqis. He has always advised the Assyrians in this sense and will continue doing so. His aim is always to make the Assyrians loyal and law-abiding citizens. He considers, however, that the local officials have not been carrying out a wise policy and he fears that the Assyrians may get out of control. He cited a number of cases in which he thought injustice had been shown.

The Assyrians have always been in the habit of coming to their Patriarch with their troubles and he feels that it is his duty to represent their grievances to Government. He stated that he had nothing to add to this.

4.   His Beatitude denied the reports that he has worked against land settlement. On the contrary he considers it vital for the Assyrians, is most anxious to see it brought about and will not do anything to make the task of Major Thomson and the Government more difficult. He does not, however, consider that the committee which has been appointed is truly representative of the community and fears that the settlement on its present lines will be a failure.

He considers:

(a) That the first action to take is to ascertain the number to be settled immediately and in the future;

(b) That land registration should be carried out as soon as possible;

(c) That those who are now in privately-owned lands and for whom Government lands can be found, should be given a title in due course after they have moved; they should not take precedence over Assyrians who have no lands and who apply for settlement on government lands;

(d) That the question of financial assistance to settlers should be considered.

I said that this could not be considered now and that I could not say whether Major Thomson would make any recommendations in this regard.

5.   His Beatitude feels aggrieved that his loyalty to His Majesty the King should have been called in question as he has frequently in the past both in action and in writing given expression of it.

(Signed) K. CORNWALLIS,
Adviser.

Baghdad, June 6th, 1933.

Baghdad,
as from the Assyrian Patriarchate,
Mosul, dated June 8th, 1933.

Dear Sir Kinahan,

I thank you for your letter of the 6th sending me a copy of the notes of my interview with you on that morning, which you have sent to His Excellency the Minister of Interior, and I thank you for the interest and labour for the affairs of my people.

On the whole the notes do correctly represent what passed between us. There are, however, some things I would like to state differently and again other things recorded.

For instance, *Paragraph 1,* the last thought. May I state no feelings influenced my reply to His Excellency. The fact is that I could not reply to the letter of the Government otherwise before consulting my people.

In *Paragraph 2* and elsewhere in these notes I would like that the word "community" be understood to mean the Assyrian people.

Paragraph 3. The importance of this paragraph would be better understood if it is realised that the Assyrians, unlike other communities, are refugees and homeless, and the idea behind the League of Nations by a homogeneous settlement is to replace their homelands and make them contented loyal subjects. This is not being done, on the contrary, after twelve years, there is not one instance where an Assyrian has received title deed substitute of his lost home. The Assyrian refugees, however, voted for the Mosul vilayet to be included in Iraq for this purpose.

With regard to the last part of paragraph 3, I would like to add that the traditional customs of the people should not be interfered with as at present. The same privileges are maintained by other tribal people in Iraq.

In conclusion, I would appeal to you to see my position as it now is, and advise me as to how I can possibly fulfil my duty to my people as well as comply with the requests from all sides.

1. Major Thomson as the Expert Adviser requests my assistance to bring about a Settlement Scheme.

2. You as the Adviser to the Ministry of Interior asked me for my views to present them to the Minister of Interior, and send you copies of my proposals to Major Thomson.

3. His Excellency the Minister who represents the Government has ordered me to retire from all temporal affairs of my people.

Therefore, under these circumstances, it becomes impossible for me to comply with any of these requests.

I have under preparation proposals for a Scheme of Settlement which will be in the interests of all concerned.

The presentation of these proposals depends on the change of the present policy.

(Signed) Mar Shimun.

Draft Letter to His Beatitude Mar Shimun
from His Excellency the Minister of Interior.

I have received your letter of the 3rd inst. and as I have informed you verbally, I consider it so ambiguous that I cannot take it as a reply to my letter of May 28th.

2.　I have, however, read your letter of May 31st, 1933, to His Majesty the King. I have also read a note by the adviser dated 7th inst., recording the result of a conversation with and your reply of June 8th to him. I have also had a discussion with you on June 8th.

3.　I take note from the above:

(a) You fully recognise that in matters of administration, Assyrians must conform to laws, regulations and manner of procedure which applies to all other Iraqis. You have always advised them in this sense, and will continue doing so; your aim is always to make the Assyrians loyal and law-abiding citizens.

(b) You consider that land settlement is vital for the Assyrians. You are most anxious to see it brought about and you assure me that you will not do anything to make the task of Major Thomson and the Government more difficult.

4.　But as regards your personal position I confirm to you what I explained in my letter No. U/1104 dated May 28th, 1933 —— namely, that it will resemble that of the spiritual heads of the other communities in Iraq, and the Government cannot delegate to you any temporal power. But as you are aware, it is the right of every Iraqi to petition the Government on any subject, and spiritual heads of communities have always been accustomed to bring to its notice the needs and grievances of their people. Therefore, if you have any complaints at any time I am ready to cause enquiries to be made.

I notice that you have complained of the policy which you say is being adopted in Mosul. The policy of the Government is perfectly clear. It is to treat the Assyrians with fairness and justice like all other Iraqis; to make them loyal and contented subjects of His Majesty the King and to effect their permanent settlement in a manner that will lead to this end. Unfortunately up to the present certain sections of the Assyrians have held aloof from Government and they have only themselves to blame if they are looked upon with suspicion. I wish however to put an end to this state of things and I sincerely hope that all Assyrians will show their loyalty by co-operating fully with Major Thomson and by giving him all the assistance for which he asks. If this is done, I have no doubt that there will be a rapid and I hope permanent improvement in the situation.

I shall be obliged if you will acknowledge this letter.

Dear Sir K. Cornwallis,

I return, herewith, the draft copies you handed to me of the proposed letter from His Excellency the Minister of Interior and my acknowledgment thereof.

I also enclose a copy of the suggested letter as modified by me after full consideration in the interests of all concerned.

I thank you very much for the trouble you are taking in this matter.

Sincerely yours,
Patriarch of the Assyrians.

Baghdad, June 13th, 1933.

DRAFT LETTER TO HIS BEATITUDE THE MAR
SHIMUN FROM HIS EXCELLENCY
THE MINISTER OF INTERIOR.

I have received your letter of the 3rd inst., and as I have informed you verbally, I consider it so ambiguous that I cannot take it as a reply to my letter of May 28th.

2.   I have, however, read your letter of May 31st, 1933, to His Majesty the King. I have also read a note by the Adviser, dated the 7th instant, recording the result of a conversation with (you) and your reply of June 8th. I have also had a discussion with you on June 8th.

3.   I take note from the above:

(a) You fully recognise that in matters of administration, Assyrians must conform to laws, regulations and manner of procedure which applies to all other Iraqis. You have always advised them in this sense and will continue doing so; your aim is always to make the Assyrians loyal and law–abiding citizens. On the other hand the Government fully realise that the Assyrians unlike other communities are refugees and homeless and the idea behind the League of Nations by a homogeneous settlement is to substitute their homelands and make them contented subjects.

(b) You consider that land settlement is vital for the Assyrians. You are anxious to see it brought about and you assure me that you will do everything possible to make the task of Major Thomson and the Government's easier.

4.   But as regards your personal position I confirm to you that it will resemble that of spiritual heads of other communities in Iraq, and that the traditional and established customs of your Assyrian people will be privileged to remain. You will have the right to petition to His Majesty the King, or His Government regarding the needs and grievances of your people.

I notice that you have complained of the policy which you say is being adopted in Mosul. I will issue instructions to the Mutassarif of Mosul Liwa to conform to the Government's policy and the contents of this letter and I hope you will make known to Major Thomson your proposals for settling the Assyrians.

The policy of the Government is perfectly clear. It is to treat the Assyrians with fairness and justice like all other Iraqis, to make them loyal and contented subjects of His Majesty the King, and to effect the permanent settlement in a manner that will lead to this end.

I, therefore, sincerely hope that you will advise all the Assyrians to show their loyalty by co-operating fully with Major Thomson, and by giving him all the assistance for which he asks. If this is done I have no doubt that there will be a rapid, and, I hope, permanent improvement in the situation.

I shall be obliged if you will acknowledge this letter.

——————————

Baghdad,
as from Assyrian Patriarchate,
Mosul, May 31st, 1933.

Your Majesty,

I humbly request leave to give Your Majesty my opinion in the following lines about the present policy of the Mosul authorities as I see it to settle the Assyrian question.

Knowing that a word from Your Majesty at this hour, to Your Majesty's Advisers could change this policy and thus bring the affairs of the Assyrians to a successful issue.

I was ordered by the Mutassarif of Mosul with great urgency to proceed to Baghdad immediately in response of an invitation from the Minister of Interior to discuss with him and Major D. B. Thomson the Foreign Expert for the new Assyrian Settlement Scheme the Assyrian affairs.

On the sixth day after my arrival in Baghdad, and after many attempts, I was granted an interview with His Excellency the Minister of Interior.

In the meantime I have word from Mosul that the authorities there are still continuing with their old policy with regard to the Assyrian question. If this is the case, it is inconsistent with the purpose of my invitation to Baghdad as explained to me.

I very much regret to have to bring it to Your Majesty's notice that during my interview with His Excellency the Interior Minister, I was informed of the unfavourable attitude of the present Government towards me personally.

If I did not participate with the present policy adopted by Mosul authorities the reason has been that policy was entirely unconstructive.

I do feel most confident that the present policy which has now for some time been carried on by the Mosul liwa authorities only as I presume and which has already proved a failure, is not consistent with the noble spirit of Your Majesty, which has more than once been most graciously expressed to me by Your Majesty personally.

I take the advantage of Your noble spirit and fatherly kindness to assure myself that Your Majesty's desire is to make the Assyrian people a contented, loyal and helpful subject people within Your Majesty's Dominion, and to attain this end I am ready as I always have been to offer my utmost services to Your Majesty.

Hoping at this late hour that some constructive scheme can be arranged, which will enable my people and myself to prove to Your Majesty's Person our loyalty and gratitude, I remain, etc.

The Residency,
Baghdad, June 18th, 1932.

Beatitude,

I have received your letter of June 17th, together with two copies of the petition of the Assyrian leaders of the same date, one of which is addressed to me and the other to the Chairman of the Permanent Mandates Commission.

This petition puts forward a number of demands of far-reaching effect and great importance and raises issues which cannot be settled without a reference to the League of Nations. It therefore is quite impossible for me to give an undertaking by June 28th, that the demands made in the petition will be approved. The petition must be forwarded to the League for consideration, and as it is demanded that the claims put forward in it must be adopted by the Council of the League, no undertaking can be given concerning them without the League's authority. I am forwarding the Assyrian leaders' petition at once to my Government for onward despatch to the League, and Your Beatitude may be assured that it will receive the earliest possible consideration.

In the meantime, your people have everything to lose from precipitate action and since, as I have shown, it is quite impracticable to make a reply to the petition by June 28th, I urge you to advise Assyrian levies to postpone the execution of their resolution to cease serving, until such time as a reply is received from the League.

If Your Beatitude does not so advise them, and if they persist in leaving the levies and joining in the national movement, to which reference is made in the last paragraph of the petition, before an answer is given to you, I must warn Your Beatitude that the Assyrians will be regarded as having offered a grave discourtesy to the League, who will have been given no possible opportunity to reply before your ultimatum expires. Moreover, in such circumstances the Assyrians could not reasonably expect to obtain any future employment in the Government services.

I must ask you to send me an immediate answer by the hand of Captain Holt.

(Signed) F. H. HUMPHRYS.

His Beatitude
The Most Reverend Eshai Mar Shimun,
Assyrian Patriarch.

No. S.O. 851.   The Residency,

Baghdad, June 22nd, 1932.

Beatitude,

I have received your letter of June 20th by the hand of Captain Holt. There occurs in this letter the following passage which I do not understand:

> "At this morning's meeting it was unanimously agreed by the leaders that a final reply could not be given to Your Excellency's letter with regard to the question of postponement of the resolution of the Assyrian levies."

Captain Holt tells me that he pointed out to Your Beatitude that, if this was not in fact the final reply, he would stay in Ser Amadiyah until he obtained it. He tells me, however, that he was informed by Your Beatitude that this was the last word of the leaders and that they refused to postpone the resignation of the Assyrian levies unless I accepted all their demands, except that relating to Hakkiari, by June 28th. I have already explained that it is not within my power to accept demands of this nature, which will have to be carefully considered by my Government in London and by the League of Nations at Geneva; nor is a representative of the Iraqi Government empowered to accept them without the approval of the Iraqi Parliament, since the demands involve alterations to the fundamental laws of Iraq in regard to minorities which can only be agreed to with the consent of the League of Nations.

I have informed Your Beatitude that I am unable to understand what the Assyrians have to gain by giving up their present service which is worth nearly a lakh of rupees a month to them, and by disqualifying themselves for further service in the future. On the other hand, they have a very great deal to lose by such short-sighted behaviour, which cannot fail to appear to the British Government and people as singularly ungrateful and inopportune.

I would finally point out that the fact that an earlier petition which was submitted by the Assyrian leaders to the Permanent Mandates Commission last November to the effect that it would be no longer possible for the Assyrians to remain in Iraq after the termination of the British mandate is still under the consideration of the League, makes it still more incomprehensible that the Assyrian leaders should expect a reply to an entirely new set of demands of the most complicated and far-reaching nature before the petition can even have been seen by the League. In giving such an ultimatum, Your Beatitude cannot fail to realise that the Assyrian leaders are putting themselves in the wrong with the British Government and the League of Nations.

There is nothing more for me to say in this matter, except to express my deep regret at the unnecessary sufferings which the Assyrians seem determined to bring on themselves. I am making arrangements to take over the duties vacated by those Assyrians who desire to leave and to entrust them to British troops until other Iraqis have been recruited to replace them.

But the door is still open.

(Signed) F. H. HUMPHRYS.

His Beatitude
The Most Reverend Eshai Mar Shimun,
Assyrian Patriarch.

High Commissioner's Office,
Baghdad, June 28ᵗʰ, 1932.

Beatitude,

In spite of everything that has occurred I am still prepared to offer following conditions for levy service.

On condition that you and the other leaders will give a solemn undertaking not again to interfere with the discipline of the Assyrian levies, and on condition that all ranks give undertakings to serve loyally and truly, levies will be maintained at present strength, until an answer is given by the League to the Assyrian petition of June 17th, or until December 15th, whichever is the earlier date. If, however, levies have definitely decided that they do not wish to serve at Basra, one company must be reduced to allow for the formation of a company of other Iraqis to take over from the Assyrians at Basra.

On receipt of the answer from the League, arrangements will be made to retain such men as it may be desired, to recruit for the forces to be formed under the Anglo-Iraqi Treaty of 1930.

It is impossible for me to give you a reply in precise terms as to what demands in the Assyrian petition will, and what will not be considered as reasonable, and in conformity with the general policy of my Government and the League. I cannot at this stage commit myself further than to inform you that such questions as recognition of Patriarch, land settlement, representation in Parliament, schools, dispensaries, retention of rifles, and conditions of service in the Iraqi forces, are recognised by me as reasonable subjects for consideration and that the earliest and most sympathetic attention to these matters will be pressed by me on the Iraqi Government, and, through my Government, on the League of Nations.

You may be assured of the sincere goodwill of the British Government and myself and of our desire to do all that is possible for the welfare of the Assyrian people. I cannot believe that you will deliberately reject my advice to give up hasty action and to await the decision of the League, so that these important issues may be discussed in a calm atmosphere.

(Signed) F. H. HUMPHRYS.

His Beatitude
The Most Reverend Eshai Mar Shimun,
Assyrian Patriarch.

The Residency,
Baghdad, June 28th, 1932.

Personal.

Beatitude,

I was very glad to receive your message this evening and as requested I am sending you a signed copy of my telegram of June 27th.

You know that I shall do everything in my power to help you and your people at Geneva. I will even do my best to find a solution in regard to Hakkiari though you will realise that this is an international question of great delicacy.

All I ask from Your Beatitude and the Assyrian leaders is that they should assist me by maintaining the levies in loyal service and the people in a calm spirit until the decision of the League of Nations has been received.

I know that I can rely on your help in this.

With my kindest regards to Lady Surma and Your Beatitude. I was so sorry that I missed seeing her in Baghdad owing to my illness.

(Signed) Francis HUMPHRYS.
High Commissioner's Office,
Baghdad, July 3rd, 1932.

Beatitude,

Thank you for your message of July 2nd. I note that you are prepared to send another letter to the levies at Hinaidi, Mosul, Diana and Sulaimania, in accordance with my draft copy of which is enclosed, after you have explained it fully to the leaders on July 5th.

It is true that my Government and myself are doing our best to obtain the reply of the League of Nations to your national petition before the termination of the mandate, which is expected to take place in September, but I know that you will understand that it is impossible for me to guarantee that the League will communicate their reply by this date. It is for this reason that I have asked that instructions should be sent to the levies to serve loyally until the receipt of the League's reply, rather than until the end of September. I have from the first impressed on Tour Beatitude the importance of delaying the decision of the levies to resign until they have had an opportunity to study the reply of the League to the national petition. I feel sure that Your Beatitude will agree with me that this is a reasonable act of courtesy, both to the British Government and the League of Nations, and it is in reality in the best interests of the levies themselves.

I promise you that I will continue to do everything I can to obtain the League's reply as early as possible. The validity of the League's decision will not be affected by the date on which it is received.

(Signed) F. H. HUMPHRYS.

His Beatitude,
The Most Reverend Eshai Mar Shimun,
Assyrian Patriarch.

STATEMENT MADE BY SAYED CHABALI HAJI
THABIT IN THE IRAQI PARLIAMENT
ON JUNE 28TH, 1933.
(VIDE *Al Istoclal,* No. 1929, of June 29th, 1933.)

Gentlemen,

I have to throw light on the public opinion, specially on that of our Press, regarding this misleading name Assyrians, which is in common use. As you are aware, this term is only recently coming into being. There is nobody who reasonably deserved this name; if there is any, we are the first to grasp it, as we are the original inhabitants of this country and take this from the physical and not political point of view. The same question arises in Egypt; it is called Pharaohs', but really Mosul is Arab even before the Islam. I regret to note that our Press still stick to this mysterious name. The group which calls itself Assyrians should be named Tyaris; they intermingle with the Assyrians and Chaldeans, this is confirmed by their being bilingual. If, for example, there is any of them who can decipher the tablets maintained in our Museum, he can make us believe that they are descendants of the Great Assyria. Proverb, "(if) he passed the examination set, he deserves honour; if he fails, he is liable to disgrace".

The Tyaris can be divided into the following sub-sections: (1) Tyari Bila, (2) Tyari Zair, (3) Tyari Jilu, (4) Tyari Bazi, (5) Tyari Dizi; they all go under the name Tyari.

These in the pre-war days inhabited in Hikkari, Juliamerk, Bash Gala, and Van in Turkish territories with their religious headquarters in Qudshanus, (2) Persia, their headquarters in Urmia, (3) Russia and (4) part of them lived in Barwari villages in the outskirts of a mountain which is named after them –– viz., Tyari Mountain in the vicinity of Amadia, and their headquarters being in Ashita where their religious leader resides, who puts his untimely claims before the Government. These villages are within the Turkish border, but some of them happily are situated in the Iraqi side; they are genuine Iraqis; they are entitled to share the benefits of our country; ours is theirs, and theirs ours.

The above-mentioned Tyaris are therefore aliens, and not former inhabitants of this country. They are nearly 20,000 who fled from Persia, Russia and Turkey, with the strong desire of the Colonial Office. When they poured into Mosul and began living by illegal means, the inhabitants there were somewhat indisposed, and cried to get rid of them; but, unfortunately, their pleadings were not listened to until some unhappy event took place in Mosul. The Mosulawis cried loudly and insisted on their being removed to their former homes or at least scattered in the villages, to avoid further accidents.

It was prophesied at that time that their settling together would jeopardise the general security and disturb peaceful citizens. The Government migrated them to Kirkuk; as though Kirkuk was not Iraq. They caused there the most bloody accident Kirkuk has ever seen, and made hundreds of our martyrs to lose their dear lives. This happened during the celebrations of "Id-al-Fatir".

I cannot help weeping when I remember that doomed event; still, some mysterious hand plays havoc and moves them to and fro. Recently one of their priests (Rev. Bedari), who resides in Mosul, published the most notorious article against the poor government. The police authorities on the spot confiscated his cursed pamphlets, but the said priest was able to dispose some fifty copies and distribute them among the prominent people. May I ask His Excellency as to the steps taken against such behaviour?

This wretched and corrupt people was housed and fed in Iraq and were expected to be loyal and dutiful subjects, but, on the contrary, after being surfeited and ungrateful to the hospitality shown by their hosts claim humorous rights. Experience, however, shows that these are armed to the teeth and are in a position to inflict the severest blow on the Government! We are not so coward but we wait to see what steps will be taken against those interlopers, what is the Government's attitude towards them in this respect, and why she keeps quiet and postpones their punishment and to make it known from what source they obtained their arms. We therefore request and recommend their being stripped of their arms forthwith, or, at least, arm their neighbours for defensive measures.

We cannot clearly understand the programme of their settling together in Zibar area. The Government further sanctioned 13,000 dinars for their settlement, and the settlement officer intends to settle some of them in Barzan area; as though we dislodged the Barzanis to make room for those, and to breed the poisonous germ in the head of the Government.

These will, at any rate, be an obstacle in the way of the Government; we therefore should scatter them in all the liwas to be able to rule them peacefully. We understand that they imagine special status, but they cannot be attained to, and we cannot at our will create a difficult situation similar to that already created in Palestine (Zionists).

Further, what is the British Consulate at Dianna? And what are the intelligence officers scattered in the country? And what is this mythical hand which turns this unseen machine? We were under the impression that this game would come to an end with the Mandate, but they wish to restart it in an independent State. We can wait no longer, everything is ripe, we request the Government to take punitive measures against them.

Gentlemen, the most important problem to solve is, to remedy this bleeding wound; to do this, we shall cry and cry loudly.

The soil of this country is formed of the bones and blood of our ancestors. How can we close our eyes and be indifferent in defending our sacred fatherland? *(Applause.)* Our ally wants many things in this country of their adoption, we must guard it against any intruders.

————

STATEMENT MADE BY MAJOR THOMSON IN THE
MEETING HELD IN THE MUTASSARIF'S
RESIDENCY, MOSUL, ON JULY 14TH, 1933.
(Vide *Al Ummal*, No. 144.)

Subject: Assyrian Settlement.

I have the pleasure to meet all the Assyrian chieftains. I had the opportunity of meeting some of them previously. I want to express myself fully. Should I fail to explain my settlement programme, I have certainly not discharged my duties satisfactorily. I wish all of you will be mindful and pay attention to the proceedings of this meeting.

Most of you, of course, understand what my duty is; the Government wants me to offer my services to help her, and that is in accordance with the pledge given by the Iraqi Government to the League of Nations. No doubt, you have heard of the final decision of the League through the Mutassarif. I want to remind you that prior to my departure from this country, whether settlement successful or otherwise, I shall write a diffused statement on this matter, and forward it through the Government to the League of Nations.

In my conversation with Mar Shimun at the beginning of June last, I discussed with him questions pertaining to settlement. In the course of my debate with him, he altogether refused discussing such matters, and also did not furnish me with names of some Assyrian notables whom I wanted to meet in Mosul or elsewhere. He refused to co-operate with me, with the sole excuse that he does not agree on the policy adopted by the Government in this respect, and forgot that I have been invited to help the Government in the settlement. I also pointed out to him that the Government quite agrees on my proposals. The next thing made him to refrain from co-operating with me was that the Government asked him not to interfere with the political affairs –– and that he will enjoy no temporal rule and the Assyrians will be dealt with directly by the Government, as he is the only spiritual head in this country who enjoys such rules. I presume he does not understand the meaning of temporal rule. I should like to explain this clearly as far as possible.

The Government requested him not to interfere with these affairs and to leave the idea of obtaining an official post with the Iraqi Government, and to avoid further interference with the Assyrians. I do not believe that Mar Shimun still sticks to his uninvited claims. I explained to him that there is nobody who enjoys both temporal and spiritual rules. He afterwards sent me a letter promising to furnish me with details of his programme and his objections to the present settlement policy. It is over a month and still no such papers have been received, and no facilities made by him in the settlement. He still holds different ideas and does not agree with the Government in the capital regarding his personal claims.

I feel it my duty to tell you that if he fully understands the final decisions of the League, and if he really works for the benefit of his people, I should say that it would have been better for him to count the personal claims as a second matter, and to follow his followers.

The most important matter is that you were not confident and were suspicious of settling. In this case a great majority of you live simply on your capital, and no doubt that capital will some day or later exhaust. Had you settled for good some four or five years ago, you would have been certainly much happier and comfortable. In case you deem it advisable that Mar Shimun's presence is a necessity in the settlement, I should request you to advise him to agree on the Government's policy and to co-operate with us without further delay.

You must remember that my presence here is solely for your settlement and to give my directions for your own benefit and must tell you that this is the only chance of seeing me here under your disposal. You should understand that there is no Government in the world who can give such privileges as those given by the Iraqi Government. You have to enjoy them forthwith.

As regards settlement, I will strive as far as possible to settle families of any tribe in one village. Some time ago, the Government wished to be furnished with lists of families who wish to settle, in order that arrangements can be made for their settlement in the villages; up to date but a few registrations have been made.

Naturally, those who have consented to settle, will be given the option to choose lands for settlements and those who delay will lose. I shall not hesitate to urge families who wish to settle in and cultivate lands to register their individuals as soon as possible. Those who are already settled in villages, but owing to material and other causes wish to evacuate them, will be dealt with later on. Certainly those who are in employment in Baghdad or elsewhere, and those who require to own lands for cultivations on large scale (*i.e.*, those who require to own lands and lease them to tenants) will also be dealt with after we have settled those who will cultivate the lands themselves.

These are the available lands for settlement — viz., Dashta-Zai, Jentazi, Kizfaghar and some more lands in the vicinity of Mosul and other villages. I must tell you that the Government sanctioned 13,000 dinars for your settlement, and that amount will be utilised for irrigation and housing purposes, I should be really delighted to see the Assyrians settle for good in these lands. I have personally made a tour on these lands, and can assure you that they are habitable, as regards land-owning rights, etc. (Government or private owned), some specimen contracts have been concluded previously, between the Government and tenants or landlords and tenants.

I will continue to help the Assyrians, and will point out to them some difficult situations arising. In conclusion, I can assure you that the Iraqi Government is prepared to help you in any way. Colonel Stafford and myself are here, and we both wish you to be happy.

I ask you to grasp what we have said, and to understand that our sole intention is to direct the Assyrians and to help them as far as possible.

———

Baghdad West,

June 7th, 1933.

Your Beatitude,

I am writing to let you know that I am leaving Baghdad this evening on my return to Mosul.

My present intention is to leave Mosul for Amadia on Saturday next, and to visit the Assyrian villages, the Deshty-zer, and other possible areas for Assyrian settlement.

When we had our talk on Monday you will remember you promised to write me a letter setting out your appreciation of the present policy for Assyrian settlement, with your remarks thereon.

You also promised to send me a list of Assyrian notables whom you would like me to see and with whom I might talk over the general situation, and who would also be willing to act on the Assyrian Advisory Committee in Mosul.

Should any of these gentlemen like to accompany me on my present tour and those in the coming months I should welcome them gladly.

I am looking forward to having the pleasure of meeting you in Mosul in the near future and of further discussing the question of Assyrian settlement.

(Signed) D. B. THOMSON.

His Beatitude Eshai Shimun,
    Assyrian Patriarch,
        Baghdad.

———————

Baghdad,
as from Assyrian Patriarchate,
at Mosul, June 7th, 1933.

Dear Major Thomson,

I hasten to reply to your urgent letter of June 7th informing me of your immediate departure for Mosul and district.

May I inform you that the statements you have recorded in this letter as from me are contrary to what I said.

I certainly did not inform you that I appreciated the Mosul policy towards the Assyrian settlement of the last months, which could be implied in your letter. I fully explained the importance of the need to change this policy.

I said if you wished I would gather together the people's appointed representatives to meet you at Mosul, or you should visit and interview the people themselves to enable you to view the situation rightly. I did not promise to write you a list of names.

I said that if you wished I would be glad to give you in writing my opinion on the present situation and this is now in the course of preparation.

I also informed you that I was awaiting an answer to my letter to His Excellency the Minister of Interior, regarding the Government's interpretation of the Patriarch's "temporal power" and its attitude towards me. My co-operation in the future naturally has to depend on that reply.

It would help me greatly if you could enlighten me as to exactly what your position is.

Sincerely yours,
(Signed) Mar Shimun,
Assyrian Patriarch.

Major D. B. Thomson,
The Expert for Assyrian Settlement,
Baghdad.

No. A/P/S/5.

Baghdad, June 21ˢᵗ, 1933.
As from the Assyrian Patriarchate,
Mosul.

Excellency,

As arranged with you this morning I am returning to Mosul to-morrow Wednesday, June 22ⁿᵈ. But I do not wish to leave Baghdad without expressing once more to Your Excellency my appreciation of your courtesy in receiving me, and of the patient hearing which you have given me.

While unfortunately there are several points in which we have not yet reached an understanding, nevertheless I wish to assure Your Excellency that the dominant desire of my heart is to see the Assyrian people content and happily settled in Iraq as loyal subjects to His Majesty the King and His Government.

Yours most respectfully.

––––––––––

No. AP/S/40.

Baghdad,
as from Assyrian Patriarchate,
Mosul, dated June 28ᵗʰ, 1933.

Excellency,

I have the honour to acknowledge your letter No.C/1239 dated June 18ᵗʰ, 1933, and in reply, I understand from my conversation with Major Edmonds, that the reference to history in my letter No. AP/S/35 of June 3ʳᵈ, 1933, has created an impression different from that which I wished to convey. I was not, of course, claiming temporal power in the sense of "temporal power" delegated to me by the Governments named, but to the traditional customs of the Assyrians which I desire to see maintained if your Excellency agrees to this would you kindly instruct the authorities concerned.

As regards the work of Major Thomson, I am of course, anxious to see it crowned with success and will do my best to co-operate if the work of settlement is carried out in a manner which to my opinion promises satisfactory results.

My ideas on the subject are set forth in my letters addressed to Sir K. Cornwallis.

With renewed assurances of my loyalty to His Majesty the King and my respects to Your Excellency.

(Signed) Eshai SHIMUN,
By the Grace of God,
Catholicos Patriarch of the Assyrians.

As from the Assyrian Patriarchate, Mosul.
Baghdad, June 29th, 1933.

To His Excellency
The Minister of the Interior,
    Baghdad.

Your Excellency,

I beg to state that the action of the Government now confirmed by your letter No. S.1273 of June 24th, 1933, detaining me in Baghdad against my will for no just cause is illegal, and that any responsibility of what may happen when the news reaches my people rests with the Government.

I also wish to point out that the methods adopted by the local officials in dealing with the Assyrians on the Settlement Policy, is contrary to the "Fundamental Law" or the guarantees given by the Iraqi Government to the League of Nations on May 30th, 1932. Therefore I am arranging to place the documentary evidence before the proper authorities.

I am quite prepared to suffer any further injustice that the Government may put on me, but in no way will I submit to the methods which have been used to make me sign documents which betray my people into accepting an unreal fulfilment of the promises and recommendations of the League of Nations.

Finally I again repeat, as per my previous correspondence with Your Excellency, and also through your British Advisers:

(a) I am willing to assist in the Settlement of the Assyrians in Iraq;

(b) After settlement I will give the required promises in writing to do my utmost to make my Assyrian people as one of the most loyal and law-abiding subjects of His Majesty and His Government;

(c) I will then make preparations in accordance with the Canons of my Church, for drafting of a law according to Your Excellency's suggestion and conformable to Article VI of the Fundamental Law.

If this is not agreeable to the Government, I claim the right to ask the League of Nations for the Alternative Settlement Scheme.

(Signed) Eshai SHIMUN,
By the Grace of God,
Catholicos Patriarch of the Assyrians.

Copies sent to the Diplomatic Representatives of:

Britain	Turkey	Belgium
America	Holland	Norway
Italy	France	Czechoslovakia
Poland	Germany	Persia.

P.S. — May I draw Your Excellency's attention to the inflammatory speech of an honorary deputy, recorded and broadcasted in *Al-Istoclal* of June 29th, and other local papers inciting hatred towards the Assyrians.

STATEMENT MADE BY KAHLIL AZMI BEG,
MUTASSARIF, MOSUL LIWA,
IN THE MEETING WHICH WAS ATTENDED BY
NEARLY HUNDRED ASSYRIAN CHIEFTAINS.
(This was held in the Mutassarif's Residency,
Mosul, July 10th, 1933.)

The cause of our meeting is the true desire of the Government to cut off the imaginations recently bred among the Assyrians and to cut off ideas which differ in form from the present situation. These were sown in the minds of some by those who began unwise activities.

(1) Not coming into touch with the Government officials has affected mostly, if we investigate the case we will find that the foundations of these misunderstandings were assumed as imitations *(sic)*. The Assyrians are the most blameworthy in this matter. For, every one knows that until recently they pretended to be living in a foreign country, and not coming into touch with Government officials, and we learn that they were uncertain in their friendly invitation, or their remaining in this country (they still are in the habit of distinguishing themselves) and are looking forward to acquire a special status, and still dream of autonomy. This, of course, cannot be attained.

As regards the decision of the League of Nations (copy of which will be given to you) and as regards the three neighbouring countries, and their attitude towards you, it was expected that something would have been done by these, but owing to the present financial difficulty,

285

they are not in a position to do anything in your case. (You will also hear to-day the policy of these three regarding your sojourn to their countries.)

(2) You must be certain that the Iraqi Government under the auspices of His Majesty King Feisal the First, are planning your future and will not hesitate in assuring your future prosperity and security. The Government are aware of the benefit she derives of your settling in the country, and have determined to treat you as she treats the inhabitants of which the country is composed, and has undertaken to look upon you with equality, and expects you to obey the laws.

(3) The Iraqi Government understands the petition of the Mar Shimun to the League of Nations, and the Government opposed such petitions as soon as she learned that these were inconsistent with her policy. The result was that the League refused such claims, and here, we are in possession of a copy of the League's decision. It will be distributed to you (by Kasha Yoseph) in Assyriac. You will observe that the League refused these claims especially in the case of autonomy, and was bound by treaty given by Iraq, to the effect that she will strive to settle all the landless who desire to settle and will not put any obstacle in the way of those who desire to leave the country. She also promised to employ those persons who are fit for Government posts as she employs Arabs and Kurds, but in some cases they cannot get these posts as they are in ignorance of either Kurdish or Arabic.

We shall leave this and turn back to the settlement question. The Government promised to employ a foreign expert to help her in settling these people, and she did this. Major Thompson has been here for more than a month. He will explain to you the very thing you and I wish to know.

Government's line. This is what the Government can do so far as settlement is concerned. The Assyrians ought to obey the rules of the country, and the Government will not tolerate, in their capacity as an independent State, to see any one in the country ignoring the laws and order, under which all the subjects are bound. But the patience extended by the Government toward the Assyrians, and the kind treatment they met with are specially due to the humane and kind attitude of a kind Government toward the refugees in her lands. But I do not mean that these shall continue for ever, for those who cannot be loyal subjects try to do worse, and do not deserve those privileges. This cannot be tolerated by any limited nation. The Government has treated the Assyrians as she treats the Arabs and Kurds through the village headmen. But the landlords are Arab shaikhs or Kurdish aghas, their title is not official, the Government do not think of the Arabs in the south who call themselves shaikhs (as a matter of fact every member in the shaikh family is entitled to be addressed as shaikh), but the Government will not appoint any shaikhs.

Recently the police authorities complained of a sudden decrease in the registration of Assyrians rifle for passes. It has been decided to decrease the number of rifles possessed by the various tribes in Iraq and to carry on this, the Assyrians must hand over some of their rifles, when the Kurds and Arabs have done the same. It must be understood that the Government is pursuing its policy like many civilised Governments and do not seek any bloodshed, but will take every possible step to solve this amicably.

Last month, the Government wished to take necessary steps against Malik Yacub and his followers as they refused to comply with the Government orders — *i.e.,* when he was summoned by the Dohuk authority, he did not come. These would have been as drastic as those taken against shaikh Ahmad of Barzan, had he not settled his question amicably. He must understand that he is not allowed to repeat such actions.

Those who agree to abide with the decision of the Government — *i.e.,* those who desire to settle in Iraq — are entitled to naturalisation certificates, but the Government will not grant her lands to those who do not mix with the Iraqis, and who are trying to get their personal ambitions.

Mar Shimun asked the authorities at Baghdad in May last, to let him have the programme as regards the settlement, when he discovered that something was mentioned regarding spiritual and temporal rules, and his stay in Baghdad for some time; he apparently does not run after his fruitless imaginations. You must understand the Government's clear policy is to recognise Mar Shimun as a spiritual head of the Nestorian Church. He will be treated as we treat the other heads of Churches in Iraq, and the Government desires to substitute a special law for the Assyrian people, as those in force for the Chaldean, Armenian and Jews, and that which comes into effect to the Yezedis, these will not permit them to carry on according to their traditions.

The Government do not agree to grant Mar Shimun temporal rule for she is not in the habit of granting such rule to any of the religious heads in Iraq, and there is no reason why we should make any exception to Mar Shimun. Before the world war, he was recognised as spiritual and temporal head of the Assyrians: this was due to the lax of the Turkish regime. Yes, there were in Iraq persons who enjoyed such rules –– *e.g.,* Dijali family of Mosul, Bab an family of Kurdistan, and A1 Sadon family (of) Basra, and many Arabs in the south. But by the declining of the Turkish regime, this rule was abolished, and reasonably that of Mar Shimun also was abolished, and has no influence whatever. Since the British occupation of Baghdad, they have conferred a temporal rule upon Mar Shimun in order to facilitate the recruiting business but this is not in accordance with the Iraqi Government and henceforth will be abolished. Any individual will be treated distinctly by Government and not through the heads who consider the peasants as their slaves, and master the results of their toil, to live easy life. We therefore repeat our word to make you understand that it is not reasonable to confer temporal rule on Mar Shimun.

It would be better for Mar Shimun to think about spiritual matters, he is an expert either in temporal or spiritual. You, who are present, and who are older than he should advise him to submit to the Government. All the Assyrians will be considered as happy sons of the country, let them go back to their work together with their brothers — the Iraqi. In the meantime I should point out that this must be taken as an advice and do not miss this opportunity. Those who like to leave this line and follow their imaginations and spend their time in idleness, will move illegal movement, let them blame nobody but themselves because they have deceived the simple-minded without paying any regard to the results. This date will be registered against those who caused this uneasiness. In any case God is above as a witness. I shall gladly answer any questions directed to me by any of you, and would like to hear something from the Administrative Inspector and Major Thomson.

Ref. to *Al Ammal,* No. 144.

SPEECH OF THE ADMINISTRATIVE INSPECTOR (COL. STAFFORD) MOSUL REGARDING THE ASSYRIANS, IN A MEETING HELD AT MOSUL, WHEN THE MUTASSARIF DECLARED THE IRAQ GOVERNMENT POLICY AND INTENTIONS REGARDING THE ASSYRIANS.

It appears to me that the Acting Mutassarif has said everything necessary regarding this case. I have a few remarks which I should like to make. I joined this liwa less than two months ago, as I was previously working in south of Iraq where very little is heard about the Assyrians. Since my arrival at Mosul I had always to deal with this case. My attention has been attracted mostly by the absence of communications between the Assyrians and the Government which resulted in misunderstanding and doubt. I am obliged to agree with the Acting Mutassarif that this is due to the Assyrians own fault. It appears that until recently they considered themselves as strangers living in a foreign country, and therefore they took to the belief that it would be better for them if they do not come in touch with the Government. Certainly this position has created ill feeling of the Government officials.

I want you all heads of the Assyrians present here to understand finally that this condition of affairs is unbearable and should end forthwith. Either the Assyrians should admit that they are Iraqi subjects, enjoying the same rights and subjected to the same laws as the other natives of the country, whether Kurds, Arabs, Mohammedans, Christians or Jews, or they should be prepared to leave the country. There is no other alternative. Major Thomson will explain to you briefly the particulars about the lands where you are supposed to live, therefore I need not say anything on this subject, but I strongly corroborate the statement that this is the last opportunity which will be given to the Assyrians who have not settled yet to get lands or rights for cultivation in this country. Everybody who instigates the Assyrians not to apply for settlement will inflict an irrevocable damage on them.

As regards the second alternative which I mentioned –– viz., leaving Iraq –– I don't think all the Assyrians understand the situation. The Iraqi Government has undertaken to give all possible facilities to those who wish to leave the country –– i.e., anybody who wishes to go will not be prevented from doing so –– but the Iraqi Government is not at all responsible to find a place for them outside Iraq and naturally she cannot do this.

In the meantime the League of Nations on their part did not promise to give them lands other than in Iraq. It is for the Assyrians themselves to arrange to get the sanction of the country where they would like to settle and to find their transport expenses. Until now no agreement of another Government was obtained for their settlement, nor is it likely that any neighbouring Government will agree to the emigration of the Assyrians in great numbers.

(1) *Turkey.* –– There is no hope whatever that Turkey will change her position with regard to the Assyrians. Turkey refuses them. It is

natural that the Assyrians are anxious to return to their own country but it should be clearly understood that this is out of the scope of our subject.

(2) *Persia.* —— The Persian Government has intimated that she accepts a few of the Assyrians under very difficult conditions: *(a)* All firearms should be handed over; *(b)* settlement will not be in one place but in very widely separated places; *(c)* they will have no rights in the land given them; *(d)* they will not be given financial assistance.

(3) *Syria.* —— As you are aware the French authorities in Syria are dealing with the Armenian emigrants, hence they have no lands which could be allotted to the Assyrians. It is true that the Assyrian young men could get employment in the Colonial French Army but such service is very difficult and has no prospects whatever. Naturally once they go the Iraqi Government will not allow them to return. This is the position regarding the neighbouring countries. If you want to be sure you can enquire here from the French and Persian consuls respectively.

In view of the present economic position of the world, no country will accept the Assyrians or any sort of immigration.

I think what I said is enough to explain that the prospects of the Assyrians is actually in Iraq. I know that the Iraq Government is very keen to solve the Assyrian problem for the mutual benefit of both. I know that all responsible Iraqis whether Ministers or officials wish to see the Assyrians living as Iraqis. It is therefore the duty of the Assyrians to participate in this feeling. If you do this I guarantee good feeling and assistance towards you, but first of all you should throw away the spirit of separating yourselves from the Iraqis. Had your children in the past learned the Arabic or Kurdish languages various employments would have been open for them.

Everybody feels and is sorry for the troubles and pains the Assyrians sustained and the Government which is not at all responsible for them means to make everything possible to relieve and help them. Don't forget that the Iraqi Government was not established long ago and Iraq did not reach a wealthy stage as yet.

The Assyrians cannot expect a better condition than that of the Kurds or the Arabs. If they want to succeed they should work hard. I hope you will all do this for your sakes and your children's sakes. The Acting Mutassarif has dealt with Mar Shimun's case clearly and I must say that what the Acting Mutassarif said is a truth which does not require any explanation. There are no two authorities in the world, spiritual and nonspiritual mixed together and it cannot be applied in Iraq. It is time for you now to decide finally whether you intend to live in Iraq or not. In my opinion and as one who seeks your benefit I say you cannot live anywhere but in Iraq.

An Outline of the Present Assyrian Situation and Its Causes.

Friday night July 21st, 1933, about 1,000 young and middle-aged men, headed by Malek Loko of Ikhuma, Shlimim and Yako, sons of Malek Ismail of Tiary and eight priests, passed the Iraq frontier, near Pesh Khabur (Zakho) into Syria. Five hundred of them were mounted and the rest on foot. They left behind them the old men, their women, children and belongings. On Monday next another group of 500 from Nahla Barwar and Mosul succeeded in passing the frontier in ferries of their own make, above Pesh Khabur. Four hundred more passed the Tigris on Wednesday July 26th, against some resistance from the Iraqi police force. On Thursday 27th the Iraqi forces got hold of the river passages from Pesh Khabur to the Turkish Border and turned back some fifty men of Gowar, arresting seven of them. This was done at the formal request of the French authorities in Syria. For four days the tribesmen camped in the open near the river waiting for more arrivals, and then moved to a village

Derek (?) some hours distant. From there they have sent a letter to the Minister of Interior (copy to Lady Surma) by a messenger, stating:

> "At the special meeting of July 10th and 11th, the Acting Mutassarif of Mosul, the Administrative Inspector Colonel Stafford and the Settlement Officer Major Thomson, have told us to get away from Iraq if we are not satisfied with the present arrangements of the Government, so we left. We ask you to let our remaining brethren join us without military interference. We will not do anything wrong to anybody nor fight your soldiers, unless we are forced to."

There is a general opinion among the Assyrians that the French Government is favourably disposed to receive them in Syria. This of course against the official denial of the French Ambassador. The French Consul here, Mr. Lucas, told me that the Assyrians who forced the frontier will be disarmed and sent back to Iraq. This to be done as soon as the French will take possession of the newly delimitated line between Iraq and Syria. The messenger assured us that the French provided the Assyrians with food and some tents.

The Assyrians who left Iraq represent 15,000 persons counting their families, thousands more are waiting for an opening in the military belt, to leave. Out of 30,000 Assyrians in Iraq, 5,000 only might remain. The villages north of Mosul are deserted, ricefields left to dry, sheep abandoned in the hands of servants, belongings are being sold by the women. It can be said that this third exodus of the Assyrians since the war, is general. The reasons for this desperate move are many. The Assyrians were promised and hoped for a special treatment if they were to remain in Iraq. They joined their little forces with the Allies and fought on the side of the British Army in Persia and Iraq. They shed their blood for the delimitation and pacification of Iraq. The long and bitter experience of the past has proved to them that they cannot live in the villages of Kurds without a special arrangement; they know that they cannot expect such assistance from a Moslem Government in case of difficulty. They know that in the last incident of Yako, the Government actually armed the Kurds against them. They were told that they will have to give up their arms before anybody else.

Sir Francis Humphrys has promised the Patriarch to help him to obtain some concessions for his people, if he would go to Geneva. The Patriarch failed to obtain any privileges in Geneva, but he was promised again to a fair settlement of his people.

When the Settlement Officer arrived, the Patriarch was put aside, and told not to interfere. His views about Iraq, while in Geneva and his hopes about the future of his people in Iraq did not please the Iraqi political men; they decided to ignore him and not recognise him as the leader of the Assyrians. The Patriarch felt offended and chose the policy of waiting and non-co-operation. The Government retaliated by inviting him to Baghdad and detaining him there. This last action brought to the memory of the Assyrians the similar detention during the war, of Hormizd brother of the then Patriarch, in Constantinople, and his subsequent death at the hands of the Turks. The feeling against the Government ran high in the villages.

The Government appointed five new leaders from different tribes, gave positions and salaries to the opposers of the Patriarch, favoured especially Presbyterian Assyrians and took into their confidence Mar Sergies Bishop of the Jilu Tribe, at present not on good terms with the Patriarch. A regular campaign against the Patriarchal authorities was conducted in the villages by the Government officials. Those friendly disposed towards the Patriarch were ill-treated, arrested, and persecuted in many ways. The chiefs of the villages were called again and again under different pretexts and told to betray Mar Shimun. The house of the Patriarch was watched and he was warned not to hold any meetings.

The Assyrians could not accept new leaders; could not resign themselves to be persecuted unjustly; could not drop so abruptly their allegiance to their Patriarch. They began to revolt. Yako, son of Malek Ismail, defied the Government in Baghiry; Malek Loko of Ikhuma resisted the Kaimakam in Dohuk, Shleman of Tiary and Kasha Ishaq, evaded arrest in Mosul. The villages began to boil with unrest. The meeting of July 10th, gathered by the Government, blasted the last hope of the Assyrians regarding their settlement. They understood that every family will be given free land for cultivation and will be helped in starting new villages. The Government made it clear to them that only a fraction of them will be settled in Dashta Zer and others will have to stay where they are. Major Thomson, the Settlement Officer, seemed to be bound to the Government's policy. The great question of settlement as cherished in the minds of the Assyrians was reduced to a mere shifting of some 600 families from one place to another.

The offensive remarks about the Assyrians in the Parliament made it clear to them that they are unwanted in Iraq. The Arabic Press by publishing articles against the Assyrians created an hostile feeling among the local population. The publishing in the American Press of the article, known to you, by the Bev. Cumberland, and its translation in the Arabic papers, filled the hearts of the Assyrians with discouragement. The Bishop in Jerusalem's determined attitude towards the Patriarch and Lady Surma, siding unconditionally with the Government's policy, made them feel that our Church is also against them. These and other of longer standing causes, forced the Assyrians to the desperate move of leaving Iraq.

Those who left will not return to Iraq. If forced, they will fight, try to go to Turkey or disperse in the mountains. If France accepts them, all others will slowly follow. The Assyrians know now that Iraqi Government does not want them and that the general public hates them. They were ready last December to go to Persia, but they preferred to give themselves up to France, which retains still the privilege of protecting the oppressed in the East.

In Syria they will know that they will have no rights to ask for privileges, or special treatment; that they will have to give up their arms; but they are ready for that in order to be able to cultivate their grounds and pasture, their cattle of peace. Still this is a slip in the British policy in the East, which will be judged severely in the annals of future history.

(The above is an unbiased report from a reliable European in the Mosul liwa.)

[Copy.]   July 23rd, 1933.

                                              Near Khaniq.

Minister of Interior,
    Baghdad.

Excellency,

As a result of Mosul meeting the Iraqi Government policy was explained to us both regarding settlement and Patriarch.

Mutassarif openly said "those unsatisfied with this policy are free to do emigrate from Iraq". Accordingly we have come to the frontier and we request the Iraqi Government not to block the road to those who want to join us.

We got no intention to fight unless forced.

(Signed)   Yacob Malik Ismiel; Malik Baito; Loko Shlimun; Malik Warda; Rais Esha; Rais Iskhaq; Malik Marogl; Tooma-D. Makhmoora; Yoshia Esho; Malik Selim; Shamasha Ismail; Rais Mikhail.

Edi K.,
Secretary of the Assyrian Emigration.

TRANSLATION OF A LETTER ADDRESSED TO HIS
EXCELLENCY THE PRIME MINISTER.

Excellency,

The Tyaris' case engages public opinion mostly, as it has developed to be the severest calamity in the future prosperity of the country, no matter settled together or scattered.

Apparently, these did not enter the country to live settled and easy life, but with other intentions. They caused unhappy accidents in Mosul and Kirkuk. This shows that these are danger anywhere or at any time.

No nation in the world has ever done such a horrible mistake as ours, we granted lands for their settlement, sanctioned thousands of dinars for their agricultural purposes, and allowed them to reap the benefit of our country. In spite of this all, they deserted the country — *i.e.,* crossed the border in a horde of over 1,300 armed men — and they continue to cross the borders. They do not contend with this, but threaten others, and are planning a natural disposition, to which they are devoted, and which was unveiled by them recently, they are badly off financially at the present moment, what will be their attitude toward the Government, if, perchance, they prosper materially and intellectually?

We have to recommend the best remedy for this disease; request the Government to expel them promptly from the lands, contrary to the League, and give them no excuse. This will avoid turmoil and disorder in the country.

(Signed) General Secretary:
HAZIB AL WATANI (Nationalist Opposition Party).

Refer to *Ikha al Watani,*
No. 419, July 30th, 1933.

II. REPORT OF AUGUST 30ᵀᴴ, 1933.

Assyrian Patriarchate,
Nicosia, Cyprus.
August 30th, 1933.

To His Excellency
 Secretary-General League of Nations,
  Geneva, Switzerland.

Excellency,

Following my report dated August 4th, 1933:

Your Excellency will have seen from that report wherein I stated that an Assyrian village was burnt down, that I was not feeling easy about the fate of my people, and that the storming of the first Assyrian village was but the symbol of further ravages and acts of violence by the Iraqi Government forces that were to follow.

My correspondence and that of my people subjected as it were to strict postal censorship in contravention to Article 15 of the Iraqi Constitutional Law and I being under Government detention, Baghdad, totally cut off from my people, it was not under the circumstances possible for me to obtain in time first-class information as to callous oppression of my people without making a searching enquiry which has now been rendered somewhat possible subsequent to my deportation from Iraq on August 18th, 1933.

It would appear that subsequent to the meetings held at the Mutassarifiyyah of Mosul on July 10th and 11th, 1933, at which meetings the Assyrians were told to leave Iraq if they disapproved the Government policy in regard to heterogeneous settlement that would have necessarily led to their complete destruction, added to this the declared policy of the Government to settle a few hundred Assyrians only thus leaving thousands of others unsettled and homeless as

Your Excellency will have observed from the copies of letters and reports before you, the Assyrian representative leaders who enjoy the confidence of almost all the members of my people decided to obey the Government instructions conveyed to them by the Mutassarif of Mosul by leaving Iraq to a place where they can live peacefully. Syria, under the French mandate, was under the circumstances the only avenue open in the face of my people.

The Iraqi Government instead of honouring its public announcement referred to above placed Mosul liwa under military occupation and began molesting groups of Assyrians who were desirous of joining the groups who had already left Iraq and safely reached their destination without firing a single shot, every group being headed by its own representative leader from every Assyrian tribe. Simultaneously with the molesting of Assyrians in Mosul, the Iraqi advance guard launched several attacks and counter-attacks on the Assyrian representative leaders who were now in a point on the Syro-Iraqi frontier on August 4th, 5th and 6th, 1933, inflicting, according to the Iraqi Government *communiqué* itself, casualties of some ninety-five Assyrians killed and a larger number of wounded; the latter I am assured were brutally killed on the battlefield.

My people whether those on the Syro-Iraqi frontier or those in Mosul had no intention whatever of fighting the Iraqi forces but the circumstances under which they found themselves forced them to defend themselves in the face of many difficulties and overwhelming odds until they finally entered Syrian territory. Had the Iraqi Government honestly kept its announcement made at Mosul and did not harass those left in Mosul and permitted them to leave peacefully to join their comrades and relatives, I am sure that not one drop of blood would have been shed. But the aim of the Iraqi Government was to inflict as many casualties as it could on my people before and after leaving Iraq.

Had the Assyrian representative leaders who left Iraq remained in Mosul, their fate would have almost certainly been tragic as has been the fate of their compatriots and relations who remained behind for all the activities of the Iraqi Government tended to show that such would be the case. And if the Assyrian representative leaders who were now on the Syro-Iraqi frontier after receiving a desperate appeal from their comrades who were being badly molested by the Iraqi army, did not go to relieve them it is almost sure that that group would have been totally wiped out.

Before there was any fighting, the Assyrian villages, at the instigation of and the encouragement by the Iraqi Government officials without distinction, were exposed to all kinds of ravages. Their sheep and cattle were carried off with impunity; cultivated lands were encroached upon and destroyed; rice and other cultivations were totally damaged; burglaries became common and anarchy universal. The Assyrians were being raided hourly and were left unprotected to the cruel treatment of the predatory Arabs at the open instigation of a fanatic Government who had three months previously prepared a plan for the total extermination of the Assyrian people by first attempting to disarm them some two months ago and then attack them.

On its return from the frontier, the Iraqi army together with that part of the force which was proceeding to Assyrian settlements shot down every non-combatant isolated Assyrian they came across. In the villages of the Qadha of Dohuk, men, women and children were turned out of their villages and shot down collectively by rifle and machinegun fire. In Simel alone, more than three hundred and fifty persons were massacred in this barbarous manner. The Iraqi army went so far as to bayonet some of these defenceless people. In the Qadha of Dohuk where the excesses were acute and the casualties among the Assyrian civil population heavier the reason was because the Assyrian settlements and villages were within the easy reach of the Iraqi army and the access to them was not difficult as these villages and settlements lie not far away from the main roads that the Iraqi army force was using.

In Amadiyah districts, individual murders became common and the property of the civil population carried away. The persecution of the Assyrians in the other settlements was of no less barbarity than in Dohuk and Amadiyah districts.

Reports to hand from various sources show that the Assyrians who have been treacherously victimised by the Iraqi Government and the police can be counted in hundreds. Thousands of Assyrians have become widows and orphans. All of these have become destitute for what little they had has all been looted. They are at present destitute and poverty-stricken and look here and there for crumbs of bread they can find.

It is however said that a certain number of Assyrians who mysteriously escaped the massacres were transported to Dohuk and each person supplied with three loaves of bread *per diem*. Diseases are reported to have already broken out among the panic-stricken Assyrian population which will soon become universal and play havoc with those who have survived only to undergo more acute sufferings. The rest of the Assyrian villages in addition to those in Dohuk and Amadiyah have been subjected to robbery and loot and a large proportion of the villages burnt down.

The number of people who have suffered terribly in every imaginable way at the hands of the Iraqi Government is estimated at eight thousand and I do not know what has happened to my people since my deportation from Iraq.

It should be borne in mind that the Assyrians up to the last moment maintained a peaceful and tranquil spirit though they were aware that the Iraqi Government was doing its utmost and leaving no stone unturned to bring about these massacres. To make sure that when the massacres would be put in operation, the Iraqi Government had long before embarked upon a scheme whereby she weeded out all the Assyrian policemen in the north and transferred them to the southern districts. Before trouble breaking out in Mosul, the Iraqi Government established temporary police posts and increased the numbers of others from among newly recruited men and posted them in every Assyrian village and settlement of importance to prevent them from giving any sort of relief to their brethren who were being massacred in the other villages. To justify this action, the Iraqi Government stated that this was necessary to protect the civil population! Travelling by day and night from Mosul to other districts was forbidden in order to hide the atrocious acts that were in process.

On May 12th, 1933, an Arab officer in Mosul was told to say that stones were thrown over his house by Assyrians. This was to enable the Iraqi commander (who subsequently issued the orders following those of Baghdad for the massacring of the Assyrian population) to raid and assassinate the Assyrian Patriarch and the other Assyrians in Mosul. It can be safely said that this case in which the Assyrian Patriarch was falsely accused was the first sign of the contemplated massacres. The Mutassarif of Mosul informed a European in Mosul that the assassination of the Patriarch and the rest of the Assyrians was within the military plan of operations.

This having failed in Mosul to produce the long-awaited sequel, the authorities in Baghdad took the matter up themselves. A perversive but a continued anti-Assyrian campaign was carried out by the medium of the newspapers throughout Iraq which went on for three months unchecked. As a matter of fact it was encouraged by the Government officials. The ill-feeling against the Assyrians became universal when certain deputies delivered fiery speeches in the Iraqi Parliament implying the necessity for the extermination of the Assyrian people. There was a general outcry through sheer fanaticism and hatred created and promoted by the Government for a holy war against the Assyrians. Demands for anti-Assyrian demonstrations were pouring in from Baghdad and Mosul at the instigation of the Government. In the case of the Kurds in Iraq who had already risen twice on a large scale in addition to several other minor risings against King Faisal's Government and his artificial but oppressive regime, there was no desire on the part of the Arabs to volunteer and support the Iraqi Government as they did in the case of the Assyrians. The case of my people was obviously different. We were looked upon as unbelievers and all means employed against us were lawful.

The Assyrians in Baiji in the employ of the Iraq Petroleum Co. were attacked and removed from their posts. The Assyrian railway employees were also all withdrawn to Baghdad.

Despite all the persecutions and acts of violence to which the Assyrians were subjected, the Assyrian levies awaited patiently in a wonderful manner that is highly commended hoping that the League of Nations and the Powers interested in my people to take drastic action against the oppressors and find a definite and final permanent solution for their future welfare. The Assyrian levy officers and men were seeing and hearing of the tragic fate of their wives, mothers, sisters, children and relatives yet they did not move to meet evil with evil. It is true that they petitioned the Air Vice-Marshal and gave him one month's notice following the terms of their contract after which date they would leave the service to go and save their people but they were disallowed to take this step. Actually through deep sorrow and grief about sixty and seventy of them were rapidly falling sick daily and were going to their doctors for medical treatment as a result of the terrible agony they were passing through.

The Assyrians in Baghdad were disarmed and had, together with those in Mosul and Kirkuk, and in all the other parts of Iraq to live under a reign of terror as they were expecting death, and a brutal death, at any moment.

Before I go any further, it would not be out of place to mention that when I last met Sir Francis Humphrys the then British High Commissioner in Iraq at Geneva at 'the Hôtel Beau-Rivage on the eve preceding the entrance of Iraq to the League of Nations he admitted that in 1931 arrangements were well in train to massacre the Assyrians had it not been for the prompt action he had taken to stop it. I thanked him most cordially but asked him what guarantees had he that could ensure the non-repetition of what we were discussing and what assurances had he to stop any attempt for such massacres in the future. He was kind enough to say that Iraq would not venture to attempt to do so as the British influence would still be great in Iraq; that he personally would have much time to devote to the Assyrian question and that he would do much more than when High Commissioner.

Whilst on this, may I draw Your Excellency's attention to His Britannic Majesty's Government's announcement before the Permanent Mandates Commission:

> "His Majesty's Government fully realise its responsibility in recommending that Iraq should be admitted to the League. . . . Should Iraq prove herself unworthy of the confidence which has been placed in her, the moral responsibility must rest with His Majesty's Government."

At 2.30 p.m. on August 17th, 1933, an Arab police inspector entered the Y.M.C.A. premises at which I was dwelling and handed me an order for my deportation from Iraq. A copy of the order in question is enclosed herewith. I will not dwell on the legality or otherwise of this arbitrary order but would simply say that it is in contravention to Article 7 of the Iraqi Constitutional Law; of the Iraqi Nationality Law and is a grave violation of the letter and spirit of the guarantees of the League of Nations for the protection of the Iraqi minorities. This order supposed to be based on an emergency law that will be passed by the Iraqi Parliament the first moment it is presented to it, has rendered the guarantees of the League of Nations null and void. Thousands of others in addition to Assyrians are liable to this arbitrary treatment and you will now realise that our fears in the past, as at present, were well founded. Iraq is not a State that can and will respect international guarantees and keep up promises and it is lamentable that my people despite their years continuous protests should have been subjected to such a Government.

Five minutes after the arrival of the police inspector with the order of my deportation in his hand, the Air Vice-Marshal dropped in to say that he had had information about the order as the Iraqi Government had furnished the British Embassy with a copy. The Air Vice-Marshal said that there were two alternatives. Either I should submit to deportation to Cyprus immediately or else the armed policemen who have formed a cordon round the Y.M.C.A. would seize me by force together with my father and brother and throw us over the Iraqi frontier. The Air Vice-Marshal was perturbed to such an extent so as to say that he was not altogether sure whether or not we could be safely transported to our new destination. As no one was allowed access to my place of residence and as I do not know Arabic, I asked the Air Vice-Marshal to give us a chance to have the order translated. This was not to be. I then asked that I should be given an opportunity to see or telephone to the British Ambassador and this was also refused.

I enclose herewith a copy of my letter dated August 15th, 1933, to the British Ambassador Baghdad. I had to submit to the order of deportation in view of paragraph (c) of the letter under reference, and particularly to have the massacres stopped as stated in the letter.

In order to give another chance to the League of Nations to intervene and fearing an undoubted clash between my Assyrian people and the levies in Baghdad on the one hand and the Iraqi police on the other if the latter would have attempted to commit

305

the usual acts of violence which they were prepared to do *vide* the statement of the Air Vice-Marshal, I agreed to proceed to Cyprus but do hereby most strongly protest against the action of the Iraqi Government. I am assured that there would have been a serious retaliation on the part of the Assyrian levies with disastrous effects to the Assyrian case as the Iraqi Government was doing all in its power and tempting the Assyrians as in previous instances to take the law into their own hands thus enabling the Government to fall on the Assyrians in Baghdad as they did in the other parts of Iraq. I was informed by authoritative persons that the Arab Government was after my blood as it is now after the blood of every Assyrian in the country. I now emphasise the fact that the life of every Assyrian in Iraq is in danger and an imminent danger. I would have personally gladly sacrificed myself in defence of my Assyrian people and would only be too glad to meet the fate of my predecessors but as the lives of my people were at stake, as are now, I have accepted the order of deportation under the strongest protest pending the intervention of the League of Nations in regard to the whole Assyrian question.

At 4.15 a.m. in the morning the Iraqi authorities handed me over to the Air Vice-Marshal and the secretary to the British Ambassador who took me, my father and brother by cars to Hinaidi. From there we were transported by air to Cyprus.

Your Excellency will have observed that the Emergency Law No. 62 for the year 1933 referred to above was purposely enacted to be applied in our case irrespective of the existence or otherwise of the guarantees of the League of Nations.

I am at present in Cyprus with my father and brother.

Two Assyrian levy officers were detailed by the Air Vice-Marshal to accompany me to Cyprus and on their return to assure the Assyrian levies and the Assyrian population now completely desperate and waiting eagerly to hear that I was free to proceed to Geneva and elsewhere and re-submit and defend the Assyrian case before the world.

Eight Assyrians have been deported to Nasiriyah, Muntafik Liwa, on the lower Euphrates and many others are being terrorised.

I was informed to-day by Mr. C. Hart Davis the District Commissioner Cyprus that addition to the Patriarchal family members that include men, women and children now on their way to Cyprus, eight other Assyrian leaders are to be deported to Cyprus bringing the number of deportees to 25. This is based on information received from London by the Government of Cyprus.

It would be quite impossible for the League of Nations to fully realise the barbarous atrocities committed against my people and the excesses used against them if no International Enquiry Commission proceeds to the spot as soon as possible to find means to stop further massacres that are bound to follow. And in order to be able to assist the Commission in its difficult task and give a full account of what has taken place, it is essential that I should be on the spot together with representative leaders recognised by the Assyrians and selected witnesses to give evidence in a healthy atmosphere under the protection of the League of Nations.

Finally, I pray Almighty God to accomplish through your intermediary the salvation of this remnant of the most martyred Christian Church and people.

(Signed) Eshai SHIMUN,
By the Grace of God, Catholicos
Patriarch of the Assyrians.

Annexes

Ministry of Interior, Iraq.
     No. S/1801.

Date 25th Rabi ul Thani 1352
     August 17th, 1933.

To Eshai Mar Shimun.

This is to notify you that the Council of State has, by virtue of the authority vested in him, decided to withdraw your Iraqi nationality and this Ministry has moreover decided that you should be deported outside Iraq.

For your information, we send you herewith a copy of the order relating to this.

(Signed) NASHAT AL SINAWI,
For Minister of Interior.

Ministry of Interior, Iraq.
     No. S/1792.

Date 24th Rabi ul Thani 1352
     August 16th, 1933.

Whereas the Council of State has decided to withdraw the Iraqi nationality from Eshai Mar Shimun in accordance with the authority vested in the Council of State *vide* Article I of the law for the withdrawal of Iraqi nationality No. 62 for the year 1933 and whereas it has appeared that the deportation of the person in question outside Iraq is in the interests of law and public security:

Therefore We, Minister of Interior by virtue of the authority vested in Us under Article II of the Law in question, order that he be deported outside Iraqi frontier.

(Signed) NASHAT AL SINAWI,
For Minister of Interior.

———————

c/o Y.M.C.A.
Baghdad, August 15th, 1933.

His Excellency,
The Acting British Ambassador,
Baghdad.

Your Excellency,

Might I recall to you our conversation of yesterday, August 14th. That the British Government had made a decision to remove the Patriarchal family, that is, myself, father, brother and Lady Surma, because:

(a) Of danger to its life;

(b) Because of the status of Iraq as an independent State, no protection could be given by the British in this country;

(c) If we left Iraq temporarily, that I should be free to proceed to Geneva, or any place where I could help my Assyrian people.

The alternative being —— that the Iraqi Government had decided to imprison us either in Nasiriyah or Rutbah, and if we state that we are not Iraqis, then they will deport us over the frontier.

You also stated that the Iraqi Government accused me of being the cause of the present situation.

As I have already answered you verbally yesterday, so I now state in writing. The Patriarchal family has no wish to avail itself of any protection apart from that afforded to the whole Assyrian people. The most urgent question at the moment is that the British Government who handed us over to Iraq should stop massacre, persecution, and extermination of the families especially when so many of the young men are now serving British interests in this country when they could be defending these helpless families. This to me is much more important than any question of personal safety.

Moreover, if the presence of the Patriarchal family of eighteen persons is in danger and thus endangers the life of the Assyrian people, because of their loyalty, then surely their removal to an B.A.F. cantonment at Mosul or Hinaidi would be sufficient protection.

If as you say the Arab Government hold me solely responsible for the present situation, and my presence in Iraq prejudices the termination of the massacre and bitter feeling, then in the interests of peace I agree to being transferred under British auspices for a period to such a place that I am free to present in person the case of the Assyrians to the League of Nations. In such a case I would need to take with me a personal attendant.

(True copy.)

(Signed) Eshai SHIMUN, *Patriarch.*

III. REPORT OF SEPTEMBER 12TH, 1933.

Assyrian Patriarchate,
Nicosia, Cyprus.
September 12th, 1933.

His Excellency,
  Secretary-General,
    League of Nations, Geneva.

Excellency,

In continuation of my report dated August 4th, my letter of the 16th and my second report dated August 30th, 1933.

FIRST DETAILED REPORT ON MASSACRE.

I forward herewith the first detailed report bearing on the massacre of the Assyrians in Iraq. You will observe that the information contained therein was collected from the persecuted persons themselves. Children have also been interrogated and it cannot be said that facts have been exaggerated. I believe that actual facts have been minimised rather than exaggerated and I hope to furnish the League of Nations with more particulars on the massacre.

The Assyrian women who have furnished this information are illiterate and it would have been impossible for any person, terror-stricken as the Assyrian women were, to note down every small detail minutely. Their evidence leaves no room to doubt the report that the actual perpetrators of the massacre were the Iraqi troops who were acting under the orders of their own officers in conjunction with the civil authorities who in their turn were linked up with higher authorities in Baghdad and Mosul. This I have emphasised in my former reports.

The Kurds.

In my radiogram of early August, I said "Assyrian women, children, included in massacre by certain Kurdish tribes armed by Government". This I think requires some explanation.

The Sar Amadiyah summer camp for the British was closed down as soon as trouble broke out and the Assyrian levies who were guarding that camp were brought down in groups by cars to the aerodrome in the vicinity of Simel and from there were transported by air to Baghdad. Except for a few minutes' stay of the levies in the Simel aerodrome, their journey to Baghdad was uninterrupted. It was they who saw Assyrian dead bodies lying on the roads between Sar Amadiyah and Simel and as they would not believe that the Iraqi army would have committed these barbarous acts, they informed me of what they saw and they were, in the absence of accurate information, under the impression that this was the work of the Kurds instigated by the Government. My information conveyed in my radiogram was therefore based on the first information report which has since been modified.

The Air Vice-Marshal.

On the day of my deportation from Baghdad, the Air Vice-Marshal, Iraq, promised me to go to the massacre zone, establish a refugee camp in Dohuk and collect all those who had lost their male relatives. I am informed that he went as far as Mosul town with other British officers but they were disallowed by the Arab authorities to proceed farther than Mosul.

If a British Air Vice-Marshal representing one of the greatest Empires and who is there to protect Iraq from external aggression is not permitted by the Arab authorities to visit an area which is a few miles from Mosul, the League of Nations will not therefore find it difficult to realise the extent of measures and precautions the Arab

312

Government has taken to prevent any observer from seeing the horrors that have been committed. Moreover, the League of Nations will also realise how difficult it has been for me to obtain even the preliminary reports.

At present, the women and children are being terrorised and coercive measures used against them —— only known to those who know the Arab methods —— to compel them to say that it was the Kurds and *not* the Iraqi troops who killed their relatives. They are being told that if they do not say so they will share the fate of their relatives.

IRAQI DELEGATION TO GENEVA.

The League of Nations representing almost all the Nations of the world will shortly be receiving some of the actual instigators of the recent horrific acts committed with extreme cruelty against the Assyrian people in Iraq. Denial of atrocities and shifting of responsibility will be their two main aims but the League of Nations will realise that an accused cannot at the same time be a witness and arbitrator. It was this procedure adopted in the past that brought about the present calamities on the Assyrians and it is neither fair nor just that this same procedure which has resulted in disaster to my people, should be applied.

I earnestly ask that the Iraqi Government, an accused at present, should have no privilege over the Assyrians before the international bar at Geneva. It should be equally treated with the Assyrians as regards procedure in the present case and the latter should be permitted to exercise the natural right of producing their witnesses to substantiate the accusations already made against the Iraqi Government. The privilege accorded in the recent past to the Iraqi Government of hearing it in person while the Assyrians were heard "on paper" only has been abused and the proverb says: "Once bitten, twice shy".

THE BRITISH OFFICIALS.

Some of the British officials have informed me that they were the servants of the Iraqi Government. These are therefore not expected to illustrate a correct picture of what has taken place unless they are prepared to adversely affect their positions which, from what I know, is doubtful.

SIR FRANCIS HUMPHRYS.

Sir Francis Humphrys, the British Ambassador, who played an important rôle in making the admission of Iraq to the League of Nations possible and who has undertaken on behalf of his Government "the moral responsibility should Iraq prove herself unworthy of the confidence placed in her", cannot either be reasonably expected to say that he misjudged Iraq after having made those eminent declarations about Iraqi fitness for independence and Iraqi tolerance.

IMPARTIAL ENQUIRY.

In view of the foregoing, the League of Nations will never be able to reach the bottom of the truth if it does not make its own enquiries independently on the spot. An enquiry by an interested party or parties will not remedy the present position nor will it enable the League of Nations to find a real solution for this acute problem. I am sure that if the League was given a chance immediately after the publication of the Anglo-Iraqi Treaty of June 30th, 1930, to make a searching enquiry into the dreadful position of the Assyrians and their complaints that inundated the League's Secretariat, stringent measures which were necessary for the real and not visionary protection of the Assyrians would have been recommended before entrusting Iraq with an unrestrained power which we all knew would be abused.

Status of the League of Nations from the Iraqi Point of View.

The Secretariat of the League of Nations will recollect the telegram sent by Yasin al Hashimi (now Minister of Finance and notoriously anti-Assyrian), Naji al Siwaidi (Senator) and Ja'far Chalabi Abu Timman in 1930 to the effect that they did not want Iraq admitted into the League of Nations. The Iraqi political circles treat the League of Nations with contempt and it is this and other reasons that have encouraged them to look upon the guarantees for the protection of the Assyrians as mere scraps of paper. Count Teleki and his Commission had prophesied in their special recommendations that this would be the case if there was no effective supervision on the spot to see that the rights and interests of the Minorities were respected and protected. The responsible Iraqis believe (and there has so far been nothing to dispel their belief) that they can persecute the Assyrians in any way they like and when it comes to judgment they will clear themselves by the simple device of withdrawing from the League.

Attached statement is only a sample that should illustrate the Iraqi public opinion. The premature emancipation of Iraq and the setting aside of the interests of the other races in the Mosul vilayet, particularly the interests of the Assyrian's, could not but have produced these deplorable results.

Iraqi Government's Allegations.

In my former reports I have explained the extensive anti-Assyrian campaign carried out against the Assyrians by encouragement of the Government. The Iraqi Government in order to further poison the minds of the Arabs fabricated a tale which was to the effect that three of their officers after being killed in battle by the Assyrians had their bodies mutilated by the latter. This allegation is devoid of foundation. It was cultivated to further arouse the ill-feeling against the Assyrians. During all our battles in the past, no such complaint was made against the Assyrians who have always proved to be noble and they have always kept up the simple laws of civilisation. The truth is this:

I was informed by Major Aldwards, commanding Assyrian levies, that the Assyrian representative leaders who were on the Syro–Iraqi frontier had captured two Arab officers and a considerable quantity of ammunition and war material and as the fight was going on, the Assyrians could not have taken their prisoners with them, and so they tied them up and left them behind in a tent by which lay the captured ammunition that included explosives. The Iraqi aeroplanes wanting to blow up the ammunition dropped bombs from the air that resulted in the death of their own officers.

The Assyrian people in Iraq and abroad are eagerly awaiting for me to be able when I obtain a *laissez-passer* from the British Government (as my Iraqi nationality has been withdrawn) to place the Assyrian case and the people's demands in person before the League of Nations when I shall be able to refute the allegations of the Iraqi Government.

I have applied to the British Government for a *laissez-passer* on receipt of which I propose proceeding to Geneva.

I pray the Almighty God that the League of Nations whose principle is justice and a support of the oppressed will this time not allow the innocent blood of my people to have been shed in vain.

(Signed) Eshai SHIMUN,
By the Grace of God, Catholicos
Patriarch of the Assyrians.

ANNEX.

First Massacre Report of Assyrians in Simel, on Friday, August 11th, 1933.

The following account of the massacre in Simel is taken from the mouths of the Assyrian women who were brought to Mosul on August 17th, 1933, as no man escaped the death to tell the story.

On August 8th, the inhabitants of the villages in the neighbourhood of Simel were notified by the police to come to Simel to be protected from Arabs and Kurds. The Assyrians from the villages of:

Sayyid Zari,	Chamma Gore,	Sarshuri,
Mawani,	Kharab Kuli,	Garpili,
Qasr Yazdin,	Dari,	Busuriyeh,
Mansuriyah,		

thereupon came to Simel with their cattle and belongings.

The following day they were ordered to surrender their arms as they were told that there was no danger if they did so, for they were under the Government protection. Yonan of Baz, the headman of the village, collected in the police station all those Assyrians who were in possession of Iraqi nationality papers and told them that they would be safe under the Iraqi flag. Eighty-two persons from the Baz tribe sat the whole day and night around the police station, some with their women and children. On August 10th, Thursday, the police returned the rifles to their owners, without ammunition, and, in the afternoon of the same day, the rifles were collected again and handed to the police.

On August 11th, Friday, Naib Chaush (police sergeant) separated the women and children below the age of ten from the men in the police station, and ordered them to scatter in the houses of the village.

317

That was early in the morning. At or about six o'clock in the morning, the Iraqi flag was lowered from the police station. Soldiers from the Iraqi army, in dark-blue shirts, appeared advancing towards Simel from the direction of Zakho road. Some Arabs of the Shammar tribe and some Kurds (of Mahmud Agha and from Slivani) entered the village. The soldiers surrounded the village and the officer in charge with two soldiers came up to the police station. The officer in charge was addressed by Goriel Shimun of Baz, brother of Yonan the headman of the village. "I am an Iraqi citizen and all those Assyrians present here are Iraqi citizens. If you so desire take me to Qaimaqam Dohuk who will show you that we are such in the Government books." The officer pretended to agree and took him down the slope. There the second soldier shot him dead from behind. This was the signal for the massacre. Soldiers in dark-blue shirts ran to the houses and killed every male child over ten years old. All the remaining men from the Baz, eighty-one in number, were killed with revolver shots. Six women trying to cover their husbands were also killed together with six babies. All the other Assyrians were killed in their houses or while attempting to escape.

The persons killed and who are known to us are:

13 from Sayyid Zari,
14 from Kharb Kuli,
 2 from Mawani,
 1 from Dohuk

The number of the killed who could not be identified runs from 200 to 250 and possibly more.

Three known women were killed with their three small babies.

One woman, Khammi, wife of Hawil being pregnant had her womb cut and the child destroyed.

Eleven known priests were killed after being tortured. Among them were two Catholics.

After killing all the men, the soldiers stripped the dead taking their things of value and then they chased the women. Arabs and

Kurds looted the village. The better-looking women were violated, stripped and let go.

Towards the sunset, the soldiers received orders to retire. The Arabs and Kurds did not cease looting. They also killed some of the wounded men who were still alive but who were already shot by the Iraqi army. Late at night they carried the cattle and went away.

For two nights and one day the dead bodies remained unburied.

On the 13th, workers arrived and dug four trenches and piled the dead bodies in them. On the 14th, Simel was again peaceful, interrupted only by the wails of the naked and hungry terror-stricken Assyrian women and children.

The Minister of Interior who was during the massacre at Mosul came to Simel accompanied by Colonel Stafford, the British Administrative Inspector, Mosul, and they saw what had taken place.

Experienced street workers were sent from Mosul to cover or clean the trace of blood.

On August 16th, four hundred Assyrian women were brought down from Simel to Mosul and placed in khans.

After the arrival of the women from Simel, two priests Qasha Yosep de Kelaita and Qasha Kina of Baz were sent among the women to persuade them not to say that the troops of the Iraqi army had done the massacre but to testify that Arabs and Kurds killed their relatives and looted the village and that the soldiers were there to protect them.

———————

SIMEL MASSACRE.

Statement made by an Assyrian Woman, Nimo Abo, resident in Simel since 1921.

On Tuesday, August 8th, 1933, all the Assyrians living near Simel were gathered together by the police to be protected by the Government.

On the same day, considerable number of Iraqi army soldiers came from Zakho to Simel and collected the rifles. These were taken by the Qaimaqam of Dohuk who, on his return took three Assyrians with him —— namely, Qasha Sada, Rais Tailo Baznaya and a third person. All the three were killed on the way near Dulib. Qasha Sada's head was cut off and his body cut into pieces.

On Wednesday, the Arabs took the sheep of the Assyrians and killed eight shepherds. Three days later the police invited three men to go with them in search of the sheep. When they were some way from Simel, the police killed them all. They must have been killed by bayonet as we did not hear any shots though we were watching.

On Friday, the police sergeant gave orders that everybody should return to their houses and that no harm would come to us. On our way, we saw the Iraqi troops entering Simel and the village was surrounded. Most of the men ran to the house of Goriel of Baz thinking that they would be safe there. Goriel told them that he was an Iraqi citizen and that his house and everybody in it would be safe. The Iraqi army officers gave the orders to begin the massacre. Soldiers started firing at Goriel's house and killed every one there. They then scattered in the village and entered the houses one by one and killed any man they found. I saw two officers taking a woman into a house. When she came out trembling and crying she told her mother-in-law that they raped her.

Many women and children went to the police station to be protected by the police. Three priests and twenty men went there also and tried to hide themselves among the women. But Naib Chaush informed the soldiers of them. The soldiers came in search of them and on finding them killed them all. Some women and children trying to cover their husbands and parents were killed.

A girl of nine years took shelter in the church. She was a Baz girl. The soldiers found her and killed her. They also took some holy books and burnt them together with the girl's body.

On Saturday some soldiers of the Iraqi army returned to the village and tried to hide the dead bodies which were left in the open. They were doing that in a great hurry as some British aeroplanes were flying above. At night many dogs visited the village. The police informed the Government about this and about one hundred workers arrived from Mosul, buried the bodies and covered every trace of blood.

We remained about five days in Simel, after which we informed the police that we cannot live there any longer in fear and hunger. Some of us then went to Dohuk and some to Mosul. In Mosul we were examined by Malek Khamo, Qasha Kina and Qasha Yosep de Kelaita who tried to make us say that the Arabs and Kurds killed us. I cursed them and told them: "How can we say that the tribes massacred our people when we have been massacred by the Iraqi army soldiers?"

————————

The following account was given by a prisoner who was to have been killed on August 14th, 1933, when an order arrived from the Minister of Interior that all killing should cease:

Many Assyrians were taken from their villages by the police and brought to Dohuk to be jailed there, for fear they might join their brethren who were to Syria.

On August 9th nine of the prisoners were taken in an armoured car and conducted to Zakho Pass. There they were killed by machine-gun fire.

On the 10th, another group of nine was taken from the prison and brought near the army camp at Aloka. On their way, two more Assyrians were caught. All the eleven were killed by the soldiers.

One wounded Assyrian was brought to the prison from Badi. The commandant of police ordered the policemen that he be thrown to the dogs. He was taken and thrown so violently against the floor and he died right there.

On August 12th, priest Dinkha with eight other men were taken from the prison and handed them to the soldiers who killed them.

On August 13th, priest Ishmail and other fifteen men were taken from the prison and killed on small hill near Dohuk.

Status of the League of Nations from the Iraqi Point of View.

On August 21st, 1933, the following statement was made in the Iraqi newspapers:

"Poland has most cruelly treated her minorities and Germany has persecuted the Jews in the extreme but Britain and the other Powers did not intervene. No foreign Power can interfere in such affairs. The relations of Britain with this country must not be more than her relations with the above Powers if our independence is on the same footing as that of Poland and the other States. . . . The Assyrians took up arms and it was incumbent on the Government to suppress it and it was also incumbent on her to take all measures to merge this group in the Iraqi unity."

On the 24th the following statement was made:

"This united public opinion that was demonstrated recently coupled with the good feeling must be preserved and strengthened for we believe that in future Iraq will be faced with incidents and many events which, if compared with the Assyrian insurrection, the latter would not but be a simple thing."

The following statement made on August 27th, 1933, in a political newspaper written and administered by Iraqi deputies was as follows:

"When those who were joyful and gay about our entry into the League of Nations, we were in the foremost of those who said this would not be of any utility or advantage. A long time had not elapsed between our entry and the withdrawal of Spain, Brazil and Japan. We would however be sorry if the colonists believe that the League of Nations can terrify Iraq. . . . Iraq as a State or rather an independent State refuses to attach any importance to anyone while dealing with its affairs and interests. The League of Nations, particularly some of its members must know that Iraq is no longer a piece-good that can be bought and sold and is no longer, as the intriguers knew it to be, a slave to be sold in the markets of Geneva. . . . If that does not suit Geneva, Paris or London, it suits Baghdad admirably."

On August 28th, 1933, the following statement was made:

"The Iraqi people was prepared to take up arms and go to the death-field but the matter was not of great importance as those insurgents who disturbed the peace and disobeyed Government were a small mean batch but the reason that led the people for such a big rising was because this batch had gone crying before the western countries that it was being ill-treated and that it was the victim of religious fanaticism. . . . We have not yet forgotten the persecution and oppression committed by Italy in Tripoli against those who wanted to defend the integrity of their country. . . . The foreign influence must be uprooted from this country. . . . The Iraqi public demand the enforcement of conscription as the public is bloodthirsty to suck the blood of the enemies. . . ."

INDEX

A

Adad (diviner of heaven and earth), 23, 48, 70, 74, 105–6, 109–10, 114, 119, 125–28

Akhe, 204, 207

Akitu House, 104, 108, 110, 113–15

Akkad, 6, 20–21, 26, 38, 40, 74

Akkadian, 6, 17, 19, 21–22, 104

alabaster, 2, 9, 42

Albaker, Ahmad Hassan, 145

alphabet, 20, 28, 30

Alqosh, 151–52

Alza, 203, 206

angels, 3, 35, 60, 62, 82, 98, 178

Antu (god), 120, 122–26, 128–29

Anu (god), 70, 114, 119–26, 128–29, 208

aqueducts, 3, 67, 79

Arabs, 180, 184, 187, 225, 239–40, 244, 251–53, 274, 287–88, 290, 292, 303, 312, 315, 318

Aramaic, 18, 28–29

Arbela, 8, 11, 136

armies, 8, 187, 206, 208, 211

aromatics, 72, 107

ascension, bride, 171

Ashur (city), 7, 12, 30, 47, 49, 51–52, 102, 215–16
    enemies of, 203, 213–14
    ziggurat of, 47, 64

Ashur (god), 58, 88–89, 113, 202–3, 205, 207–8, 214
    power of, 205, 208
    worship of, 206–8

Ashuraye, 6, 52, 164

Ashurbanipal (Assyrian king), 21, 25–26, 38

Ashurbanipal II (Assyrian king), military campaign of, 89

Ashur-dapur-Il (king of Assyria), 215

Ashurism, 7, 48–49, 52–53

Ashur-Marduk-sallim-ahhe, 131

Ashurnasirpal II (Assyrian king), 48–49, 57–58

Assad, Hafez al-, 144

Assur, 1, 11, 62, 109

Aššur, 21, 23, 25, 70–73, 105–11, 114–19, 131, 133–34
    gate of, 111, 116

Assur, *See also* Ashur (city)

Aššur, *See also* Ashur (city)

Assyria, xxiv, 6–9, 11–12, 44, 48–49, 56, 97, 102, 105–6, 135–36, 148, 151, 164, 202–3, 213–15
    alphabet of, 20, 28, 30
    ancestors of, 6
    ancient, 17, 132
    artifacts of, xxi, 48, 57, 82, 89

ABOUT THE AUTHOR

Chief operations officer Venesia Yacoub currently oversees eight midsize companies. Her background is in business analysis, financial services, and business management. Previously she was in a management role at a brokerage firm where she acquired knowledge in various complex trading systems and stock markets. Prior to that, she worked in a payroll services firm and she has also worked in the banking sector.

Venesia is Assyrian, and she was five years old when her family left Iraq. She grew up in Ontario, Canada, and she attributes her family's strong values and upbringing in upholding their annual traditions and to still have the ability to speak Assyrian today. Her dream is to visit her homeland one day.